DATE DUE

JE 11 '03			

DEMCO 38-296

RATIONALITY REDEEMED?

Routledge
New York and London

RATIONALITY REDEEMED?

Further Dialogues on an Educational Ideal

Harvey Siegel

Published in 1997
by Routledge
29 West 35th Street
New York, NY 10001

Published in
Great Britain by
Routledge
11 New Fetter Lane
London EC4P 4EE

Copyright © 1997 by
Routledge
Printed in the
United States of America
on acid-free paper.

Library of Congress Cataloging-in-Publication-Data

Siegel, Harvey. 1952–
    Rationality redeemed? : Further dialogues on an educational ideal
/ Harvey Siegel
        p.   cm.
    Includes bibliographical references and index.
    ISBN 0–415–91764–6 (alk. paper). — ISBN 0–415–91765–4
(pbk. : alk. paper)
    1. Education—Philosophy.   2. Critical thinking.   3. Reasoning.
4. Critical pedagogy.   I. Title.
LB14.7.S54   1996
370'.1—dc20
                                              96–24011
                                                 CIP

CONTENTS

PREFACE

The chapters which follow are based, either mainly or in part, on earlier publications of mine. Some have been only minimally edited; others have been substantially revised. I am grateful to the editors and publishers of the journals and collections involved for permission to reprint this previously published material.

Chapter 1, "Epistemology, Critical Thinking, and Critical Thinking Pedagogy," appeared in *Argumentation*, vol. 3, #2, 1989, pp. 127–140.

Chapter 2, "The Generalizability of Critical Thinking," first appeared in *Educational Philosophy and Theory*, vol. 23, #1, 1991, pp. 18–30. It was reprinted under the title "The Generalizability of Critical Thinking Skills, Dispositions and Epistemology," in Stephen P. Norris, ed., *The*

Generalizability of Critical Thinking: Multiple Perspectives on an Educational Ideal, New York: Teachers College Press, 1992, pp. 97–108.

Chapter 3, "Teaching, Reasoning, and Dostoyevsky's *The Brothers Karamazov*," appeared in P. W. Jackson and S. Haroutunian-Gordon, eds., *From Socrates to Software: The Teacher as Text and the Text as Teacher*, Chicago: Eighty-Eighth Yearbook of the National Society for the Study of Education, 1989, pp. 115–134.

Chapter 4, "Not By Skill Alone: The Centrality of Character to Critical Thinking," appeared in *Informal Logic*, vol. 15, #3, Fall 1993, pp. 163–177.

Chapter 5 combines two publications: (1) "Why Be Rational? On Thinking Critically About Critical Thinking," appeared as the "Institute for Critical Thinking Resource Publication, Series 2, #1," 1989, Montclair State College, pp. 1–15 (a shortened version appeared in Ralph Page, ed., *Philosophy of Education 1989* [Proceedings of the Forty-Fifth Annual Meeting of the Philosophy of Education Society], Champaign: Philosophy of Education Society, 1989, pp. 392–401); and (2) "Rescher on the Justification of Rationality," appeared in *Informal Logic*, vol. 14, #1, Winter 1992, pp. 23–31.

Chapter 6, "Critical Thinking and Prejudice," was prepared at the invitation of the Anti-Defamation League for its sponsored conference on critical thinking and prejudice in 1986. A later version was presented, under the title "Argumentation and Prejudice," at the Wake Forest Conference on Argumentation and Democracy in Venice, Italy in June 1992, and is to appear in the Proceedings of that conference, edited by M. D. Hazen and D. C. Williams (in press).

Chapter 7, "The Rationality of Reasonableness," appeared in Margret Buchmann and Robert E. Floden, eds., *Philosophy of Education 1991* (Proceedings of the Forty-Seventh Annual Meeting of the Philosophy of Education Society), Champaign: Philosophy of Education Society, 1991, pp. 225–233.

Chapter 8, "The Limits of A Priori Philosophy," appeared in *Studies in Philosophy and Education*, vol. 11, #3, 1992, pp. 265–284.

Chapter 9, "Gimme That Old-Time Enlightenment Metanarrative: Radical Pedagogies (and Politics) Require Traditional Epistemology (and Moral Theory)," appeared in *Inquiry: Critical Thinking Across the Disciplines*, vol. 11, # 4, May 1993, pp. 1, 17–22. It was presented as a keynote address at, and was reprinted in W. Oxman and M. Weinstein, eds., *Critical Thinking as an Educational Ideal: Proceedings of the 1992 Fifth Annual Conference for Critical Thinking*, Upper Montclair, NJ: Institute for Critical Thinking, Montclair State College, 1993, pp. 27–36. It was also presented at the 1993 annual conference of the Philosophy of Education

Society; a shorter version appeared under the title "Gimme That Old-Time Enlightenment Metanarrative (Response to Weinstein)," in Audrey Thompson, ed., *Philosophy of Education 1993* (Proceedings of the Forty-Ninth Annual Meeting of the Philosophy of Education Society), Champaign: Philosophy of Education Society, 1993, pp. 37–40.

Chapter 10, "'Radical' Pedagogy Requires 'Conservative' Epistemology," was presented as an invited address to the Philosophy of Education Society of Great Britain at New College, Oxford on April 10, 1994, and appeared in the *Journal of Philosophy of Education*, vol. 29, #1, March 1995, pp. 33–46.

Chapter 11, "Knowledge and Certainty; Feminism, Postmodernism, and Multiculturalism," appeared in W. Kohli, ed., *Critical Conversations in Philosophy of Education*, Routledge, 1995, pp. 190–200.

Chapter 12, "What Price Inclusion?," was presented as the Presidential Address of the Philosophy of Education Society in San Francisco, March 1995, and appeared in Alven Neiman, ed., *Philosophy of Education 1995,* Champaign: Philosophy of Education Society, 1995, pp. 1–22. It appeared as well in *Teachers College Record*, vol. 97, #1, Fall 1995, pp. 6–31.

The Epilogue, "Why Care (about Epistemology, Justification, Rationality, etc.)? A Brief Metaphilosophical Excursus," began as a section of the paper which here constitutes Chapter 12, and appeared in the previously published versions of that paper.

I would also like to thank here the many friends and colleagues who commented on earlier versions of the chapters (and who are explicitly acknowledged in the text); the two anonymous reviewers for Routledge, whose excellent suggestions have made this a more coherent and manageable work than it would otherwise have been; and Jayne Fargnoli and Charles Hames, my editors at Routledge, whose enthusiasm, wisdom and good cheer made working on this project a pleasure.

THAT OLD-TIME ENLIGHTENMENT METANARRATIVE

Rationality As An Educational Ideal

Peace rules the day, where reason rules the mind.
—William Collins

IN THE EIGHT YEARS since *Educating Reason* (Siegel 1988) was published, I have tried to develop and defend the view presented in it—that rationality, and what I call there its "educational cognate," critical thinking, constitute a fundamental educational ideal. In part that development and defense was prompted by issues not explicitly addressed in the book. In part it was prompted by the acute criticism the book attracted. And in part it was prompted by broader, "anti-Enlightenment" currents in philosophy of education and in general philosophy. This volume collects the several essays in which that development and defense take place. It also brings together several essays in which I have tried to engage authors who advocate radically different approaches to philosophy and philosophy of education, including those of narrative, contextualism, feminism, multiculturalism, and postmodernism.

In this Introduction I first offer a brief general statement of the view, set out in *Educating Reason*, that the fostering of rationality and critical thinking is the central aim, and the overriding ideal, of education.[1] I then briefly review the following chapters, indicating the ways in which they develop that view, defend it, and engage alternative views and discourses. Before doing so, I should explain an ambiguity in the title of this Introduction. The "old-time Enlightenment metanarrative" that I defend can be taken, narrowly, as the idea that rationality is an ideal appropriate to all education and students. More broadly, it can be taken to be a wide-ranging set of theses concerning the role of reasons in human life, the importance of individual autonomy, the centrality of considerations of justice to the evaluation of actual and possible social arrangements and relationships, the value of knowledge, the importance of believing responsibly, i.e. in such a way that beliefs are informed by and based upon relevant evidence, and so on. The distinction between these narrow and broad senses of that old-time narrative, while clear enough conceptually, tends to break down dialectically, since the defense of the narrower version seems inevitably to involve both the moral and the epistemological dimensions of the broader one. In the chapters which follow, I endeavor to defend both the narrow and more broad versions of the Enlightenment ideal of rationality.

THE BASIC POSITION

On the conception of critical thinking set out in *Educating Reason*, the critical thinker is one who is *appropriately moved by reasons*. Critical thinking involves skills and abilities which facilitate or make possible the appropriate assessment of reasons; it involves dispositions, habits of mind, and character traits as well. I briefly address these two dimensions of critical thinking in turn.

A critical thinker is one who has significant skill and ability with respect to the evaluation of reasons and arguments. For to say that one is *appropriately* moved by reasons is to say that one believes, judges, and acts in accordance with the probative force with which one's reasons support one's beliefs, judgments, and actions. A critical thinker must have, then, both a solid understanding of the principles of reason assessment, and significant ability to utilize that understanding in order to evaluate properly beliefs, actions, judgments, and the reasons which are thought to support them. This dimension of critical thinking may be called the *reason assessment* component of critical thinking.

There are at least two general sorts of principles of reason assessment: general, or subject-neutral principles, and subject-specific ones. General, subject-neutral principles are the sort that apply and are relevant to many different contexts and types of claim; their applicability is not restricted to some particular subject area. Principles of logic—both formal and informal—are subject-neutral principles, as are the principles typically taught in traditional critical thinking courses. Utilizing statistical evidence well, properly evaluating observational evidence, recognizing fallacious reasoning such as begging the question: all these involve subject-neutral skills and abilities of reason assessment. A critical thinker must be the master of a wide variety of subject-neutral principles of reason assessment.

Some principles, however, apply only to rather restricted domains; in those domains, though, they are central to proper reason assessment. Such principles are subject-specific: they guide the assessment of reasons, but only in their local domain. The critical thinker must have some knowledge of specific domains in order properly to assess reasons in those domains; grasp of subject-specific principles of reason assessment requires subject-specific knowledge. For example, in order to evaluate the claim that my symptoms provide evidence that I have malaria, I must know some medicine; in order to evaluate the claim that because the sun is in position P I should use shutter speed S, I must know something about photography. The principle "Yellowish tinged skin indicates liver malfunction" will properly guide judgments and decisions in the doctor's office, but not in the banana section of the local produce market. In general, then, principles of reason assessment can be both subject-neutral and subject-specific, and the critical thinker must manifest a mastery of both sorts of principle. This is because the ability to assess reasons and their warranting force is central to critical thinking.[2]

In addition to skills and grasp of principles of reason assessment, the critical thinker must also have certain attitudes, dispositions, habits of mind, and character traits. This complex can be called the "critical spirit" component of critical thinking. It is not enough that a person be *able* to assess reasons properly; to be a critical thinker she must *actually engage* in competent reason assessment, and be generally disposed to do so. She must habitually seek reasons on which to base belief and action, and she must genuinely base belief, judgment and action on such reasons. She must, that is, be appropriately *moved* by reasons: given that there are compelling reasons to believe, judge or act in a certain way, the critical thinker must be moved by such reasons to so believe, judge or act. She must, that is, have habits of mind which make routine the search for reasons; she must, moreover, be disposed to base belief, judgment and action on reasons according to which they are sanctioned. The critical thinker must *value* reasons and the warrant they provide. She must, attendantly, be disposed to reject arbitrariness and partiality; she must *care* about reasons, reasoning, and living a life in which reasons play a central role.[3]

Thus far, I have tried to emphasize two points. First, reasons have *probative* or *evidential force*, and the critical thinker must be proficient at evaluating the probative force of reasons. This is required for the critical thinker to be *appropriately* moved by reasons. Second, reasons have what might be called *normative impact*: they guide rational belief, judgment and action, and the critical thinker must be so guided if she is to be appropriately *moved* by reasons.

Probative force and normative impact are both key features of reasons. They are each captured by the conception of critical thinking offered, according to which the critical thinker is appropriately moved by reasons. On this conception, both skills and abilities of reason assessment, and the attitudes, dispositions, habits of mind and character traits constitutive of the critical spirit, are crucially important dimensions of critical thinking.[4]

In *Educating Reason* (1988, pp. 55–61) I offered four reasons for thinking that critical thinking, as just conceptualized, constitutes a fundamental educational ideal: respect for students as persons; self-sufficiency and preparation for adulthood; initiation into the rational traditions; and democratic living. I won't review the discussion of these four reasons here, except to say that in my view the fundamental justification for regarding critical thinking as an educational ideal is the first, moral one: conceiving and conducting education in ways which do not take as central the fostering of students' abilities and dispositions to think critically fails to treat students with respect as persons, and so fails to treat them in a morally acceptable way. This alleged justification is obviously "Enlightenment" or "Modernist" in its invidualistic orientation, just as the conception of critical thinking allegedly justified by it is equally modernist in its valorization of rationality. Criticism of this dimension of my conception of critical thinking, and the case for regarding it as a fundamental educational ideal, will take center stage in the chapters in Part Two below.

This conception of critical thinking links naturally with argumentation. For good argumentation involves good reasoning, and so the skilled assessment of the probative force of reasons; it also involves the normative impact of reasons, insofar as a good arguer is one who is not only skilled at argumentation, but who also regularly engages in high quality argumentation and is appropriately directed—moved—by it.[5] It links directly with epistemology as well, since rationality is, at bottom, an epistemic notion. Almost all of the chapters collected here deal in one way or another with the specifically epistemological dimensions of my account of the educational ideal of critical thinking: some develop it further; some defend it from criticisms; and some engage the work of authors who embrace alternative positions, which alternative positions and perspectives almost always hinge on matters epistemological. (Naturally, several chapters do two or all three of these at once.)[6]

THE CHAPTERS WHICH FOLLOW

The chapters in Part One, "Development and Defense," aim primarily at developing and defending the just-reviewed account of critical thinking/rationality and its status as an educational ideal; those in Part Two, "Dialogue," attempt to place that account in the context of alternative discourses and visions of education and its philosophy, and to consider some of the many contemporary philosophical voices which either radically reconceive that ideal or reject it outright, and which manifest radically different approaches to philosophy and philosophy of education.[7] In labelling Part Two "Dialogue," I hope to convey the invitational nature of these chapters. I claim no special expertise with respect to these various alternative philosophical approaches. But I think it vitally important that philosophers and philosophers of education who embrace one or another of these approaches talk to each other, learn from each other, and engage in honest, fair-minded evaluations of the strengths and weaknesses of the various alternative approaches to and discourses concerning our common subject.[8] As I hope the discussion in Part Two makes clear, in my view these varied approaches do indeed have important strengths (as well as weaknesses). I have endeavored in these chapters to enter into genuine dialogue—sometimes critical, to be sure, but no less genuine—with those colleagues who do not approach philosophy as I do. I deeply hope that they are read as invitations to further dialogue.

These two categories ("Development and Defense" and "Dialogue") are fluid and partly overlapping; the placement of several of the chapters in one of the parts rather than the other is somewhat arbitrary. For example, Chapters 7 and 8 could easily have been placed in Part One, since they develop and defend my position (as well as consider the strengths and weaknesses of alternative approaches); Chapter 4 could have been placed in Part Two, since it is a systematic engagement with a critic who raises fundamental doubts not only about my substantive position, but about my basic philosophical approach to issues concerning the nature and value of critical thinking (as well as a straightforward defense of my position and approach). I hope that the fluidity of these parts, and the occasional near-arbitrariness of my decision to place a given chapter in a given part, will not distract the reader. As a rule, the chapters in Part One extend and defend my earlier treatment of the educational ideal of critical thinking/rationality; those in Part Two seek to confront that treatment with some radically alternative positions and approaches, and to engage those alternatives in dialogue.

Since those alternative positions do not always concern themselves with critical thinking per se, but nearly always concern themselves with epistemology and with criticisms of Enlightenment conceptions of rationality, the chapters begin by focussing on critical thinking and gradually move beyond that educational notion to the broader epistemic one of rationality. Despite this gradual shift in emphasis as the chapters progress, the educational and epistemological concerns are throughout inexorably intertwined; one cannot, on my view, engage in serious philosophy of education without equally seriously attending to matters epistemological.

Chapter 1 relates the ideal of critical thinking/rationality to underlying epistemological issues, and defends a particular set of epistemological views, concerning truth, justification, and relativism, which harmonize most effec-

5

tively with that ideal. Specifically, I argue there for a fallibilist but absolutist conception of truth: absolutist in that the truth of a proposition, sentence, belief or claim is independent of the warrant or justification it enjoys on the basis of relevant evidence, and fallibilist in that our judgments concerning truth are always open to challenge and revision; for a view of justification as a fallible indicator of truth; and for the rejection of epistemological relativism. Since, as noted above, many challenges to my view of critical thinking, and many alternative perspectives in contemporary philosophy and philosophy of education, are based upon differing views on these matters, epistemological issues arise throughout the subsequent chapters. In this respect, Chapter 1 sets the stage for much of the subsequent discussion.

Chapter 2 directly addresses the widely discussed question of generalizability, and defends the view that critical thinking is in three important respects generalizable. Specifically, I argue that the skills and criteria of reason assessment—the main locus of extant debate concerning the generalizability of critical thinking—are partly generalizable; and that the epistemology underlying critical thinking, and the critical spirit—two dimensions of the generalizability issue which are under-addressed in the literature—are both fully generalizable.

Chapter 3 offers an analysis of teaching, and of Dostoevsky's great novel *The Brothers Karamazov*, in an attempt to explore the ways in which literature can both teach and enhance reasoning and critical thinking. Here I develop the "probative force/normative impact" distinction, and introduce the notion of "felt reasons"—both of which I hope serve to clarify and broaden my earlier discussions of critical thinking. It is perhaps worth noting that the discussion in this Chapter indirectly but sympathetically responds to the recent concern, especially among feminist scholars, with *narrative* and its educational and philosophical ramifications. (This theme is continued in my response to Lynda Stone in Chapter 11.)

In *Educating Reason* I emphasized the centrality to the ideal of critical thinking of the "critical spirit," a complex of dispositions, attitudes, habits of mind, and character traits. In Chapter 4, I defend the claim that the latter complex is central to the educational ideal of critical thinking against the criticism, put forward clearly and forcefully by Connie Missimer, that critical thinking is best understood in terms of reasoning skills alone, without reference to character. In responding to Missimer's deep and searching criticisms of the "critical spirit" component of critical thinking, I hope to have both clarified and further justified its rightful place at the center of that educational ideal.

Chapter 5 deals with the difficult but fundamental problem of justifying our commitment to rationality. It attempts to provide a nonquestion-begging, noncircular answer to the question "Why be rational?" I hope that this chapter

6

further develops and deepens the discussion of these matters offered in the Postscript to *Educating Reason*.

Chapter 6 applies my view of critical thinking to the difficult social problem of prejudice, in an effort to shed light on the cognitive aspects of that problem, and considers the ways in which enhancing the former might reduce the latter.

As previously noted, Chapter 4 responds to Connie Missimer's criticisms of the character component of my conception of critical thinking. Chapters 7 and 8 respond to two critics who challenge my views of rationality and epistemology, respectively. In responding to Nicholas C. Burbules and Mark Weinstein, I hope to have more clearly articulated and more adequately defended my positive views, and also to have raised some questions concerning their alternative positions.

Chapter 7 develops further the conception of rationality I have endeavored to defend. It rejects an overly formalistic conception, and also rejects the "contextualist" conception of "reasonableness" recommended by Burbules, in favor of a substantive, epistemic conception which avoids the defects of both an overly formalistic and an overly contextualist understanding of rationality. In Chapter 8 I respond to Weinstein's "antifoundationalist" and other criticisms of the epistemological views set out in *Educating Reason* (and also in *Relativism Refuted* [Siegel 1987]). These two chapters fill out the general epistemological stance which is basic to my overall view.

All of the chapters mentioned thusfar are based firmly in the "Enlightenment" philosophical tradition, and aspire to establish univocal analyses of rationality and of the educational ideal of critical thinking—analyses which pay scant attention to the differences among the "concrete others" who are our students (and ourselves). But this sort of universalistic analysis has been subjected to increasing criticism in recent years, and many sorts of critics—antifoundationalist, contextualist, feminist, multiculturalist, and postmodernist, in particular—reject the very sort of project which my earlier books, and the chapters just mentioned, have endeavored to carry out. How, in these postmodernist times, can one seriously propose the fostering of rationality—an Enlightenment notion if ever there was one—as a universal educational ideal? The final four chapters attempt to address this question. In so doing, they attempt to put in perspective some dimensions of the postmodernist challenge to more modernist ways of conceiving both education and its philosophy.

Chapter 9 is a response to another important paper by Mark Weinstein. In it I try to show that the feminist and postmodernist critiques of modernist philosophy and/of education, while powerful, can be—and indeed must be—reconciled with their modernist targets, if those critiques are to maintain their normative force. I argue, that is, that these critical movements require for their

7

success the very Enlightenment views, concerning rationality in particular and epistemology in general, that they attempt to overthrow; and that their criticisms have force only to the extent that they presuppose the very Enlightenment notions, ideals and "metanarrativist" techniques they seek to challenge. In this way I suggest that these critiques, while profoundly important, are less revolutionary then they are sometimes presented as being.

Chapters 10, 11, and 12 continue and expand upon this line of response to these several challenges to the Enlightenment ideal of rationality and its attendant epistemology. Chapter 10 deals, in a general way, with "radical" challenges to Enlightenment philosophy and philosophy of education and their epistemological presuppositions. Chapter 11 responds to Lynda Stone's feminist critique, and René Arcilla's multiculturalist and postmodernist critique, of that epistemological stance. As in the previous chapter, in these chapters I attempt to show that these various criticisms succeed only to the extent that they are restrained or limited by the recognition that they depend for their success on key aspects of the epistemology their critiques target. Chapter 12 is addressed to one shared aspect of these critiques: that modernism practices a problematic form of exclusion, and that the moral requirement to include those "others" who have been excluded establishes the deficiencies and inadequacies of the epistemology of the Enlightenment. Here too I try to show that this criticism is misguided, and that the moral argument for inclusion—which I endorse—not only does not challenge, but in fact itself presupposes, that very epistemology.

The six chapters in Part Two (and the Epilogue), then, attempt to embrace what is right in contemporary contextualist, feminist, multiculturalist, and postmodernist critiques; to demonstrate some of the ways in which these critiques do not succeed; and to indicate the dependence of the partial success of these critiques upon the very Enlightenment conceptions and ideals that they attempt to challenge. My hope is that these chapters will help to clarify the issues between more traditional philosophers and philosophers of education and their critics, and will place these critiques in a general perspective that will permit a more nuanced appreciation of both their strengths and their weaknesses.

The development of the positions detailed herein, especially in the six chapters included in Part Two (but also Chapter 4), has obviously been stimulated to a great degree by the powerful criticisms my earlier efforts have received. I am particularly grateful to my friends and critics Nick Burbules, Connie Missimer, and Mark Weinstein, whose collegial but hard-nosed and forceful criticisms have forced me to think through more deeply issues that I had earlier only incompletely addressed; and to Burbules, Weinstein, Lynda Stone, and René Arcilla, whose efforts have helped me to see more clearly the relations between my own work on rationality, and the various critiques of both that notion and of the general philosophical problematic in which I live and work. These colleagues have expanded my philosophical horizons; for that I will always be grateful, however much we continue to disagree.

I am also indebted to the many friends, colleagues and critics who have commented upon various versions of the several chapters; they are specifically acknowledged therein.

DEVELOPMENT AND DEFENSE

part one

EPISTEMOLOGY, CRITICAL THINKING, AND CRITICAL THINKING PEDAGOGY

Here's an object more of dread,
Than aught the grave contains,
A human form with reason fled,
While wretched life remains.
                    —Abraham Lincoln

BEING A CRITICAL THINKER requires basing one's beliefs and actions on reasons; it involves committing oneself to the dictates of rationality. The notions of "reason" and "rationality," however, are philosophically problematic. Just what is a reason? How do we know that some consideration constitutes a reason for believing or doing something? How do we evaluate the strength or merit of reasons? What is it for a belief or action to be justified? What is the relationship between justification and truth? Why is rationality to be valued?

Questions such as these are central to epistemology. Because they are abstract and difficult, their relevance to education for critical thinking is not always appreciated. But so long as critical thinking is thought of as centrally involving *reasons* and *rationality*, these questions are basic to the critical thinking student's understanding of her subject matter. Without having some epistemological understanding of notions such as reason, rationality, knowledge, truth, evidence, warrant, justification, and so on, the critical thinking student has at best a superficial grasp of her subject. It is central to critical thinking education that students develop some understanding of the epistemology underlying critical thinking.

In this chapter my task is two-fold. First, I will examine the epistemology underlying critical thinking, and argue that taking critical thinking seriously requires the taking of particular, albeit contentious, positions with respect to certain standard epistemological issues. (For example, I will argue that a commitment to education for critical thinking requires a rejection of epistemological relativism, and the embrace of an "absolutist" conception of truth.) Second, I will argue that the explicit consideration of such epistemological questions as the nature of reasons, truth and rational justification should be regarded as a basic component of critical thinking education. That is, I will argue that epistemology should be a fundamental part of any educational effort to foster critical thinking. In making these arguments, I hope to clarify both the epistemology underlying critical thinking and the relevance of that epistemology to critical thinking pedagogy. (Because of their interrelatedness, epistemology and pedagogy will be intertwined in what follows.)

CRITICAL THINKING AND THE EVALUATION OF REASONS

To be a critical thinker one must be able, at least, to evaluate the evidential or probative force of reasons.[1] That is, the critical thinker must be able to tell whether a putative reason is a genuine one; whether it strongly or weakly supports some claim or action for which it is offered as a reason; and whether she ought, on the basis of the reason under consideration, to accept the claim or perform the action in question. The beliefs and actions of the critical thinker, at least ideally, are *justified* by reasons for them which she has properly evaluated; when the beliefs and actions, in other words, are based on good reasons. But when are reasons good ones? How do we distinguish good reasons from not-so-good ones? How do we know, for example, that

    p: abortion is baby-killing

is a *bad* reason for

    q: abortion is morally wrong;

while

    r: a fetus is sentient and has a concept of self,

if justified, would be a *good* reason for *q*? In this example our evaluation of the force of reasons *p* and *r* for claim *q* is straightforward: *p* is a bad or weak reason for *q* because *p* begs the question against those who think that abortion is morally permissible since a fetus is not in relevant respects like a baby and so has no "right to life"; while *r*, if itself justified, would be a good reason for *q* because we think that beings who are sentient and have a concept of self do enjoy such a right, and that it is morally wrong to deny that right.[2] So the belief that q, i.e. that abortion is morally wrong, is justified when (and only when) there are good reasons which support it.

It is obvious that more needs to be said concerning the goodness of reasons. r, we said, would be a good reason for q *if justified*;[3] that is, we ought to believe that abortion is morally wrong (so far as this particular argument is concerned) only if we are justified in believing, i.e. have good reason to believe that it is the case, that fetuses are sentient and have concepts of self. But since there is good reason to think that r is false, r does not constitute a good reason for believing that q. r's unjustifiedness counts against its force as a reason for q, just as

s: Reagan had a deep understanding of foreign policy issues

is not a good reason for

t: We would have been better off if Reagan had
   continued on in the presidency after 1988

because there is good reason to think that s, like r, is false. If the belief that s were justified, s would be a consideration which favored an extended Reagan presidency; but if s is not justified it offers no support for t.[4]

Belief in some claim (q or t) is justified when there are good reasons which support that claim, and the belief is based on those reasons. We have just seen that one criterion by which we assess the force of reasons is their justifiability: r would be a good reason for q, except that r is itself unjustified, i.e. there is good reason to think that it is not true; similarly, s is not a good reason for t since there is good reason to believe that it is not true.[5] But it is clear that this is only one criterion by which we evaluate reasons. Another which we have seen is that of question-begging-ness: just as a reason carries no weight if it is itself unjustified, it carries no weight if it begs the question.

But how do we know that these are legitimate criteria of reason assessment? What are the criteria of reason assessment? Where do these criteria come from, and how are they themselves justified? How do we tell, in general, whether some putative reason u is a good reason for some claim (or action) v?

Full answers to these fundamental questions are beyond both my ability and my available space. But some things can be said. First, it should be noted that there are a variety of types of criteria by which we assess reasons. Some are general, in that they apply to many diverse subject matters and circumstances. Our earlier example of begging the question illustrates this: a reason which begs the question—that is, one which assumes the very point for which it purports to be a good reason—is a bad reason, with no probative weight. This is true no matter what the context or subject matter happens to be. Begging the question functions as a general criterion of reason assessment, in that any putative reason which begs the question will fail to be a good reason, i.e. will fail to provide

15

warrant or justification for the claim for which it purports to be a reason. Logic—both formal and informal—provides a large set of general criteria by which reasons are evaluated.

Other criteria are not so general, but are subject-specific. One needs to know some developmental psychology (and some philosophy), for example, in order to evaluate the claim that fetuses have a concept of self; one needs to know this in order to evaluate claims like "A fetus' performing behavior *B* is evidence that the fetus has a concept of self." Similarly, to evaluate the claim that the sun's being in a certain position is a reason for setting the shutter speed at *S*, one needs to know something about photography; to tell whether or not one's symptoms constitute good evidence that one has malaria, one needs to know some medicine. So some criteria by which reasons are properly assessed are subject-specific, while others are subject-neutral.[6] (Often it is not easy to tell whether a putative reason is a good one, even when the relevant criteria are clear; evaluating reasons is often problematic. But to the extent that one is a critical thinker, one believes and acts on the basis of reasons which one evaluates, in accordance with relevant criteria, as best one can.)

How are criteria of reason assessment themselves justified? How do we know, for example, that a reason is a bad one because it begs the question, but not because it is more than five words long? There is no short, snappy answer to this question. In order to justify a claim about something's being a legitimate criterion of reason assessment, one has no choice but to appeal to epistemology—that is, to the general theory of knowledge, truth, reasons, justification and evidence.

Moreover, when we help students to become critical thinkers—by helping them to understand and apply appropriate criteria of reason assessment, and by encouraging them to seek reasons by which to justify candidate beliefs and actions—we in effect invite them to demand reasons for accepting as legitimate the criteria of reason assessment we are teaching them. In encouraging students to become critical thinkers, then, we encourage them to pursue epistemological questions concerning reason assessment and critical thinking for themselves. That is, we encourage them to be critical thinkers about critical thinking itself. We must do this if we are consistent; otherwise, we would be saying to students: "Be critical and demand reasons regarding all aspects of your life—regarding political views, scientific and literary beliefs, personal relationships, etc.—but just take our word for it that 'begging the question' is a fallacy, and that a reason which begs the question is not a good one." This sort of message is incompatible with sound critical thinking instruction, for it in effect invites students *not* to be critical thinkers about the very thing we think it is so important for them to become. So critical thinking pedagogy requires that we allow and encourage students to think critically about critical thinking itself. This involves thinking critically about the justification of standards of reason assessment, which in turn involves considerations of epistemology—for example, it involves the consideration of views about the nature of reasons and justification, such that according to such views reasons which beg the question do not (or do) constitute good reasons—and it involves the consideration of reasons for and against those epistemological views themselves. Thus a self-consistent critical thinking pedagogy necessarily invites students to consider epistemological questions underlying critical thinking. (I shall return to this point below.)

THE EPISTEMOLOGY UNDERLYING CRITICAL THINKING

Our trail has led thus far to the conclusion that sound critical thinking pedagogy requires attention to the epistemology underlying critical thinking. So what is that epistemology? What epistemology are we committed to when we favor the ideal of critical thinking; when we think it good to be a critical thinker and encourage our students to become critical thinkers? While I don't pretend to have anything like a full conception of an epistemology underlying critical thinking to offer, I do think that a commitment to critical thinking requires that we take particular stands on some contentious epistemological issues.

The Relationship Between Rational Justification and Truth

The first concerns the nature of rational justification, and the relation between such justification and truth. We saw earlier that for r to count as a reason for q, r must be justified. What about q itself? Must q be true if belief in q is to be rational? The answer, required by a commitment to critical thinking, is negative: it can be rational to believe that q even if q is false. The rationality of believing q is independent of q's truth.

Examples make this initially paradoxical stance plausible. In the heyday of Newtonian mechanics, for example, there was excellent reason for regarding that theory as true; it was certainly rational to believe it. We now regard Newton's theory as false (on the basis of evidence and theoretical considerations not available to scientists in the nineteenth century). So a Newtonian in, say, 1850, was perfectly rational in believing what was/is in fact false. The same could be said of belief in air which had negative weight, and of belief that the Earth was flat, in earlier centuries. In general, there can be good reasons/powerful evidence which supports belief in that which is false.

By the same token, it is quite possible for evidence to point against that which is true; that is, it can sometimes be rational to disbelieve that which is true, and believe that which is false. This can be illustrated by a famous anecdote concerning Bertrand Russell. In his widely broadcast BBC radio debates with Father Copleston on the existence of God, Copleston asked Russell what he would say to God if, despite all the evidence against His existence cited by

Russell during the course of the debate, Russell arrived at the pearly gates upon his death and discovered that, evidence to the contrary notwithstanding, God did in fact exist. Russell replied that he would ask the Creator "why He had made the evidence for His nonexistence so compelling." In this reply Russell makes clear that, despite the strength of the considerations favoring God's nonexistence, it is possible that He exists, despite the evidence, all the same. Other examples illustrate the same point. It may be true, for example, that Oliver North truly believes in the ideal of government by law, and that the United States Congress has a legitimate role to play (along with that of the Executive) in the establishment of foreign policy, despite the powerful evidence that North does not believe these things; similarly, it frequently is true of some people that they have not suffered heart attacks, despite the pain in the arm, tightness of chest, and shortness of breath that suggests that they have. It may be true, despite evidence to the contrary, that fetuses have a concept of self. In all these cases, a claim can be true (that God does exist, that North does believe, that the patient is not a heart attack victim, that fetuses have a concept of self, that aspirin does not lower the probability of stroke) despite powerful evidence to the contrary. And earlier we saw that a claim can be false, despite strong evidence in its favor. In short, the lesson here is that truth is *independent* of rational justification: we can be justified in believing that q even though q is false; and we can be justified in rejecting q as false even though it is true.

The idea that truth and rational justification are independent is contentious philosophically: it contradicts Dewey's view of truth as "warranted assertibility"; and it is rejected by contemporary philosophers like Hilary Putnam (1981, pp. 55–56), who rejects a "radically nonepistemic" conception of truth and argues that truth should be understood as "ideal rational acceptability," and Michael Dummett (1980), who denies that truth can be coherently conceived of as independent of all possible verification. These contemporary philosophers pose difficult challenges to the thesis that truth is independent of rational justification; in the end, theorists of critical thinking have either to defeat these antirealist arguments (which suggest that truth and rational justification are not independent), or else adjust the "independence thesis" to reflect the sense in which truth and rational justification are not independent. Whatever the ultimate resolution of this philosophical controversy might be, however, it is clear what line those committed to critical thinking must take. So long as critical thinking involves believing on the basis of reasons, and so long as particular claims which students are considering must be assessed in accord with the reasons which students actually have or can get (and so said students are not working with Putnam's *idealization* of rational acceptability), then the power of reasons to sustain a conclusion must be seen as always open. Even very powerful reasons for or against some claim q can be wrong, misleading, or overturned by evidence not yet available. In teaching students to be critical thinkers, we do not in the first instance instruct them to believe only what is true. Of course we do think that believing on the basis of reasons is a reliable guide to believing what is true, at least generally. Nevertheless, in teaching students to be critical thinkers, we encourage them to believe (and act) on the basis of reasons which are properly evaluated. In doing so we let the truth fall where it may, and regard the student who justifiedly believes q, which is false, despite the evidence in its favor, as a more successful critical thinker than the student who believes not-q, which is true, despite the evidence to the contrary. Critical thinking involves believing rationally, on the basis of reasons; such belief must, from the point of view of our theoretical understanding of critical thinking, be conceived of as independent of truth.

Rational Justification and the Spectre of Relativism

Critical thinking, I have been suggesting, fundamentally involves believing and acting on the basis of reasons; it involves, that is, rational justification. But in some circumstances it is not clear whether beliefs or actions are rationally justified, because it is not clear what counts as a (good) reason in those circumstances. Consider the debate between Galileo and some of his opponents concerning telescopic evidence for the existence of Jovian moons.[7] Galileo claimed that there was very good reason to believe in the existence of moons orbiting the planet Jupiter, namely, observations of the moons made with the use of the recently invented telescope. Galileo held that telescopic observation provided compelling evidence of the moons' existence. His opponents, on the other hand, regarded telescopic observation as problematic, absent a theoretical understanding of telescopic operation which gave us some reason to regard telescopic images as veridical; moreover, they claimed to have very good reason for thinking that the moons didn't exist, reasons furnished by Scripture and by the writings of Aristotle. So: Galileo claimed that telescopic observation provided good reason for believing that the Jovian moons existed, while his opponents demurred; his opponents thought that Scripture and Aristotle provided reason for thinking that the moons did not exist, while Galileo demurred. The dispute concerned not only the existence of the moons. It involved as well a higher-order dispute concerning the nature of evidence for the existence of the moons. Galileo and his opponents disagreed about what counted as good reason for/against the existence of the moons.

This kind of dispute raises the spectre of relativism. For it suggests that what counts as a reason is relative to persons, frameworks or perspectives: telescopic observation provided good reason for Galileo but not his opponents; the writings of Aristotle provided good reason for his opponents but not for Galileo. Thus a candidate reason's status as a good reason depends on who is doing the judging.

Such a relativism of reasons[8] is incompatible with education for critical thinking. In such education our aim is to help students develop the ability to evaluate arguments and the probative force which putative reasons have, and to encourage students to believe and act on the basis of reasons—to be *appropriately moved by reasons*. This presupposes that reasons have probative force, and that it is possible to misevaluate reasons. Otherwise, there would be no point in helping students develop the ability to evaluate reasons properly, for it would be impossible for students to evaluate them improperly or wrongly. So consider a standard case of evaluating reasons in the critical thinking class: evaluating the argument of the newspaper editorialist. If the goodness of reasons is relative, then when I convict the editorialist of begging the question, and students do not see the example as one which is question-begging—or do not regard begging the question as fallacious—I cannot say that the students are being uncritical or failing to think critically. For if reasons are relative, then the argument must be said to be weak according to my conception of the goodness of reasons, stronger according to the students' conception. If the goodness of reasons is relative, then we cannot say that one assessment of an argument is better than another; worse, we cannot legitimately think that our argument assessment rules and criteria are superior to our students' untutored rules and criteria (or denial of such). Thus there would be no cogent rationale for teaching students how to assess reasons and arguments; no motivation for education aimed at the improvement of critical thinking.

Consequently, critical thinking demands a rejection of relativism. If we think there is some point to helping students become critical thinkers, we must think there are criteria, binding upon all reasoners, in accordance with which the strengths of reasons and arguments are appropriately determined, and we must think that it is a good thing for students to master and utilize those criteria. This is not to deny that there are cases, like Galileo's, in which it is genuinely difficult to evaluate the strength of reasons and the appropriateness of particular criteria of reason-assessment. But, as Popper says, we should not "exaggerate a difficulty into an impossibility." (1970, p. 57) It does not follow, from the fact that in some cases it is genuinely difficult to reach rational agreement, that rational evaluation of the force of reasons or the strengths of arguments is impossible—either in such cases, or in general.

So critical thinking is incompatible with, and must defeat, relativism. Fortunately, relativism can be defeated. Elsewhere (Siegel 1987) I have presented arguments against relativism; I will not rehearse those arguments here. Instead, I wish to recommend two pedagogical strategies which I have found useful in overcoming students' predisposition to relativism.

The first is to present to students the familiar self-refutation argument against relativism, aimed at their own articulation of the relativistic thesis. Suppose you and your class are discussing an editorial concerning abortion, and you suggest that the editorialist has begged the question by suggesting that abortion is wrong because it is baby killing. Your student (the relativist) responds by saying something like:

> For *you* that reason begs the question and is a bad reason. But for the editorialist it is a good reason. There is no right or wrong, either about abortion or about what constitutes a good reason for abortion. It's all just opinion.

Your task is to help the student to see that such a relativistic stance is indefensible.[9] A useful way to do this is to help the student see the dilemma she faces when she applies her relativism to itself; that is, to help the student see that her relativism is self-defeating. Your reply:

> What about your own claim that there is no right or wrong concerning what constitutes a good reason: Is it right, or just your opinion?

To make the point clearly, it is useful to isolate and name the relativistic thesis, to make for easy and clear reference. So you might put on the board:

> *A*: There is no right or wrong concerning the constitution of good reasons. Such judgments are just opinions; probative force is in the eye of the reasoner.

or some other sentences which the student agrees capture her claim. (It is typically useful to get as close as you can to the student's own words.) Then ask:

> Is *A* right, or just your opinion?

Using this technique provides the opportunity to teach something about reference, about the use/mention distinction, and about other philosophical issues relevant to the cultivation of critical thinking. But its main advantage is that it vividly displays to the student the dilemma her relativism creates for her. For if she says "*A* is right," she has given up her relativism by claiming that the truth/justifiability of at least this claim, *A*, is not relative; while if she says "*A* is just my opinion," she has granted to you and everyone else the right to reject *A*. Students who tend to relativism usually (at least in my experience) recognize the unsatisfactoriness of these two answers; they realize that their relativism is problematic. And given the frequency with which students espouse relativistic positions, it is generally very instructive to discuss the merits and defects of relativism: it is a subject in which students are typically very interested. Examining relativism—an epistemological topic if ever there was one—both engages students' attention and interest, and also helps to overcome a major obstacle to the effort to encourage critical thinking. Here is a real opportunity to teach students something important. It is of basic concern to critical thinking, for relativism threatens to undermine educational efforts aimed at fostering critical thinking. And it is fundamentally epistemological. Here we see again both an important component of the epistemology underlying critical thinking, and the proper place of epistemology in the critical thinking classroom.

The second pedagogical strategy I wish to recommend is simply this: *model critical thinking, not relativism.* In examining issues and arguments, be honest with students. Tell them what you think of reasons offered, and why. Make claims, and give reasons and evidence for your claims. Take stands, and defend them. Perhaps most important of all, give them up when appropriate—that is, when reasons opposed to your view are more powerful than your own. In demonstrating to students that it is the convicting force of reasons to which you are committed, you help make clear to them the regard you have for critical thinking, i.e. for belief and action based on the proper evaluation of reasons, and for the disposition to be moved by reasons. Such modelling of critical thinking, in conjuction with reasoned arguments in favor of it, can help students to develop the skills and especially the dispositions and character traits associated with that ideal.[10]

Truth and Justification

The third area in which critical thinking commits us to epistemological stances involves truth and the relationship between truth and justification. (This actually is a continuation of the first topic above.)

As I have been arguing, it is not truth which is critical to critical thinking, but rather justification. Truth, I have suggested, must be seen by the critical thinking theorist as *independent* of justification. Nevertheless, it is important to see that, despite the independence I argued for above, the two are related. For claims which are rationally justified are claims which we have reason to regard *as true.* This is a familiar epistemological point: if r provides a reason for q, r provides a reason for thinking that q is true, since to believe that q just is to believe that q is true. This, as we used to say in the bad old days of ordinary language analysis, is part of what we *mean* by "p is a reason for q." In the good new days, we generally make the point this way:

> To the extent that we are rational, each of us decides at any time t whether a belief is true, in precisely the same way that we would decide at t whether we ourselves are, or would be, warranted at t in having that belief . . . we are irrational if we have at t one way of assessing warrant and another way of assessing truth. If we are rational we must assume . . . a correlation between warrant-conferring rules and true beliefs—as, indeed, we all do—in order to identify true beliefs. (Firth 1981, p. 19)

In other words, we have no immediate or privileged access to the truth; we "get at" the truth by assessing warrant. We take justification to be a sign of truth. Truth thus functions for us, as Kant might say, as a *regulative ideal*: the *upshot* of justification is a prima facie case for truth.

This prima facie case is defeasible, however; what is justified now can be overturned (both by additional evidence and by further reflection), and become unjustified, later. Thus we come to the doctrine of *fallibilism*: while there is truth, there is no certainty; we get at truth by way of warrant and justification, and these are always open for further consideration.[11] We must distinguish between truth and our *estimate* of the truth; between *p*'s *being* true and our *thinking* that it is. We don't make *p* true by believing that *p* is true. Here is the sense in which truth and justification are independent, and in which truth is "absolute."[12] Nevertheless, regarding *p* as true is strictly a function of our regarding *p* as justified, for there simply is no other way in which we can responsibly judge truth.

Critical thinkers, then, are good at assessing justification, at estimating truth. This is because critical thinkers are skilled at evaluating the probative force of reasons and evidence, and it is reasons and evidence which confer warrant and justification. This is the route to true as well as justified belief. But it is a crucial lesson for the critical thinker that that route is defeasible; that her estimate of the truth of *p* at time *t* is distinct from *p*'s truth. It is a crucial lesson, in other words, that truth is independent of us, but that we strive after it by way of assessing warrant and justification. In helping students to become critical thinkers, we help them to become estimators of the truth, not determiners of it. Learning this lesson helps students to see both that truth is not up to us, but also that our estimates of the truth can be more or less cogent and careful; that, as Firth suggests, our estimates of the truth will be guided by our judgments regarding rational justification. And these judgments are enhanced by the skills and abilities (and dispositions and character traits) constitutive of critical thinking.[13]

WHY BRING EPISTEMOLOGY INTO THE CRITICAL THINKING CLASSROOM?

I have been arguing that critical thinking requires that we take particular stands on certain epistemological issues, and also that critical thinking instruction is enhanced by the explicit treatment of epistemological questions. One might balk at this latter suggestion, however. After all, there is already more to do in a critical thinking course than there is time for, one might object. More pointedly, to do epistemology in a critical thinking course is to change it to an epistemology course and to cease doing critical thinking. I should like to conclude by responding to these criticisms, and by offering some general reasons for thinking it a good idea to enhance critical thinking pedagogy with epistemology.

First, I think it is a good idea to incorporate epistemology into the critical thinking course because of its effect on students. Students (in my experience at least) like it, and find it both challenging and interesting. It helps counteract the "remedial thinking" image of the course. Epistemology *motivates* critical thinking students. (Indeed, I thought seriously about giving this chapter the title "Motivating Critical Thinking Students with Epistemology.")

Second, including epistemology in the critical thinking course gives the course some substance, some intellectual weight. It makes the course not *only* a "skills" course.

Third, epistemology is required if students are properly to understand much of what is being taught. Why should they avoid fallacies?[14] Why should they go to the trouble of reconstructing the argument of the newspaper editorialist, or of gathering evidence for their own positive views? Such questions as these, which are perfectly appropriate in the context of a critical thinking course, can only be answered by appealing to considerations epistemological.

Fourth, it helps students to see that critical thinking—both its substance and its justification for inclusion in the curriculum—turns ultimately on philosophy, and specifically epistemology. This affords the student a much deeper appreciation of the nature and point of critical thinking (and its instruction) than would be available to her otherwise.

These should suffice to answer the objections to incorporating epistemology into the critical thinking course noted above. The "no time" objection is met once it is clear how central to critical thinking epistemology is; how epistemology sheds light on such staples of instruction aimed at the fostering of critical thinking as the fallaciousness of fallacies and the desirability of evaluating arguments by assessing the probative force reasons and premises offer for conclusions. The second objection, that epistemology just is not critical thinking, is answered similarly. Once it is seen how critical thinking and its instruction presuppose contentious epistemological stances, how epistemology is basic to the theory of critical thinking, and how it contributes (both motivationally and intellectually) to educational efforts aimed at enhancing critical thinking, epistemology's centrality to critical thinking, and place in educational efforts aimed at promoting it, is clear.

There is one final reason for including epistemology in the critical thinking course which I would be remiss if I did not mention, for in its way it is the most important reason of all. Because epistemology underlies critical thinking, challenging the latter requires attention to the former. And because critical thinking involves fundamentally the evaluation of reasons on which belief and action are grounded, being critical about critical thinking requires examination of the epistemology underlying it. In incorporating epistemology in the critical thinking course, we offer students the opportunity to challenge critical thinking; in doing so we are true to its basic principles. Those

principles include the right of the student to examine claims and their putative justifications for herself. Applying this right to the course itself, the student is entitled to question, examine and evaluate both critical thinking
instruction and its presuppositions. Thus including the epistemological under-
pinnings of critical thinking in educational interventions aimed at the fostering and enhancement of critical thinking allows for the application of critical
thinking to critical thinking itself. This is precisely what adherence to the ideal
of critical thinking demands.[15]

THE GENERALIZABILITY OF CRITICAL THINKING

Has anyone ever acquired intelligence through
logic? . . . Is there more of a hotchpotch in the
cackle of fishwives than in the public disputa-
tions of men who profess logic? I would prefer a son of mine to learn to talk in the tavern
rather than in our university yap-shops.
——Michel de Montaigne

chapter 2

WHETHER OR NOT CRITICAL THINKING is generalizable depends, of course, on
what critical thinking is. There are many extant accounts of critical thinking;
these accounts differ from one another in a variety of ways. However, most of
the main accounts, including those of Ennis, Paul, McPeck, and Lipman, agree
at least to this extent: critical thinking has (at least) two central components:
a *reason assessment* component, which involves abilities and skills relevant to
the proper understanding and assessment of reasons, claims, and arguments;
and a *critical spirit* component, which is understood as a complex of dispositions, attitudes, habits of mind, and character traits.[1] Assuming that these two
are indeed central components of critical thinking, the question concerning
the generalizability of critical thinking can be usefully broken down into two
separate and more manageable questions, concerning the generalizability of
each of the two components. Most discussion of the generalizability of critical

thinking has concerned the reason assessment component; advocates and opponents of generalizability have debated whether the skills and criteria which constitute (part of) the reason assessment component are subject-specific, or rather are subject-neutral and capable of application across specific subjects or domains. There has been very little discussion of the generalizability of other dimensions of the reason assessment component. There has also been very little discussion of the generalizability of the critical spirit component. Both of these last two issues deserve more attention then they have received.

In what follows I hope to do three things. First, I will address the much discussed question concerning the generalizability of the skills and criteria which constitute an important part of the reason assessment component of critical thinking. Second, I will address the infrequently discussed question concerning the generalizability of other aspects of the reason assessment component. Third, I will address the infrequently discussed question concerning the generalizability of the critical spirit component of critical thinking. I will argue that all three questions should be answered in ways which provide comfort to the "generalists": those who hold that critical thinking is at least in some important respects generalizable. In the first section I will argue that the skills and criteria which constitute a portion of the reason assessment component are partly generalizable. On this question I think that the generalists and the "specifists" are both importantly right. In the second section I will argue that another aspect of the reason assessment component—the *epistemology underlying critical thinking*—is fully generalizable. In the third section I will argue that the critical spirit is also fully generalizable. In so arguing, I hope both to clarify further the extant debate concerning the generalizability of the skills of reason assessment, and also to point to two other important aspects of critical thinking which are generalizable. In so doing, I hope to broaden the focus of the initial question concerning the generalizability of critical thinking.

Before beginning the substantive discussion, I wish first to note an ambiguity which plagues much of the extant discussion concerning the generalizability of critical thinking. Principles and criteria of reason assessment may or may not be generalizable in the theoretical sense that they are general and so *applicable* across a wide range of cases or domains. Alternatively, they may or may not be generalizable in the practical sense that it is *pedagogically useful* to teach them, or expect them to transfer, across a wide portion of the curriculum. These issues are obviously distinct: the practical question concerning how we best teach for critical thinking is different from the abstract, theoretical question concerning the nature and applicability of the skills and criteria of reason assessment. McPeck and other specifists deny generalizability in both senses; Ennis and other generalists endorse generalizability in both senses. But McPeck's arguments against generalizability are typically addressed to the theoretical issue, while Ennis' arguments are typically addressed to the practi-cal, pedagogical one. (Ennis' advocacy of the "mixed" approach [Ennis 1989] is clearly addressed to the practical, pedagogical question of how best to teach for critical thinking.) This accounts, I think, for some of the cross-purposes, speaking-past-one-another character of the generalizability debate. In what follows my arguments for generalizability are aimed at the theoretical issue of applicability; I do not here address the pedagogical issue, though I agree with Ennis about it in the main. But it is important to realize that even if princi-ples of critical thinking are *general* in the sense that they are, theoretically, broadly applicable, it does not follow that they enjoy a high degree of transfer or are, pedagogically, usefully *generalizable*.[2]

THE GENERALIZABILITY OF THE SKILLS AND CRITERIA OF REASON ASSESSMENT

Rather than rehash old discussions, I will concentrate in this section on Robert Ennis' (Ennis 1989) recent discussion of this issue. Ennis' paper is, I think, enormously helpful, and, as advertised, it provides important clarifica-tion of several matters central to the generalizability issue. Since I agree with most of Ennis' discussion, I will only briefly describe his clarificatory achieve-ments. Where we disagree, I will argue that the situation is even more rosy for the generalists than Ennis supposes.

Ennis points out that "subject" is ambiguous in that it can mean either "topic" or "school subject"; while it is true that critical thinking is always thinking about some topic, it is false that it is always about some school sub-ject. Noting this ambiguity helps to block the erroneous inference: critical thinking always concerns some subject (topic); therefore teaching for critical thinking must take place in the context of teaching some (school) subject. Ennis also points to the vagueness of the terms "domain," "field," and "sub-ject," and notes that arguments for the subject specificity of critical thinking often founder on this vagueness. "Epistemological subject specificity"—the idea that different fields utilize different, incompatible criteria for the deter-mination of the goodness of reasons, so that what counts as a good reason in one field does not so count in another, and therefore that principles and skills of reason assessment must differ from field to field and so be taught in the con-text of the subject matter of each field—fails because of the vagueness of "field." If "field" is construed broadly—e.g., if "science" is a field—then it turns out that that field does not have principles of reason assessment unique to itself, since what counts as a good reason in science (for example, that the putative reason in question provides the best explanation of the phenomenon under consideration; or that it significantly increases the probability of the hypothesis being considered) often counts as a good reason both in other fields and in countless ordinary, everyday life contexts. Moreover, if "field" is construed broadly in this way, principles of reason assessment will differ across various sub-regions of the field (for example, a causal explanation may constitute a good reason in biology, but not in quantum mechanics). In these cases, reasons and principles of reason assessment are not field specific; and the thesis of epistemological subject specificity is false.

On the other hand, if "field" is construed narrowly, such that virtually every topic of inquiry is a "field" unto itself (e.g., the "field" of radio design, or radio tuning, or radio turning-off/on, or radio turning off, or radio turning off for a single radio), then the thesis of epistemological subject specificity is only trivially true, since a reason in one "field"—e.g., turning off my Sony portable radio because leaving it on might wake the baby—fails to be an equally powerful reason in the alternative "field" in which it is your Radio Shack tabletop model radio that needs to be turned off, only because of a willful neglect of common circumstances which make for the existence of good reasons across these artificially disparate "fields." Either way we interpret "field," then, the thesis of epistemological subject specificity—the claim that "in different fields 'different things constitute good reasons for various beliefs'"[3]—does not survive critical scrutiny.

Ennis agrees with McPeck that reasons and principles of reason assessment vary from field to field;[4] it is on this point that Ennis and I disagree. He regards this principle of "interfield variation" as "plausible" on the following grounds:

> (a) Mathematics has different criteria for good reasons from most other fields, because mathematics accepts only deductive proof, whereas most fields do not even seek it for the establishment of a final conclusion; (b) in the social sciences, statistical significance is an important consideration, whereas in many branches of physics it is largely ignored; (c) in the arts, some subjectivity is usually acceptable, whereas in the sciences, it is usually shunned. (Ennis 1989, p. 8)

Here Ennis I think fails to pay sufficient heed to his own earlier arguments concerning the vagueness of "field." For example, a growing portion of mathematics accepts nondeductive proof in the form of "brute force" computer programs which establish theorems by systematically examining enormous numbers of possible cases. In such cases we rely on inductive evidence that the computer functioned as planned, because the results of the programs are not checkable by human scrutiny for deductive validity—we rely, in effect, on inductive evidence concerning one computer-generated result proffered by another. Mathematicians have come to rely more and more on nondeductive reasons for accepting theorems as "proved." The famous computer proof of the Four Color Map Theorem is only one of many examples of such nondeductive proof (Tymoczko 1979). Contrary to Ennis' suggestion, reasons do not have to meet a single criterion—namely, that of deductively guaranteeing that for which they are reasons—in order to count as good reasons in mathematics. Mathematics is not a unitary "field" across which the same principles of reason assessment hold.[5]

Similarly, statistical significance is an important consideration in some but not all branches of the social sciences. (It is relatively unimportant, for example, in archeology, in some branches of economics, and in some branches of sociology.) The social sciences, too, fail to constitute a "field" across which specific principles of reason assessment univocally hold. Similar remarks could be made concerning the arts.

The point is not that these three areas are too large and varied to be properly considered as "fields"; for, even across such large fields as these, certain criteria for the constitution of good reasons are shared. For example, both in branches of mathematics (number theory, logic, proof theory, etc.) and in branches of the social sciences (e.g. economics and portions of sociology) good reasons must deductively establish their conclusions; in some social sciences and also in some areas of physics and engineering—and even in some approaches to literary analysis—some specific level of statistical significance is an important criterion which putative reasons must meet to be good. Moreover, in ordinary life contexts both of these criteria of reason assessment might be appropriately applied. The point, rather, is that criteria of reason assessment are complex and varied, and do not line up in any neat way with "fields," however the latter are individuated. The thesis of "interfield variation"—i.e., the thesis that certain criteria of reason assessment apply only within or across certain well-defined "fields," but that such criteria necessarily differ across fields—is false. Criteria of reason assessment are much more complicated than the thesis of interfield variation suggests. Some such criteria are very narrow in application; others are very broad and apply in virtually any context or "field."[6]

This point deserves additional comment. Ennis holds that "[e]pistemological subject specificity notes that there are significant interfield differences in what constitutes a good reason" (Ennis 1989, p. 9). Even if this were true—that is, even if it were true that differences in criteria of reason assessment varied systematically across fields—it would be a mistake to regard such a fact as establishing, as specifists such as McPeck (1981) and Toulmin (1958) regard it, that different fields have *their own epistemologies*.[7] It should rather be taken as a sign that different sorts of claims require different sorts of evidence for their establishment, but that these differences do not systematically vary across fields. To promote such differences into the status of "alternative epistemologies" is both to suggest systematic variation where there is none, and to ignore the crucial point that what varies is what it takes to establish claims of various sorts. Let us grant the undeniable: it takes *this* sort of evidence to establish *this*

31

sort of claim, and *that* sort of evidence to establish *that* sort of claim.[8] To say that we therefore have *two different epistemologies* at work here is to fail to distinguish between different epistemologies, and different criteria of reason assessment. When we have two different criteria of reason assessment, which we utilize to establish two different sorts of claims, we nevertheless have only one epistemology. In both cases, a good reason is that which warrants a conclusion. The *epistemology* across these alternative and varied criteria of reason assessment is the same.

Consider cases. My fuel gauge reading "E" (for empty) provides good reason for thinking that I am out of gas; the illuminated "idiot light" on my dashboard provides good reason for thinking that my door is ajar or my battery dead. This doesn't mean that fuel tanks and batteries have "different epistemologies." The very same sorts of reasons provide warrant in all sorts of different contexts (e.g., gauge readings of all sorts); standards of reason assessment stretch beyond "fields," whether construed as broadly as science or as narrowly as idiot lights. Moreover, differences in appropriate criteria of reason assessment do not translate into different epistemologies. Across alternative criteria of reason assessment is a unitary epistemology: reasons are good reasons if (and only if) they afford warrant to the claims or propositions for which they are reasons. Alternative criteria come into play according to the sort of claim under consideration, but they do so under the auspices of a common epistemology. Epistemology involves the study of the determination of the goodness of reasons. There are all sorts of good reasons—causal, inductive, explanatory, purposive, deductive, etc.—but they all share this crucial epistemic feature: they provide warrant for that for which they are reasons.

One might think that the preceding argument amounts to little more than a turf war over the word "epistemology," but it is not. Rather, it underlines two points which are central to the debate concerning the generalizability of critical thinking. First, while there are indeed different criteria of reason assessment by which we evaluate the power and convicting force, the goodness, of reasons, those criteria do not vary in any systematic way with "fields," however that latter notion is construed. All these alternative criteria—from "does the reason deductively establish the conclusion?" to "does the proposed explanation provide the best explanation of the phenomenon in question?," from "is this a representative sample?" to "is this the relevant sort of idiot light, such that its being illuminated indicates such-and-so?"—apply across a wide variety of school subject and/or ordinary life contexts. Second, we are entitled to regard these various criteria as appropriate criteria of reason assessment, and to appeal to them in order to establish or determine the goodness of putative reasons, only because they are sanctioned by a common epistemology: a theoretical understanding of the nature of reasons, according to which putative criteria are recognizable as appropriate criteria of reason assessment. To fail to acknowledge that even narrow, field- or context-relative criteria of reason assessment depend upon a common epistemology in order to count as appropriate criteria of reason assessment, is to ignore the possibility that putative reasons may only mistakenly be regarded as warrant-conferring.[9] To appeal to "epistemological subject specificity" in order to argue against the generalizability of critical thinking is to ignore the distinction between putative principles of reason assessment and the overarching epistemology which sanctions those principles as legitimate. It is to grant to "fields" the power to legislate the goodness of reasons within their own domains which they do not by themselves possess. A field may be the *partial* arbiter of the goodness of reasons within its domain, but it is not, and cannot be, the *sole* arbiter. To regard it as such is to reduce epistemology to a rubber stamp subject with no critical leverage or normative force of its own; it is to deny the very possibility that a field could be mistaken in regarding a putative criterion as legitimate within its domain.[10]

What are the ramifications of all this for the generalizability of critical thinking? The ramifications are favorable, on balance, for the generalist. The specifist's argument that critical thinking is not generalizable because of "epistemological subject specificity" fails: neither the skills nor the criteria of reason assessment line up neatly according to "fields," however broadly or narrowly these are defined; moreover, the plethora of criteria of reason assessment—though very varied in character, and ranging from the very narrow to the quite broad—are united by an underlying epistemology, which sanctions these criteria as legitimate. With all this, the generalist should be pleased.

I have not shown, however, that there are no skills or criteria of reason assessment which are narrow or subject-specific. There remains room to acknowledge the specifist's point, and to allow that some skills and criteria of reason assessment are narrow and specific. In this sense, both the generalist and the specifist are right.[11] Which criteria are specific, or best taught in the context of a school subject, I take to be an open question; I join Ennis in calling for empirical research into these matters. But I think that Ennis grants the "specifists" too much, in granting plausibility to "epistemological subject specificity." I hope to have strengthened Ennis' case against the specifist—I endorse his arguments against conceptual subject specificity, and I hope to have provided reason for being more skeptical of epistemological subject specificity than he apparently is—and to that extent, to have strengthened the case for the generalizability of a significant portion of the reason assessment component of critical thinking.[12]

THE GENERALIZABILITY OF THE EPISTEMOLOGY
UNDERLYING CRITICAL THINKING

I have been arguing against epistemological subject specificity, claiming mainly that skills and criteria of reason assessment do not, in general, function only within the context of specific subjects, fields, or domains. In making this argument, I have made reference to the unitary epistemology which I claim underlies and sanctions our regarding criteria of all sorts as appropriate criteria of reason assessment. I wish now to deepen the discussion of this underlying epistemology. I want to claim that this epistemology is an important part of the reason assessment component of critical thinking, and that it is fully generalizable. If I can make good on this claim, I will have strengthened further the generalist's position.

What is the epistemology underlying critical thinking? There is more to be said in answer to this question than I can say here. But briefly, the answer is this: as long as there is a reason assessment component to critical thinking, so that critical thinking is conceived as thinking which is appropriately guided by reasons, then critical thinking must be understood as requiring an epistemology which does justice to the central notions of reasons and rationality. Such an epistemology must (1) maintain a distinction between rational justification and truth, and hold that the critical thinker might justifiably believe that which is false, and unjustifiably believe that which is true. In other words, the epistemology underlying critical thinking must maintain a "radically nonepistemic" conception of truth, and hold that truth is independent of rational justification. (The theory of critical thinking, moreover, must regard critical thinking as aiming at rational justification rather than truth.) In addition, (2) it must reject relativism, and hold that (the goodness of reasons and) the rationality/justifiability of particular beliefs is "absolute" in that it does not vary across persons, times, cultures, and so on, but rather depends only on relevant criteria of reason assessment and the evidence for those beliefs at hand. Finally, (3) the epistemology underlying critical thinking must recognize (despite their independence, just noted) the following connection between truth and rational justification: the *upshot* of rational justification is a prima facie case for truth; rational justification is a *fallible* indicator of truth.[13]

The epistemology underlying critical thinking thus involves particular, and in some circles contentious, positions regarding reasons, criteria of reason assessment, rationality, rational justification, and truth. This epistemology requires an "absolutism" with respect to reasons and justification, a "radically nonepistemic" conception of truth, and an embrace of fallibilism. There is obviously much more to be said concerning all these points. However, I hope that I have elsewhere[14] secured the case for my claim that this complex of epistemological theses is required for a coherent conception of critical thinking, at least if critical thinking is to be regarded as a defensible educational ideal.

It should be clear that this epistemology is best seen as constituting part of the reason assessment component of critical thinking, since it underwrites our understanding of the proper assessment of reasons and our conception of reasons, rationality, and rational justification. It is a dimension of the reason assessment component of critical thinking which has nevertheless been neglected in most discussion of the generalizability of critical thinking, for that discussion has centered on the subject specificity of particular skills and principles of reason assessment and has mainly ignored the epistemology underlying those principles. We have before us, then, a portion of the reason assessment component of critical thinking which is distinct from the portion discussed in the preceding section concerning the putative subject specificity of particular skills, principles and criteria of reason assessment. We must therefore consider whether or not this newly introduced part of the reason assessment component, the part I have been calling "the epistemology underlying critical thinking," is generalizable.

Is the epistemology underlying critical thinking generalizable? Yes, it is a fully generalizable part of the reason assessment component of critical thinking. This epistemology provides the theoretical underpinning of our understanding of the principles and criteria of reason assessment to which we appeal when thinking critically. It is shared throughout the domains or fields in which critical thinkers assess reasons; it underlies our best conception of what critical thinking is. Indeed, this epistemology is presupposed by that conception of critical thinking; without it, we can make no coherent sense of critical thinking as an educational ideal concerning the proper assessment of reasons. The epistemology underlying critical thinking constitutes a part of the reason assessment component of critical thinking which is fully generalizable.[15] This, I take it, is good news for the generalist.

THE GENERALIZABILITY OF THE CRITICAL SPIRIT

There is yet a further component of critical thinking—the "critical spirit"—which has been by and large ignored in recent discussion of the generalizability of critical thinking. That it has been so ignored is surprising, given the near-unanimity of opinion in the theoretical literature concerning the centrality to critical thinking of the critical spirit.[16]

The "critical spirit," as I am using the term, refers to a complex of dispositions, attitudes, habits of mind, and character traits. It includes dispositions, for example the dispositions to seek reasons and evidence in making judgments and to evaluate such reasons carefully in accordance with relevant principles of reason assessment; attitudes, including a respect for the importance of reasoned judgment and for truth, and a rejection of partiality, arbitrariness, special pleading, wishful thinking, and other obstacles to the proper exercise of reason assessment and reasoned judgment; habits of mind consonant with these dispositions and attitudes, such as habits of reason seeking and evaluating, of engaging in due consideration of principles of reason assessment, of subjecting proffered reasons to critical scrutiny, and of engaging in the fairminded and non-self-interested consideration of such reasons; and character traits consonant with all of this. People who possess the critical spirit *value* good reasoning, and are disposed to believe, judge and act on its basis. It is this genuine valuing, and the dispositions, attitudes, habits of mind, and character traits which go with it, which constitute the core of the critical spirit.[17]

Is the critical spirit, so conceived, generalizable? It clearly is. The valuing of good reasoning and the desire and disposition to exercise reasoned judgment is not restricted to any domain or field; nor does it differ in character or substance from field to field. The dispositions, attitudes, and habits of mind constitutive of the critical spirit apply *generally*; the character traits constitutive of the critical spirit, like all character traits properly so called, are general and not restricted in application. It is only the fact that the debate over generalizability has been conceived as concerning skills and principles of reason assessment, rather than critical thinking more generally, that the generalizability of the critical spirit component of critical thinking has not been apparent. Once the question of the generalizability of this component of critical thinking is raised, however, it is answered in the obvious way: The critical spirit is *fully* generalizable.

CONCLUSION

I have argued that much of critical thinking is generalizable. First, I have joined with Ennis in arguing that "epistemological subject specificity" fails to secure the specifists' position. While it is true that there are many and varied criteria of reason assessment, some of which apply only to particular sorts of claims (which may but needn't occur only within some specific field), there is no systematic alignment of those criteria with particular subjects, fields, or domains, however those notions are defined or their referents individuated. What counts as a good reason for some claim depends not on the field in which the claim is made, but on the type of claim it is and the possible sorts of evidence to which one might legitimately appeal in attempting to establish it. The criteria to which we turn in order to evaluate the strength of the reasons and evidence offered for particular claims are neither bound to nor sanctioned by particular fields. They are not bound to such fields except in special, atypical cases in which the sort of claim being made can only be made in some particular field. Far more typical are criteria which extend across both fields and everyday reasoning: criteria of deductive validity, inductive strength, observational adequacy, explanatory power, etc. Nor are specialized criteria of reason assessment sanctioned solely by the fields to which they apply. If they were, there would be no possibility of critical scrutiny concerning the appropriateness of such criteria: each field would in such cases declare certain sorts of reasons to be good, and other sorts to be bad, but there would be no possibility of a field's being mistaken about its own understanding of its criteria of reason assessment. But that such mistakes are not only possible, but actual, is manifest—all we need to do in order to see this is to contemplate important, long-standing, difficult-to-resolve controversies concerning any intrafield debate.[18]

McPeck and other specifists are right in pointing out that subject specific *content knowledge* is frequently necessary for thinking critically within a subject. But this point adds little to the specifist's case: it is independent of epistemological subject specificity, on which the specifist's position depends and which, we have seen, is dubious; moreover, it is compatible with the generalist's position, and indeed is acknowledged by most generalists (e.g. Ennis 1989).

Moreover, the specifist fails to acknowledge the generalizability of the epistemology underlying critical thinking skills and criteria. Even if it were the case that criteria of reason assessment varied systematically by field, it is nevertheless also the case that the appropriateness of such criteria is determined not solely by the field in which the criteria are operative, but rather by (in addition to intrafield considerations) a more general theoretical understanding of the goodness of reasons, and of related issues concerning truth, fallibilism, rationality, and the like. This general theoretical understanding—the epistemology underlying critical thinking—is central to the coherent conceptualization of critical thinking, and is fully generalizable across the varied subjects, domains and fields to which critical thinking is relevant.

So too is the critical spirit component of critical thinking. The critical spirit is also fully generalizable across the varied landscape of critical thinking.

37

I hope, then, to have shed some additional light on the extant controversy concerning the generalizability of critical thinking, a controversy prompted by the argument against generalizability put forward on the basis of the thesis of "epistemological subject specificity." This thesis is vague, as Ennis suggests, almost certainly false, as I have argued, and the source of much mischief concerning our understanding of critical thinking and its generalizability. I hope, in addition, to have pointed to two aspects of critical thinking which have been wrongly neglected in the debate concerning generalizability. Both aspects—the epistemology underlying critical thinking, and the critical spirit—are integral to our overall conception of critical thinking. Both are fully generalizable.

While it is true, then, both that certain specialized criteria of reason assessment are restricted to particular fields, and that specialized content knowledge is frequently required in order to think critically, it seems nevertheless to be the case that critical thinking is overwhelmingly generalizable.

TEACHING, REASONING, AND DOSTOYEVSKY'S
THE BROTHERS KARAMAZOV

It is wrong always, everywhere, and for everyone, to
believe anything upon insufficient evidence.
— W. K. Clifford

The man who listens to reason is lost. Reason
enslaves all whose minds are not strong enough to
master her.
— George Bernard Shaw

chapter 3

PERHAPS THE GREATEST PHILOSOPHICAL NOVEL of the Western tradition, Fyodor
Dostoyevsky's *The Brothers Karamazov* raises and treats such fundamental issues
as the existence of God, the problem of evil, the relation between religion and
morality, the nature of morality, the relation between psychology and philosophy, the relations between motivation, explanation and justification, the conflict between reason and faith, the nature and power of rationality, and the role
of reason in human life. Dostoyevsky's great work does not simply raise such
issues, however. In treating them, it teaches us about them; we learn from the
novel, and understand more after reading it than before.

We might wonder how this teaching gets accomplished. After all, none of
the major characters are teachers, at least as that term is traditionally understood; there are no Gradgrinds or Miss Jean Brodies here. *The Brothers
Karamazov* teaches us, but it is not easy to say how. My aim in this chapter is

to examine the nature of the teaching of this text. In doing so, I will appeal to some philosophical accounts of teaching. But my main concern will be with the text itself: with the lessons it teaches us; and with the way those lessons are taught. I hope that the discussion will point beyond Dostoyevsky's novel, and suggest more general lessons concerning the pedagogical possibilities of (philosophical) fiction. In particular, I will urge that reasons and the fostering of rationality are central to teaching and to education more generally; that fiction affords access to a particular class or type of reasons—"felt" reasons — that are basic to rationality and that fiction is particularly well-suited to exploit and utilize; and that understanding the nature and role of such felt reasons in *The Brothers Karamazov* allows us to understand the brilliant way in which Dostoyevsky, who is himself the masterly teacher of this text, teaches us through it. In arguing for these points, I will be offering answers to several questions concerning the ways texts teach, including these: How can fiction teach? What are the pedagogical possibilities of fiction? What sorts of lessons can be taught? How can a work of fiction teach us contradictory lessons, as when different characters express contradictory viewpoints? How are the lessons of fiction, or literature more generally, different from more usual sorts of lessons? In answering these questions, I will be utilizing Dostoyevsky's novel to illustrate claims concerning successful fictional texts more generally: claims concerning the sorts of lessons they teach, and also the way in which those lessons are taught.

40

LESSONS OF THE TEXT
What is Taught, and How?

The Brothers Karamazov is so rich in philosophical wisdom that it is difficult to know where to begin an account of its lessons. Space permits consideration of only a small sample. My purposes will be served by focussing on Ivan's atheism and his struggle to adjudicate between belief and unbelief, and on Alyosha's fideistic response to Ivan.

Ivan Karamazov is a tortured atheist. He is an atheist in the straightforward sense that he denies the existence of a traditional god. But he is tortured because he wants, and in some sense needs, there to be such a god.[1] In Ivan we have the embodiment of the conflict between belief and unbelief. And we learn much from Dostoyevsky's portrayal of the confict.

Why does Ivan reject god? He offers at least two reasons. First, he is much moved by the problem of evil.[2] He cannot see how a loving god could permit the horrible and seemingly senseless suffering of which he cannot help but be aware. Ivan is particularly moved by the gratuitous suffering of children, victims who, because they are children, cannot in any way deserve to suffer or be guilty of any acts which warrant it. Ivan's chilling depiction of evil moves us in a way that few philosophical discussions could:

By the way, not so long ago a Bulgarian in Moscow told me . . . of the terrible atrocities committed all over Bulgaria by the Turks and Circassians who were afraid of a general uprising of the Slav population. They burn, kill, violate women and children, nail their prisoners' ears to fences and leave them like that till next morning when they hang them, and so on—it's impossible to imagine it all. And, indeed, people sometimes speak of man's "bestial" cruelty, but this is very unfair and insulting to the beasts: a beast can never be so cruel as a man, so ingeniously, so artistically cruel. A tiger merely gnaws and tears to pieces, that's all he knows. It would never occur to him to nail men's ears to a fence and leave them like that overnight, even if he were able to do it. These Turks, incidentally, seemed to derive a voluptuous pleasure from torturing children, cutting a child out of its mother's womb with a dagger and tossing babies up in the air and catching them on a bayonet before the eyes of their mothers. It was doing it before the eyes of their mothers that made it so enjoyable. But one incident I found particularly interesting. Imagine a baby in the arms of a trembling mother, surrounded by Turks who had just entered her house. They are having great fun: they fondle the baby, they laugh to make it laugh and they are successful: the baby laughs. At that moment the Turk points a pistol four inches from the baby's face. The boy laughs happily, stretches out his little hands to grab the pistol, when suddenly the artist pulls the trigger in the baby's face and blows his brains out. . . . Artistic, isn't it? Incidentally, I'm told the Turks are very fond of sweets. (Dostoyevsky [1958], pp. 278–9)

This passage is only one of several that could be cited here to good effect. Ivan is full of stories of the torture of children.[3] It is for him the most troubling sort of suffering; a vivid type of evil most difficult to reconcile with the existence of god. And Ivan stops short a common variant of the "free will defense" theodicy with the following plaintive worry:

Can you understand why all this absurd and horrible business [i.e. the suffering Ivan has just depicted] is so necessary and has been brought to pass? They tell me that without it man could not even have existed on earth, for he would not have known good and evil. But why must we know that confounded good and evil when it costs so much? Why, the whole world of knowledge isn't worth that child's tears to her "dear and kind God!" I'm not talking of the sufferings of grown-up people, for they have eaten the apple and to hell with them—let them all go to hell, but these little ones, these little ones! (p. 283)

Ivan thus rejects the idea that knowledge of good and evil is somehow worthy of the suffering that pays for it, as theodicists sometimes suggest. It is, as he says, simply not worth it. But there is a further point regarding suffering that Ivan makes, a point which in its way is more powerful still. It is this: any successful theodicy must maintain a fully adequate conception of the horror of suffering. Belittling it, for example by noting its short duration in time compared to the infinitely long eternal bliss awaiting us in heaven, or arguing that suffering can be accounted for by noting its necessity, will not do. One must, according to Ivan, cling to the fact of suffering; explaining it does not explain it away. Unspeakable suffering is part of the fabric of our world; our understanding of the world must fully acknowledge both its ubiquity and its horror. (pp. 283–288) But such a world is not only incomprehensible to Ivan's "Euclidean mind"; it is also morally unjustifiable and unacceptable. So Ivan rejects this world which god offers him:

> We cannot afford to pay so much for admission. And therefore I hasten
> to return my ticket of admission. . . . It is not God that I do not accept,
> Alyosha. I merely most respectfully return him the ticket. (p. 287)

The problem of evil, and the ubiquity of suffering, thus constitute a powerful set of reasons for Ivan to reject belief in an all-loving god, to "return the ticket." But Ivan offers another complex of reasons as well. These occur in the context of the celebrated "Grand Inquisitor." In his story, his "poem," of the Grand Inquisitor, which Dostoyevsky regarded as "the culminating point of my literary activity,"[4] Ivan complains bitterly of god's refusal or failure to provide for humans on earth for the sake of a terrible freedom which guarantees human unhappiness; he laments again the enormous price god asks us to pay for our faith.

Ivan presents, then, a powerful case for atheism. Yet, despite himself, he is tortured by his atheism. Ivan wants, desperately wants, for there to be a god. Why? Ivan is much moved by moral sentiments, and is painfully aware of the possibility that if there is no god, then "everything is permitted." This is a pervasive theme in Dostoyevsky's work: god is necessary to ground morality. Yet god's existence cannot be reconciled with the contrary evidence which is evident to Ivan's "Euclidean mind." And so Ivan is consumed by his conflict between belief and unbelief; as the novel draws to a close Ivan is driven mad by his philosophical, yet visceral, ambivalence.[5] It is difficult to imagine a philosophical idea or dispute portrayed more powerfully in a work of fiction. Dostoyevsky makes the philosophical issue come alive, and demonstrates the enormous role it can play in a life—not just in an armchair or at the blackboard. *The Brothers Karamazov* teaches a very powerful lesson concerning the place of philosophy in individual human lives.

Even Alyosha, Ivan's younger brother and the main representative and

42

defender of faith in the novel, occasionally doubts god's existence.[6] Nevertheless, Alyosha, who Dostoyevsky regards (perhaps problematically)[7] as the hero of the novel,[8] rises above his doubts and, unlike Ivan, embraces both god and the suffering world of god's creation. Alyosha (and Father Zossima) is (are) not stupid or unaware of Ivan's reasons for his atheism; nor does he reject or try to rebut those reasons. He simply accepts them. And he accepts god's existence, and goodness, as well. For Zossima, the quiet joy of faith is sufficient to dispel both Ivan's atheistic arguments and the torture of his soul; for Alyosha, god's existence, goodness and salvation are accepted, and made basic to his life, despite their admittedly problematic status from the point of view of a "Euclidean mind," i.e. from the point of view of reason. Alyosha's faith thus stands in the novel as an answer to Ivan's atheism.

In this way Dostoyevsky portrays not only the conflict between belief and unbelief, but also the more general conflict between faith and reason. Again, his portrayal is masterly: in the character of Ivan the force of reason comes alive with dramatic intensity and urgency; in Alyosha the strength of faith and the possibility of a higher wisdom which elevates faith over reason are also powerfully presented. And of course we know, both from the text and from other sources, that Dostoyevsky stands firmly with Alyosha and faith. By the end of the novel Ivan, though sympathetically presented, is driven mad by reason and his tortured conflict; Alyosha ends not only on his feet but as the object of the final spoken dialogue of the novel, "Hurrah for Karamazov!," shouted by the boys who have come to love him. To the critics, moreover, who suggest that Dostoyevsky lost his way in siding with Alyosha's simplistic faith instead of with Ivan's powerful atheism, the author sneers:

> The dolts have ridiculed my obscurantism and the reactionary character of my faith. These fools could not even conceive so strong a denial of God as the one to which I gave expression [through Ivan] . . . The whole book is an answer to that. . . . You might search Europe in vain for so powerful an expression of atheism. Thus it is not like a child that I believe in Christ and confess Him. My hosanna has come forth from the crucible of doubt.[9]

There are many other philosophical questions explored in *The Brothers Karamazov* besides the ones so far discussed. In addition to theism versus atheism and faith versus reason, the novel raises questions about the relationship between reason and emotion,[10] between religion and morality, and even about the willingness of belief.[11] I beg the reader's pardon for not discussing Dostoyevsky's treatment of these further questions, and of Mitya, Smerdyakov, and the rest of Dostoyevsky's fabulous cast of philosophical characters. Instead, I wish to redirect our attention to the pedagogical questions with which we began. What is taught, in the novel, and how are we taught? I have suggested that we are taught many lessons: that god's existence is irreconcilable with the suffering of children; that it is possible to accept Ivan's atheistic arguments and still accept god; that the relationship between religion and morality is fundamental; that philosophical perplexity is and ought to be, as Socrates suggested, at the center of human life; and so on. Now this raises a problem. For not only are some of these lessons controversial; some contradict others—for example, we cannot accept both Ivan's atheistic lesson and Alyosha's theistic one—and so some must be false. (Moreover, there is excellent reason, independent of contradiction, for regarding some of these lessons as false: for example, the thesis that religion grounds morality.) Does it make sense to say that in reading *The Brothers Karamazov* we are taught falsehoods? How can contradictory lessons be taught? What, more generally, is the relationship between teaching and truth (falsity)? In order to answer such questions as these, we must step back from the novel and say something about the nature of teaching. I beg the reader's indulgence, then, for the following detour from Dostoyevsky's text, through the seemingly distant terrain of philosophical considerations concerning teaching. I hope that when we rejoin the main route of our journey, the relevance of the detour will be apparent.

THE RATIONALITY THEORY OF TEACHING

What is it to teach? Which characteristics of teaching episodes should we applaud; which should we condemn? What should teachers strive to achieve? What should they strive to be? Should teaching be conceived primarily as a matter of modelling? Must teaching be didactic? Socratic? Should it inspire by example? There is no shortage of answers to such questions. Many such answers, however, are bad ones. I wish to recommend a conception of teaching in which rationality is central; this conception is known in the philosophy of education literature as "the rationality theory of teaching." Perhaps the best way to approach the rationality theory is by contrasting it with another theory, popular in some educational circles. I refer here to what may be called (to name its fault) the "teacher as automaton" conception.

According to the "teacher as automaton" conception of teaching, the teacher is not thought of as an intellectual engager of the student, who encourages and honors the student's developing critical awareness or engages the student's intellect with her own. Rather, the teacher is thought of as a quasi-programmed technician, capable of exemplifying specific standard behaviors but not of utilizing judgment. Because of the widespread embrace of the teacher as automaton conception—as manifested in educational panaceas such as performance/competency based teacher education and "teacher-proof" curricula—it is perhaps worth a brief look at the difficulties which accrue to that conception.

Can the teacher be thought of as a mindless accomplice in the carrying out of education programs conceived by others? She can—the evidence is that she is often so conceived—but not unproblematically so. Israel Scheffler, who criticizes this conception, characterizes the teacher according to it as

> a minor technician within an industrial process. The overall goals are set in advance in terms of national needs, the curricular materials prepackaged by the disciplinary experts, the methods developed by educational engineers—and the teacher's job is just to supervise the last operational stage, the methodological insertion of ordered facts into the student's mind. Teacher competence is to be judged (at most) in terms of academic mastery and pedagogical dexterity, and teacher education becomes identified with training in the subject, coupled with training in the approved methods of teaching. (Scheffler [1973], p. 61)

As Scheffler's discussion makes clear, there is much to disapprove of here. First, the conception of the teacher as a mindless technician or automaton is a degrading one; the clear suggestion is that students have to be protected from their teachers, for their teachers lack the wherewithal to conceive and participate in interactions which will be of benefit to the students. The idea of "teacher-proof" curricula, however well-meaning and concerned about students the proponent of that idea might be, is insulting to teachers. But the problems with the "teacher as automaton" conception go far beyond the drawbacks of being degrading and insulting to teachers, important as these problems are. That conception presupposes as well an inadequate conception of students, and of education more generally.

Should teachers be thought of as performers; as persons who have mastered certain specific behavioral repertoires? It would be comforting if teachers could be happily so thought of, for it would make the task of education easier: figure out what students should learn; determine which teacher performances or behaviors facilitate such learning; and train teachers to master those behaviors. The world, alas, is not so simple as this educational vision suggests; nor is the vision itself defensible. First, it is not the case that certain behaviors routinely result in predictable outcomes. Identical teacher behaviors may, in diverse circumstances, give rise to radically different student outcomes. Speaking sharply may helpfully chasten an unruly student on one occasion, but further antagonize a similar student on another; repeating the item to be learned in slightly different language may helpfully reinforce an idea for a student and so foster learning in one case, yet bore another student to tears and so discourage learning in another. It is simply a mistake to think that any particular set of behaviors or performances, no matter how subtly conceived or context-specifically specified, can be "programmed into" the teacher with the

45

result that those behaviors or performances will reliably foster learning or desirable dispositions or habits of mind. Teachers must, on the contrary, be able to "read" students and situations, and use their judgment, in order effectively to determine both the activities which will most likely further educational aims and the way in which those activities ought to be carried out. Teacher judgment, moreover, while central to effective teaching, cannot be reduced to or conceived in terms of behavior or performance.[12]

Perhaps more importantly, the conception of teacher as automaton also presupposes that *students* are automata, and that educational content is programmable. For the idea that certain teacher behaviors will reliably result in predictable student outcomes presupposes that students bring nothing (or without exception bring the same predictable, manipulable things) to the teacher-student interchange, and passively await restructuring as the result of the exposure to teacher behavior. Such a view of students utterly misses the fact that students are persons, with hopes, fears, desires, interests, dispositions, talents, and potentials, who interpret and react to teachers in highly individual ways. To view students as amenable to shaping by teacher behavior is to view students as inert objects; it is to deny their humanity.[13]

To view students in this way is also to misconceive the nature of educational content and the point of teacher-student interaction. Students can be seen as capable of benefiting from mindless teacher behavior only if that benefit consists in the learning of facts and information and the mastery of specific behaviors. For if the student is programmable, then educational content must admit of being put in program form. This view of educational content, however, ignores our most cherished aspirations for students. For we want students not only to master specific behaviors and bits of information; we want them, more importantly, to be certain sorts of persons—to have certain sorts of dispositions, habits of mind, attitudes, and characters, in addition to a wide variety of skills, abilities, and significant knowledge. All of this requires a view of students which takes much more seriously the independent intellectual life of the student than the "student as programmable automaton" conception does. And this, in turn, requires a far richer conception of the teacher than the "teacher as automaton" conception. For the teacher must herself live a far more complex intellectual life than that conception allows, if she is to interact educatively with students who themselves live such lives. Taking seriously the idea that students ought to be helped to foster the abilities, dispositions and character traits associated with the critical thinker requires a conception of the teacher which places her independent judgment and rationality at the center of her activities as a teacher. The critical abilities and propensities of teachers and students, and their stature as educational desiderata and centrality as elements of educational content, doom any conception of teachers which portrays them as mindless automata, technicians, or preprogrammed performers.

The rationality of teachers must be acknowledged as central to their identity as teachers, and to any adequate conception of teaching.[14]

Thus we come to the rationality theory of teaching, which places the offering and exchange of reasons at the center of teaching activities:

> To teach ... is at some points at least to submit oneself to the understanding and independent judgment of the pupil, to his demand for reasons, to his sense of what constitutes an adequate explanation. To teach someone that such and such is the case is not merely to try to get him to believe it: deception, for example, is not a method or a mode of teaching. Teaching involves further that, if we try to get the student to believe that such and such is the case, we try also to get him to believe it for reasons that, within the limits of his capacity to grasp, are *our* reasons. Teaching, in this way, requires us to reveal our reasons to the student and by so doing, to submit them to his evaluation and criticism. ... To teach is thus ... to acknowledge the "reason" of the pupil, i.e. his demand for and judgment of reasons ... (Scheffler [1960], pp. 57–58, emphasis in original)[15]

According to the rationality theory of teaching, then, teaching is best regarded as a very special mode of belief-inculcation. We can inculcate beliefs in many different ways—e.g. by torture, brainwashing, lying, conditioning, propaganda, manipulation, indoctrination, peer pressure, etc.—but for acts of belief-inculcation to count as teaching acts, the offering of reasons, the fostering of reason-assessment abilities and reason-honoring dispositions, and the respecting of the demand of the student for reasons to justify and guide belief and action, must be taken as central.

This is a superficial account of the rationality theory of teaching, to be sure. In the present context, a fuller discussion would be inappropriate.[16] I wish now to return to *The Brothers Karamazov*, equipped with the rationality theory of teaching, in order to pursue further our earlier questions concerning the pedagogical dimensions of that work.

FELT REASONS

We left off our discussion of the novel by asking whether it made sense to say that it taught us contradictory, and so false, lessons. Given the rationality theory of teaching, the answer is clear, and clearly affirmative. For we are given reasons —powerful reasons—for the several lessons offered. It is an epistemological commonplace that justified beliefs can be false; that p's being backed by good reasons is compatible with p's being false.[17] So it makes perfectly good sense to say that we learn lessons, for example, concerning both atheism and theism; concerning both the power of reason and the force of faith. We learn about these positions, and about the reasons which support them, even though we know that not all the positions learned about—all the lessons learned—can be true.

Upon reflection, this is not surprising. In a typical philosophy class, for example, we might be taught, and learn, about reasons which support realism as well as reasons which support constructive empiricism, or which support free will as well as determinism. That is, we can learn that mutually incompatible positions each enjoy the support of good reasons; insofar as we adopt the rationality theory of teaching, such learning can be said to be the result of teaching. For on that theory, teaching requires the giving of reasons for views entertained, so that such views enjoy at least some substantial measure of justification. Teaching does not, however, require that that which is taught be true. Thus it permits that we can be taught that which is false.

The rationality theory of teaching thus resolves the difficulty of the novel teaching contradictory, and so false, lessons. For on that theory it is possible to teach lessons which are in some measure supported by reasons. Some such lessons may be false, and some such may contradict others. Given the rationality theory of teaching, then, there is no problem in saying that *The Brothers Karamazov* teaches us powerful lessons, some of which contradict others, and some of which are false.

But the rationality theory needs to be expanded, or supplemented, in order fully to account for Dostoyevsky's power as a teacher, and to answer the other questions raised earlier concerning the lessons of philosophical fiction. For "reasons" must be understood more broadly than simply as considerations which stand in logical, or epistemological, or propositional relationships to lessons taught, if we are to identify the special genius of Dostoyevsky's teaching in *The Brothers Karamazov*, or satisfactorily answer the questions concerning fiction and pedagogy raised earlier. In order to do all this, I wish to introduce the notion of *felt* reasons.

The reasons that Dostoyevsky presents to us through his characters for the various lessons taught in the text are not particularly original or forceful, if taken out of the context of the novel. To take just one example, the reasons offered by Ivan for doubting the existence of a good or loving god—reasons which focus on the existence of evil, and especially on the unnecessary pain and suffering of innocent and undeserving children—are old and familiar to students of philosophy. Philosophers as early as Epicurus raised precisely Ivan's reasons in arguing against the existence of an all-powerful, all-good god; and throughout the history of philosophy the problem of evil has played a central role in deliberations concerning god's existence. What is so powerful, then, about Dostoyevsky's presentation of the problem of evil?

The answer, I think, has to do with the visceral quality reasons sometimes have; with the impact that reasons sometimes have on us as feeling persons. We *feel* the force of reasons in some circumstances in entirely different ways than we feel the force of (what are propositionally) the same reasons in other circumstances. This can be illustrated simply by considering the differences in our reactions to the problem of evil as it is treated in, for example, Hume's *Dialogues Concerning Natural Religion*, or the essays (besides Dostoyevsky's) in Pike's (1964) *God and Evil*, and in *The Brothers Karamazov*. While all three treatments are powerful in their way, there is a visceral, or felt, quality to Dostoyevsky's treatment which is manifested to a lesser extent in (or absent entirely from) the others, and indeed is absent more or less universally throughout standard philosophical treatments of the problem of evil. It is to this visceral quality of some reasons that I wish to point with talk of "felt reasons."

I want to suggest that the conception of reasons we utilize in characterizing the rationality theory of teaching, and the role of reasons in education more generally, be broadened to include felt reasons. For felt reasons, I want to argue, have a particularly important role to play in education, especially in education which aims at the fostering of rational dispositions, attitudes and abilities in students. I want to suggest, further, that it is the special characteristics and possibilities of felt reasons which underlie the particular forcefulness of teachings such as Dostoyevsky's, and that, more generally, it is felt reasons which are at the heart of the particular and unique pedagogical virtues of fiction, and the notion through which we best answer the questions raised at the outset concerning the pedagogical possibilities of fiction. Let me develop these two suggestions in turn.

I have argued above that a central aim of education is the fostering of rationality in students, and that a well-educated student/person is one who is, at least, *appropriately moved by reasons*. In the course of arguing for this view, I have urged that students be helped to develop the skills, dispositions and attitudes which enable them to be so moved. On this view students ought to be helped to develop appropriate skills of reason assessment, so that they can competently evaluate putative reasons and distinguish good reasons from weak or spurious ones; they should also be encouraged to develop attitudes of reasonableness and the disposition to be moved by reasons so evaluated: to be disposed to seek reasons on which to base beliefs and actions; and to believe and act on the basis of reasons they have themselves submitted to rational scrutiny. On this view of education, it is crucial that students become sensitive to reasons. In speaking of enhancing the "reason-sensitivity" of students, I mean to suggest simply that students be helped to understand that reasons are sometimes powerful directors of belief and action, and have enormous probative and normative force. For example, in recognizing that the problem of evil provides a very good reason for doubting the existence of an all-powerful, all-good god, we ought to recognize that continued belief in such a god—absent countervailing considerations in favor of such a god's existence, or opposed to the force of the problem of evil—is not appropriate. Thus we should be *appro-*

priately moved by reasons: we should believe and act on the basis of proper evaluation of the probative force of reasons bearing on the relevant possibilities for belief and action. But we should be appropriately *moved* by reasons as well: once we have examined the relative strengths and weaknesses of reasons relevant to possible beliefs and actions, we should believe and act accordingly. Felt reasons are relevant to both these dimensions of the role of reasons in education.

The *appropriateness* of being "appropriately moved by reasons" involves ascertaining the evidential or probative force of reasons offered for some claim, belief, or action; I am *appropriately* moved by reasons if my assessment of alternative beliefs and actions and the reasons offered to support them correctly evaluates the evidential or probative force those reasons in fact have. I am appropriately *moved*, on the other hand, if my actual beliefs and actions properly reflect the probative force of reasons: if my beliefs and actions accord with the weight of reasons relevant to candidate beliefs and actions; if I recognize the normative force that the reasons in question have. Thus appropriateness involves the assessment of evidential or probative force and the proper weighing of reasons, while movement involves the recognition of the normative force or impact of reasons. This distinction between the *probative force* and the *normative impact* of reasons is crucial, I think, to a proper understanding of the complexity of being "appropriately moved by reasons." Let me attempt to clarify it by noting the relationship of felt reasons to each disjunct.

Felt reasons are relevant to our being *appropriately* moved by reasons in that they can sensitize us to the idea that reasons have different probative weights (and so normative force). A fundamental lesson of an education aimed at the cultivation of rationality is that reasons differ: not all putative reasons are genuine ones; good reasons are more powerful than bad ones; and some putative reasons are spurious and have no evidential or probative force at all. To learn this lesson is immediately to recognize the importance of evaluating reasons: to inquire into the merits and strengths of reasons offered in support of candidate beliefs and actions. This lesson then paves the way for the study of the appropriateness of reasons, and for the development of skills of reason assessment. In sum: felt reasons, by impressing upon us the force that reasons sometimes have, can help to convey to students the fundamental lesson that the relative merits of reasons differ, and so to shed light on the importance of becoming a practiced and competent evaluator of reasons and their evidential/probative force. They can thus shed light on the importance of being *appropriately* moved by reasons.

Felt reasons are even more crucial, I think, to our coming to understand the importance of being appropriately *moved* by reasons. They can help us, that is, to grasp the *normative impact* of reasons. Ivan helps us to see why we should not believe in god, given the suffering of innocent children. Alyosha helps us to see how belief in god is possible, despite Ivan's worries. The point here is simple—felt reasons can move students, and in doing so convey the lesson that reasons have normative impact and should be seen as "movers" of belief and action—but it has, I think, an important educational ramification. We should take as an important educational objective the enhancing of the "reason-sensitivity" of students; that is, we should strive to help them to be open to, and to recognize, reasons. The sensitizing of students to the nature, force, and role of reasons, and the circumstances in which reasons have force and relevance, should be seen as a basic educational activity, and one in which felt reasons have a special role to play.

This point may be illuminated through an analogy with moral education. It is a commonplace that a major goal of moral education is the enhancement of moral sensitivity and empathy, so as to foster the appreciation of moral reasons. Seeing a consideration as a powerful moral reason often depends on being able to empathize with those in the moral situation at hand, or on being aware of and sensitive to the legitimate interests and needs of moral agents. Being insensitive thus harms one's ability to grasp, and participate in, morally charged situations. So an important dimension of moral education is the fostering of the sensitivity required to appreciate properly moral reasons. Similarly, I want to suggest, education ought to foster students' sensitivity and openness to reasons more generally: to help develop the abilities and dispositions to recognize reasons, to seek them, to evaluate them, and, most importantly in the present context, to be moved by them. For just as the student whose lack of moral sensitivity renders her a less competent moral agent and a morally less well-educated person, a student who lacks sensitivity to reasons generally, and especially the disposition to be appropriately *moved* by reasons, is similarly hampered and ill-served by her education. And felt reasons, I am suggesting, can be particularly useful in conveying the lesson that reasons appropriately *move* persons. They can help students to recognize and be open to reasons, and also to be moved by them.[18]

How can felt reasons sensitize students to reasons and their normative, directing character; their moving force? Most fundamentally, felt reasons can have this effect when characters are convincingly and sympathetically portrayed as persons who are themselves so moved.[19] In showing the reader that a character (with whom the reader is already familiar) is herself moved by some reasons, and in showing the way that the character regards those reasons as warranting movement, an author is not simply evaluating the probative or evidential force of those reasons. (Indeed the author may not be doing this at all.) The author is, rather, connecting those reasons to characters who feel their force. The reader, in this sort of circumstance, sees the relationship drawn between the reasons and a person, a personality, who recognizes the relevance of those reasons to her own beliefs and actions, and modifies those beliefs and actions in light of those reasons. Thus Ivan's life is more or less completely colored by his worries about evil; his reasons for rejecting god are so deeply felt that they make any stance besides rejection impossible for Ivan to adopt. This rejection ends up tragically in Ivan's case, but that merely underscores the force his reasons have to move him. Alyosha's reasons for accepting god, despite evil, also function in the novel to move him to act, and live, in accordance with them. In general, fiction can, and good philosophical fiction does, illustrate the force that reasons have to move people who feel that force. In so doing, fiction can convey, perhaps more effectively than other media, the fundamental lesson that reasons can and do—and *should*—move people to whom they are relevant.

But what are "felt" reasons? Are they some weird sort of abstract entity, altogether different from more garden variety sorts of reasons? I would be remiss if I did not close this section by pointing out that felt reasons are not different in kind or ontological status from ordinary propositional reasons. Felt reasons, rather, are ordinary reasons whose power to move people is made obvious or manifest by the way in which those reasons, and the person for whom they are reasons, are portrayed. Felt reasons are not a different *kind* of reason; they are rather a particular kind of *presentation* of reasons. In having their moving force portrayed, felt reasons can be helpful in generating in students a sensitivity to reasons, and a recognition of their normative, directing power; they can help, consequently, in developing in students the disposition to be moved by reasons. And as I have suggested, this disposition is basic to education. Literature is perhaps the most effective way of teaching this lesson and of developing this disposition. So literature can contribute to education by utilizing felt reasons so as to foster a general disposition to be moved by reasons.[20] We need, still, to connect this discussion of felt reasons more directly to Dostoyevsky's great novel. To this let us now turn.

TEACHING, REASONS, AND *THE BROTHERS KARAMAZOV*

We have seen that it makes perfect sense to say that *The Brothers Karamazov* teaches us contradictory lessons. Who teaches us these lessons? In one sense, it is the characters themselves who are the teachers. Ivan teaches Alyosha about the force of the problem of evil. Alyosha in turn teaches Ivan something of the nature of faith and mystery.[21] And of course both of them teach us, the readers. While none of the characters in the novel portray classroom teachers, many of them are self-conscious "lesson-conveyers" and are rightfully thought of as teachers, though not as classroom teachers. There is no compelling reason to be fussy about bureaucratic form; while there are no characters in the novel who occupy the social role of teacher, it is clear that many of them are nonetheless teachers. So it makes perfectly good sense to regard Dostoyevsky's characters as the teachers in this text.[22]

On the other hand, it is clear that Dostoyevsky himself is the teacher of this text. The author of a text that teaches teaches her readers, utilizing the text as a vehicle for the lessons taught. This is especially clear once we ask how the text teaches. For this sort of text, the lessons are taught primarily through the use of the pedagogical device[23] of felt reasons—a device not available to non-novelists, or to lesser ones. No matter how good a Philosophy 101 teacher I am, I cannot, by discussing arguments for and against atheism (for example), convey what it feels like to suffer Ivan's torment, nor Zossima's simple faith, nor Alyosha's somewhat less simple faith.[24] Such awareness of felt reasons, though perhaps not central to the philosophy class, should nevertheless be regarded as relevant to a full understanding of the matter at hand. Felt reasons, in other words, are reasons; it is the special virtue of the philosophical novel that it can effectively convey such reasons. In so doing it deepens our understanding of whatever issue we are fretting over. Thus Dostoyevsky's novel contributes mightily to our understanding of (e.g.) the problem of evil—even though in the end it still falls to philosophers (or, more exactly, competent evaluators of philosophical reasons), equipped with the understanding gleaned from efforts like Dostoyevsky's, to determine the force of reasons, felt and other, regarding faith and evil.

The novel, I am suggesting, can add to our understanding of philosophical issues, by making clear to us the motivations and felt reasons undergirding alternative views. A very fine novelist can make such reasons come alive, and drive home sorts of reasons not open to more conventional modes of teaching. In a masterful philosophical novel, such as *The Brothers Karamazov*, the contributions the novel makes to our understanding can be great indeed. We do learn—a lot—from Dostoyevsky's novel. Not only do we learn from the novel, we are taught by it. Who then is the teacher? The answer should be clear. Characters who are teachers may be teachers in texts. But authors are teachers *of* texts. Dostoyevsky himself is the masterful teacher of this text.[25]

How does Dostoyevsky teach us? By offering felt reasons: by portraying characters who are themselves moved by reasons, Dostoyevsky moves us. He conveys to us the probative force and normative impact which reasons have; this is the broad role I have argued that felt reasons can play in an education centered on the fostering of rationality and critical thought. He conveys to us as well the particular force which the reasons offered in the text have; in this way Dostoyevsky teaches us lessons concerning theism, evil, faith, reason, and so on. We are moved by Ivan's reasons, and Alyosha's reasons, as they are themselves moved by each other's.[26]

What does Dostoyevsky teach us? Obviously, he teaches us lessons concerning atheism, theism, faith, morality, psychology, and the nature and scope of reason itself. Educationally, he teaches us that these "big" questions and issues are crucial to life, and so ought to be part of a general education; they *should* be considered in ordinary classrooms.[27] These lessons are significant, and are not to be dismissed. His ultimate lesson is, however, different. In telling his tale, Dostoyevsky masterfully demonstrates literature's ability to bring reasons to life, to make us *feel* the force of reasons. In so doing, he makes philosophical questions come alive. The ultimate lesson of this novel—presented so powerfully that even the most casual reader cannot help but be grabbed by it—is that philosophy itself lives, and enriches life. *The Brothers Karamazov* teaches us, in a way that even Socrates couldn't, that philosophy matters. It is Dostoyevsky's genius that he could teach us this lesson that way.[28]

NOT BY SKILL ALONE

The Centrality of Character to Critical Thinking

Men are apt to mistake the strength of their feeling
for the strength of their argument. The heated mind
resents the chill touch and relentless scrutiny of logic.
—William Gladstone

... [T]o call an argument illogical, or a proposition
false, is a special kind of moral judgment.
—Charles Sanders Peirce

chapter 4

IN HER CHALLENGING PAPER (1990), Connie Missimer argues that "a view
dominant among theoreticians of critical thinking" (145),[1] according to
which critical thinking involves not only thinking skills, but character traits,
attitudes, dispositions, habits of mind and character traits as well—which
complex I have labelled above the "critical spirit"—is badly flawed. Missimer
contrasts this dominant view, which she labels the "Character View," with her
preferred alternative conception of critical thinking and the critical thinker—
which she labels the "Skill View"—according to which critical thinking is a
matter of skill alone, and does not involve any aspect of the critical spirit.[2]
Missimer argues that the Character View has important defects, that the Skill
View has important advantages over its rival, and that therefore the Skill View
is a more adequate conception of critical thinking than the Character View.

In what follows I examine Missimer's arguments against the Character

View, and in support of the Skill View. I argue that most of those arguments fail, that Missimer fails to address important arguments against the Skill View and in favor of the Character View, and that the dominant view is justifiably dominant, in that it is a more adequate conception of critical thinking than Missimer's recommended alternative.[3]

WHAT'S WRONG WITH THE CHARACTER VIEW?

According to Missimer, the Character View suffers from a number of defects. First, the various dispositions and character traits which make it up, and the interrelationships between them, are not adequately specified. Second, those dispositions and character traits are characterized differently by different theorists, with the result that different accounts of the Character View appear to be inconsistent with one another. Third, and most important, the Character View appears to have the unpalatable (to Missimer) result that a significant number of "celebrated" (147) and "great" (148) thinkers, indeed "intellectual giants" (145), turn out on it not to be critical thinkers at all. Fourth, the Character View "smuggle[s] in moral prescriptions" (145) to its conception of critical thinking, thus making those prescriptions liable to uncritical acceptance. Let us consider these alleged defects in turn.

The Relevant Character Traits Are Inadequately Specified

Missimer is I think right about this. To take her examples (146), it is unclear how much patience a reasoner must have, or just how impartial a reasoner must be, in order for her to be rightly said to possess the relevant character traits. But it is far from clear that this is a serious criticism of the Character View. For one thing, such traits as these are notoriously difficult to measure or quantify; as Aristotle urged, we ought not to strive for a standard of precision inappropriate to the subject matter involved. For another, the having of these character traits is clearly a matter of degree; the Character View typically treats them as ideals to be aimed at, and as only imperfectly achieved even by superior critical thinkers (Siegel [1988], p. 47; p.153 note 34). In so far as having them is a matter of degree, that it is difficult to say how much is enough is a point which the proponent of the Character View can acknowledge with equanimity; this difficulty is completely compatible with that view.

Missimer also claims that having or not having these character traits "tell[s] us nothing about the *quality* of [a person's] thought" (146, emphasis in original). This charge is ambiguous. If read as a comment on a person's reasoning *process*, then having or not having them *does* tell us about the quality of that process: a process of reasoning which fails to manifest impartiality is of lower quality than a comparable process which (to a greater extent) does. If read as a comment on the *product* of that process, or about a person's reasoning conceived as a relation among sentences or propositions, then Missimer is right:

my thinking may be highly skilled, and of high quality, when understood in this propositional way, even though I failed to be (e.g.) impartial in my reasoning process. But this is in no way troublesome for the proponent of the Character View. Indeed, it is explicitly recognized in the distinction between the critical spirit and reason assessment components of critical thinking (Siegel [1988], Chapter 2), the very point of which is to note that reasoning can be of high quality in the latter sense while being of low quality in the former.

Thus this first criticism of the Character View fails seriously to challenge that view. Its proponents can quite happily regard the need for further specification of the dispositions, attitudes, habits of mind and character traits constitutive of the critical spirit, and their interrelationships, as a proper subject of further philosophical research, rather than a significant objection to it. They can and should also agree that issues of character are irrelevant to the determination of the quality of the (propositional) products of thought.

These Character Traits Are Characterized Differently by Different Theorists

Here too Missimer is I think right, but only innocuously so. The fact that different theorists characterize the features of the critical spirit differently is no more bothersome to the Character View than the fact that different theorists characterize the skills which are constitutive of critical thinking differently should be seen as problematic for the Skill View.[4] Proponents of the Skill View need not say that theorists who advocate that view are unanimously agreed as to the precise specification of those skills; similarly, proponents of the Character View need not pretend they share a complete, detailed characterization of the character traits which are constitutive of it. Here, as earlier, disagreement is rightly regarded as a call for further reflection, not for the abandonment of the view. If so, then the fact that some rival characterizations of the Character View conflict in no way challenges that view.

Moreover, at least some of the sorts of conflict which Missimer here discusses rest upon a misunderstanding of the character traits involved. In her Susan/Margaret case (146), it is unclear how Missimer is understanding "respect for [a] considered argument," since the Character View values the character trait of respect when applied to persons—we respect a person's right to formulate her own independent judgment; we respect her right to demand reasons, etc.—but not when applied to "considered arguments," especially ones which we think "contain distortions." Indeed, it is unclear what "respect for a considered argument" might mean, other than that an argument should be esteemed in accordance with its merits—which is exactly the attitude recommended by the Character View. Furthermore, a critical thinker who appropriately feels "revulsion at her earlier argument" because she now realizes that that argument contains distortions can also, on the Character View, "experience surprise or delight at the new theoretical possibilities that she now sees"

(146). Missimer suggests that on that view, if one feels the former one is some-how not allowed to feel the latter. But the Character View in no way prohibits or disapproves of the latter experience.[5] Missimer concludes: "It is difficult to see why we must conclude that Susan was not thinking critically just because she failed to respond in a manner prescribed by a version of the Character View" (146). But it is not difficult to see this at all: to the extent that Susan failed to respond appropriately to her reflective circumstances—in Missimer's example, to the extent that Susan did not revise downward her estimate of the adequacy of her earlier argument, in response to her discovery that that argu-ment contained distortions—to that extent, she is thinking uncritically. But that downward revision, and concomitant feeling of revulsion, is completely compatible with Susan's also experiencing surprise or delight at the new pos-sibilities she now sees. Again, no difficulty is raised here for the Character View.[6]

Great Thinkers With Venal Characters Are Not Critical Thinkers

Here we come closer to the heart of Missimer's opposition to the Character View. Missimer argues that that view is deficient because it yields the unpalat-able result that "great thinkers" and "intellectual giants" who have "venal" characters (147) are, because of their venal characters, *uncritical*, despite their superior intellects and intellectual achievements. She holds that there is better evidence that the intellectual merits of a thinker, and her status as a critical thinker, are independent of that thinker's character; her major argument against the Character View is just that it has the seemingly absurd consequence that character defects tell against a thinker's status as a critical thinker. Thus, since thinkers of the stature of Newton, Russell, Rousseau, Marx, Galois, Harvey, Bacon, and Freud are "acknowledged great thinkers" (147), but some of these "celebrated thinkers were venal" (147), then—since venal characters fail to meet the character requirements deemed by the Character View to be necessary for critical thinking—these acknowledged great thinkers fail to qualify as critical thinkers. This, Missimer suggests, is tantamount to a reduc-tio ad absurdum of the Character View.

There is much amiss with this argument against the Character View. First, that view does not hold that a thinker has to be completely moral, or have a perfect character, in order to qualify as a critical thinker. As we have seen, hav-ing the relevant character traits, and indeed being a critical thinker, is on that view a matter of degree. So no argument which goes from "S has a defective character" to "S is therefore not a critical thinker" or "S does not qualify for the label 'critical thinker'" will go through. The most that can be said is some-thing like: To the extent that a thinker suffers from relevant character defects, to that extent that thinker fails to be a critical thinker. For being/not being a critical thinker, on the Character View, is a matter of degree.[7]

Second, and more importantly, Missimer writes as if the Character View holds that *all* character traits are relevant to a thinker's status as a critical thinker, so that a person who speaks rudely to others, or is overly insensitive to the plight or feelings of others, or plays the horses with the family savings, is deficient as a critical thinker. This is a serious distortion of the Character View. Of course if the person in question is thinking about the goodness or justifiability of those very character traits, then to the extent she maintains clearly defective traits, her having them reflects deficient, and to that extent uncritical, thinking. But in general, the character traits deemed by the Character View to be important to our conception of critical thinking are not the entire panoply of such traits, but rather only *those which are involved in our efforts to think critically.* Thus traits such as a willingness to follow an argument where it leads, a disposition to demand evidence for candidate beliefs, a propensity to weigh relevant evidence fairly, a tendency to believe in accordance with such evidence, a frank acknowledgement of fallibility, a willingness to take seriously the arguments of others which challenge one's own basic beliefs and commitments, and the like, are the traits emphasized by the Character View as relevant to one's status as a critical thinker. Other traits, such as fiscal irresponsibility, rudeness, etc., while admittedly defective, are not relevant to that status—except, as already noted, in the special case in which one is thinking about the evaluative status of those very traits.

Once this point is grasped, most if not all of Missimer's examples of great thinkers with venal characters miss their intended target, since the venal character traits Missimer points to are not traits relevant to those thinkers' status as critical (or as great or celebrated) thinkers. Missimer is quite clear that the thinkers she has in mind are those "whose thinking has by common consensus demonstrated great critical acumen" (147). She thus regards Newton's sensitivity to criticism, Russell's lying about his earlier views concerning a preemptive nuclear war against Russia, and Feynman's playfulness, rudeness, and hedonism, as evidence against the adequacy of their characters, and thus as evidence, on the Character View, against their status as critical thinkers. More outrageously, the venality of Rousseau's self-servingness, paranoia, and superiority complex; of Marx's anti-Semitism, tendency to cheat tradespeople, and treatment of his servant; of Galois' hotheadedness; of Harvey's temperamentality and eccentricity; of Bacon's coldness and betrayal; and of Freud's misrepresentations, distortions, self-serving clinical advice, and secrecy—all this venality, Missimer suggests, forces the conclusion (on the Character View) that these luminaries were not critical thinkers, despite their obvious intellectual achievements. But they were critical thinkers, and obviously so, Missimer suggests. Thus the Character View, which forces the opposite conclusion, is (by contraposition) mistaken.

To see what is wrong with this argument, we need only recall her own claim that these thinkers are those "whose thinking has by common consensus demonstrated great critical acumen" (147). What makes them critical thinkers, on Missimer's view, is their extraordinary intellectual achievements: Newtonian physics; *Principia Mathematica* and other logical and philosophical contributions of Russell; quantum chromodynamics; Rousseau's Social Contract theory; *Das Kapital* and the theory of Communism; the mathematical theory of equations; the theory of the circulation of the blood; Freudian psychology; etc. Now, were these intellectual achievements marred by the venal traits just mentioned? On the whole, obviously not, Missimer and I are agreed: however horrible to his servant Marx was, however paranoid Rousseau was, however rude Feynman was, their intellectual achievements are not marred by these character traits. That is because, on the Character View as much as on Missimer's, those traits are irrelevant to the excellence of those achievements, and so are not decisive with respect to the status of those thinkers as critical thinkers. The traits Missimer's argument seizes upon are not the traits which the Character View regards as centrally relevant to one's status as a critical thinker.[8]

On the other hand, if Newton's scientific achievements did not manifest a willingness to follow the arguments wherever they led; if Russell's great logical and epistemological works did not manifest a disposition to demand evidence for candidate beliefs; if Feynman's theorizing did not exhibit a tendency to believe in accordance with relevant evidence; if Rousseau's or Marx's social-philosophical writings did not manifest a frank acknowledgement of fallibility, and therefore a systematic scrutiny of their own arguments (and potential counter-arguments) in an effort to render those arguments as powerful as they could; if Harvey's, Bacon's, and Freud's great works did not manifest a willingness to take seriously the arguments of others which challenged their own basic beliefs and commitments;[9] if these thinkers weren't disposed to weigh relevant evidence, to consider the totality of relevant evidence, and to judge in accordance with that evidence—if *these* character flaws were manifested by these thinkers, then we would have every reason to call their status as critical thinkers into question, despite the quality of their achievements. The plausibility of Missimer's argument hinges on her reliance on character traits which are to a significant degree irrelevant, according to the Character View, to the status as critical thinkers of persons who have those traits. Once the right set of character traits are considered, that plausibility collapses.

The case against the Character View suffers further when it is recalled, as noted above, that the Character View acknowledges at its heart the distinction between the process by which a potentially critical judgment is reached, on the one hand, and the relationship between a judgment and its supporting reasons, construed propositionally, on the other. Let us agree for the sake of argument that the theories and arguments set forth by these thinkers, which constitute their major intellectual achievements, are of exceedingly high quality and originality. Does it follow that the status of these thinkers *as critical thinkers* is assured? To answer this question affirmatively, as Missimer does, is to deny that the process by which an achievement of significance is achieved is relevant to a thinker's status as a critical thinker. All that counts for the determination of that status is the product achieved. But as argued above, a worthy product can be achieved by the most uncritical of means: a theorist can fail to consider all relevant evidence, evaluate evidence inappropriately, fail to take seriously potentially important criticism, even fail to think at all.[10] Thus the propositional worthiness of an achievement is for Missimer the *only* relevant criterion for determining one's status as a critical thinker. But if it is agreed that a propositionally worthy achievement can be reached by inappropriate or less than wonderful means, and that a thinker's process of reasoning is relevant to her status as a critical thinker—as the Character View insists—then it will not do to rest that status entirely on the quality of the end product itself. But it is that to which the Skill View is committed.[11]

Once it is clear that a piece of thinking, construed propositionally, can be of high quality without the thinker in question having reasoned, procedurally, particularly well, the supposed advantages of the Skill View disappear. I have suggested above that on the Character View the "great thinkers" Missimer discusses turn out to be, on the whole, highly critical thinkers, at least with respect to the products of the thinking on which that greatness rests. But it would be no embarrassment for the Character View if such thinkers turn out on occasion to be less than exceptionally high quality critical thinkers, or even highly uncritical thinkers. For, as just noted, one's status as a critical thinker depends not only on the (propositional) products of one's thought. It depends as well on the process of that thought. It is here that considerations of character arise. That persons of venal character have sometimes thought well, and produced exceptionally high quality thought, is a result that proponents of the Character View can happily accept. So is the result that some persons who have produced such thought are relatively uncritical thinkers. The Skill View regards a thinker's status as a critical thinker as being determined entirely by the (propositional) quality of produced thought. Once process is acknowledged as relevant to that determination, as I have argued it must be, the Character View is home free.

For all the reasons adduced in this section, I conclude that the biographical evidence Missimer raises to challenge the Character View fails seriously to challenge it. Before closing this section, however, I must address one final objection Missimer offers.

If this evidence fails to upend the Character View, is there any evidence which could? Or is that view, Missimer asks, itself immune from criticism, and so at odds with its own embrace of fallibilism? Good question: if no evidence could count against the Character View, even in principle, then Missimer would be right that that view would be of dubious merit. But she is not.

First: it is clear that on the Character View it is possible for evidence to count against judgments of criticality. If we find, in examining the work or character of presumed critical thinkers (like the folks on Missimer's list of examples), either that their work was propositionally inadequate, or that the process by which they achieved that product was problematic, or that they harbor problems of character of the sort specified, then we would have evidence challenging their presumptive status as critical thinkers. So such judgments are clearly open, on the Character View, to evidential support and challenge.

What of the Character View itself: is *it* open to evidential challenge? Yes—although not the sort of challenge Missimer here considers. That view is a philosophical one; it is open to all the sorts of challenges to which philosophical theses are generally. It can be challenged by internal inconsistency; by defect in supporting argumentation; by counterexample; by criticism levelled by or poor comparison with alternative theoretical views; by failure to mesh with other plausible views; etc. The Character View is not immune to challenge. On the contrary, Missimer is here challenging it, and the Character View must meet that challenge. If her challenge is successful, then Missimer will have defeated it. I have been arguing that her challenge does not succeed, but not that no challenge can in principle do so. That View is not immune from challenge, and so is not in conflict with its own embrace of fallibilism.

That it is open to challenge is compatible with its being not open to certain *sorts* of challenge. I offer additional reasons below for thinking that the Character View is not open to the sort of empirical challenge Missimer mounts.

Important Ethical Issues Are Placed Beyond the Boundary of Critical Thinking

Finally, Missimer argues that the Character View "smuggle[s] in moral prescriptions" to its conception of critical thinking, thus "leaving ethics [outside] the scrutiny of critical thought" (145). It thus prohibits "free ethical theorizing" (151).

This objection can be dealt with briefly: the allegation is simply false. According to the Character View, *everything* is open to critical thought and "free theorizing," including the nature of critical thinking and the ethical dimensions thereof. Proponents of the Character View do not regard their own views of critical thinking, in particular the ethical dimensions of them, as themselves immune from critical scrutiny. Why Missimer thinks they (i.e. we) do is a mystery to me, since she quotes two of them to the contrary (Scheffler on 151; me on 153, note 24).[12]

According to the Character View, critical thinking is justified as an educational ideal in part on moral grounds. Indeed, I have argued that education aimed at the fostering of critical thinking is morally obligatory (1988, Chapter 3). If that argument is successful, then that sort of education is obligatory. But whether or not that argument is successful, and so whether or not that sort of education is obligatory, are of course questions which are completely open to further critical scrutiny. So are questions concerning the (moral) character of putative critical thinkers. Thus Missimer is mistaken when she suggests that

> [o]ne way is to teach critical thinking as though it were *necessitated by* (a version of) morality, for instance justice, humility and so forth. This method seems to entail an uncritical acceptance of those morals, since they have been defined as necessary for critical thought in the first place. This uncritical "morality of critical thinking" seems to be what the Character View espouses. (151, emphasis in original)

First, as just noted, the Character View in general, and its moral dimension in particular, are open—as everything is—to critical scrutiny, according to the proponents of that view.[13] Contrary to Missimer, there is nothing *uncritical* about the "morality of critical thinking" espoused by the Character View; nor is it immune from critical scrutiny. Moreover, this supposed uncriticality is a product of confusion. The first sentence of the just-cited passage suggests that a particular moral viewpoint implies that education aimed at the fostering of critical thinking is morally required. That is indeed what I argue (1988). But the second sentence of that passage suggests instead that that particular moral viewpoint is itself entailed by critical thinking, since that viewpoint is "necessary for critical thought in the first place." This is a fundamental confusion; the second sentence reverses the direction of implication of the first. Contrary to this mistaken allegation, it is part and parcel of the Character View that students "decide for themselves whether specific virtues are important in life (or necessary for critical thought)" (151). Thus Missimer was wise to write "*seems* to entail," rather than "entails," at the outset of the second cited sentence. The entailment she imagines here is not an entailment endorsed by the Character View.[14]

I conclude that none of Missimer's objections to the Character View are telling. Let us briefly turn our attention to the supposed advantages of the Skill View.

WHAT'S RIGHT ABOUT THE SKILL VIEW?

Missimer argues that the Skill View enjoys certain advantages when compared with the Character View:

> . . . the evidence in its favor would appear to be stronger; it has the advantage of theoretical simplicity; and it does not smuggle in moral prescriptions, leaving ethics instead to the scrutiny of critical thought. Finally, it

63

> is arguable that an historical version of the Skill View can show critical thinking to be more exciting than any version which the Character View has offered thus far. (145)

What shall we say of these alleged advantages?

We have already addressed the first and third of these. As argued above, the biographical evidence Missimer presents on its behalf fails to support the Skill View, and fails to challenge the Character View; and the claim that the Character View "smuggle[s] in moral prescriptions" and in doing so places ethics beyond "the scrutiny of critical thought" is false.

It is true that the Skill View is simpler than the Character View—it recognizes only the skill component of critical thinking, whereas the Character View recognizes both that component and a character or critical spirit component as well. Does this simplicity of the former view constitute an advantage over the latter? It does so only if the case is made that the skill component is the only component of critical thinking. I have argued here that that case has not been made, and that there remain good reasons to regard character traits as an essential component of critical thinking. (I shall add a further argument to that effect below.) If so, then "the advantage of theoretical simplicity" (151) turns out rather to be the disadvantage of oversimplification.

What, finally, of Missimer's contention that one version of the Skill View is "more exciting" than extant versions of the Character View? The exciting version she has in mind is one in which students are exposed to the historical "accretion of reasoned judgments on a myriad of issues by many people over time. This conception entails the notion that contrasting arguments on issues are vitally important to intellectual progress" (150). This conception is exciting largely for its pedagogical virtues:

> One can offer this historical view as an argument that the skill of critical thinking has wrought immense good—and encourage students to argue against this view. The point is for students to consider past examples of critical thinking while practicing the skill. According to this version of the Skill View, if students get a glimpse of the wealth of theories which exist in every discipline and activity, they will be more likely to start on a lifetime intellectual journey. (150)

I quite agree with Missimer about the pedagogical virtues of this sort of historical study—indeed, I recommend much the same role for the history of science in my discussion of science education. (Siegel (1988), Chapter 6) But is this an advantage which the Skill View enjoys over the Character View? No. What Missimer has here is an exciting way to *teach* for critical thinking. But this is irrelevant to the question of how best to *conceptualize* critical thinking.

The Character View can readily acknowledge that Missimer's suggestion constitutes an "exciting" way to foster critical thinking. The suggestion on the table conflates two distinct questions: What is the best way to conceptualize critical thinking?; and What is the best way to teach so as to foster critical thinking? The Character View has no special answer to the latter question; neither, I would have thought, should the Skill View. The dispute between these two views concerns the former question, not the latter.

Missimer seems to think that the Character View recommends teaching for critical thinking by preaching about the moral virtues of particular character traits (e.g. 149), and by studying the characters of thinkers: she recommends her "exciting" suggestion by noting that "[i]t focuses on great arguments, past and present, not on the arguers" (151). The clear suggestion here is that the Character View recommends teaching for critical thinking by studying arguers rather than arguments. This is absurd. Arguing that character is central to an adequate *conception* of critical thinking in no way amounts to the quite different idea that the study of character must be an essential aspect of the *pedagogy* of critical thinking. Missimer's discussion of excitement simply confuses these two concerns. Once they are distinguished, this supposed advantage of the Skill View disappears. Indeed, what is called here a "version of the Skill View" (151) is no such thing, if that view is a view about the proper *conception* of critical thinking. It is rather a suggestion—a good one, I think—about critical thinking pedagogy.

I conclude that Missimer has not provided any good reason to think that the Skill View enjoys any significant advantage over the Character View.

THE MAIN, BUT UNMENTIONED, ARGUMENT
FOR THE CHARACTER VIEW

A striking fact about Missimer's discussion is that it does not even acknowledge, let alone seriously consider, the main extant argument for the Character View. That argument (cluster) suggests that the Skill View fails adequately to characterize critical thinking, and that the Character View provides a more adequate characterization.

The argument is made in different ways by different proponents of the Character View. Perhaps the best known version is Richard Paul's. Paul distinguishes between "weak sense" and "strong sense" critical thinking, and argues that the former, which is very much like the Skill View, is an inadequate conception of critical thinking because it entails that sophists—thinkers "who are adept at manipulating argumentative exchanges in such a way that they can always 'demonstrate,' or at least protect from challenge, those deep-seated beliefs and commitments which they are not willing to explore or reject"— are full fledged critical thinkers. (Siegel [1988], p. 11) But Paul suggests that such thinkers, however skilled, should not be so regarded:

65

> I take it to be self-evident that virtually all teachers of critical thinking want their teaching to have a global "Socratic" effect, making some significant inroads into the everyday reasoning of the student, enhancing to some degree that healthy, practical and skilled skepticism one naturally and rightly associates with the *rational* person. This necessarily encompasses, it seems to me, some experience in seriously questioning previously held beliefs and assumptions and in identifying contradictions and inconsistencies in personal and social life. (Paul [1982], p. 3, emphasis in original)

Paul goes on to argue, in this and many other papers, that an adequate conception of critical thinking must go beyond skills, and include the dispositions and character traits relevant to the use and appreciation of those skills. His idea that critical thinking is importantly "Socratic," in a way which demands that critical thinking involves in particular ways the character or "critical spirit" of the thinker, is (I would have thought) one of the few generally accepted theses among otherwise contentious critical thinking theorists. In any case, on Paul's view the weak sense critical thinker is a skilled critical thinker. But she is nevertheless not a fully adequate critical thinker. What is missing is her failure to appreciate the importance of those skills and their relevance to her overall system of belief, and so her failure to utilize her skills in ways which impact on herself. That is to say, what the weak sense critical thinker is lacking is exactly the attitudes, dispositions, habits of mind and character traits regarded by the Character View as an essential component of an adequate conception of critical thinking.

Israel Scheffler makes a similar point, when he writes:

> we talk of "citizenship" as if it were a set of skills, whereas our educational aim is, in fact, not merely to teach people *how* to be good citizens but, in particular, to *be* good citizens, not merely *how* to go about voting, but *to* vote. We talk about giving them "the skills required for democratic living," when actually we are concerned that they acquire democratic habits, norms, propensities. To take another example, we talk of giving pupils the "ability to think critically" when what we really want is for them to acquire the habits and norms of critical thought. (Scheffler [1960], pp. 98–9, emphases in original)

Scheffler's claim is that skill is not enough; that the "habits and norms of critical thought" are essential to an adequate understanding of critical thinking as an educational ideal. He offers a powerful and systematic conception of education which he thinks entails that conclusion.

Both of these proponents of the Character View offer arguments against the adequacy of the Skill View conception of critical thinking, and in favor of the Character View. I have as well. None of these arguments are discussed in Missimer's article. She writes that versions of the Character View "have been advanced without much analysis" (145). Nothing could be further from the truth.

Missimer makes the point (which, with minor qualification, I accept) that a person could not be skilled at critical thinking without having practiced it: "'pure skill' in the sense of skill devoid of practice does not exist—no person could be a critical thinker who had never, or only infrequently, thought critically, just as we know of no mathematician who had never, or only infrequently, done mathematics" (150).[15] She (apparently) infers from this that the kind of person Paul and Scheffler mention—that is, a person who is able to reason skillfully but does not—is a conceptual impossibility. But this inference is erroneous; in any case there are countless counter-examples to which one could appeal. Grant that skill requires practice. It is nevertheless the case that many people who are practiced in and skilled at critical thinking nevertheless fail, at least occasionally but often routinely and systematically, to think critically. One can be practiced in and skilled at critical thinking but routinely and importantly fail to engage in it. If so, then Missimer's point about practice will not suffice to mute Paul's and Scheffler's complaint that such a person is fundamentally deficient with respect to critical thinking. That deficiency, as they (and I) argue, is best understood as one of character.

67

CONCLUDING DIFFICULTIES

I have argued that Missimer's criticism of the Character View fails, and that her advocacy of the Skill View fails as well. I would like simply to conclude on that note. But there are several further points which I am obliged to mention, even though I cannot discuss them fully here.

The Skill View Actually Involves Character

The Skill View recommends instilling the "disposition/habit to think critically" (149); according to that view this disposition/habit, and the relevant attitude toward it, is a necessary condition of being a critical thinker, since "[t]o be considered a critical thinker you must do a lot of critical thinking *as a result of having wanted to*" (149, emphasis added). If so, then the Skill View actually accepts the central tenet of the Character View.

The Relevance of Empirical Evidence to the Justification of a Conception of Critical Thinking

Missimer argues that justifying one or the other of these conceptions of critical thinking depends on empirical evidence: "even in the realm of choosing among ideals we are cast back upon some kind of appeal to experience as arbiter; intellectual history has shown that gathering evidence is less risky than relying on opinion alone" (146–7). I wonder what branch of intellectual history Missimer has in mind here: which philosophical dispute about ideals (say of justice, or political organization, or knowledge) has been settled, or even importantly addressed, by some kind of appeal to experience? Despite her discussion on these pages, the sort of evidence she appeals to is, as argued above, not relevant to the settling of this dispute. Moreover, her claim that in the absence of appeals to experience we are "relying on opinion alone" betrays a quite radical rejection of philosophical argument as a possible source of evidence for conclusions about ethical, epistemological, educational or other ideals. This rejection involves deep metaphilosophical issues (e.g. concerning naturalism) which Missimer neither acknowledges nor addresses. To say that *empirical* evidence is irrelevant to the settling of this dispute is *not* to say that "evidence here is irrelevant" (146) *simpliciter*. Her rejection of the very possibility of nonempirical evidence is extremely contentious and (I would say) problematic, but it is unargued for.[16] The autonomy of philosophy cannot so easily be dismissed. In any case, the character traits advocated by the Character View do not spring from "opinion alone"; rather they spring from philosophical, specifically moral, epistemological and educational, theory.

Causes and Conceptions

Missimer suggests in several places that the Character View invokes dispositions and character traits in order to explain causally episodes of critical thinking; she suggests that that view fails because these dispositions and traits fail to so explain (148, 149, 150). This is a fundamental confusion. The Character View is not claiming anything in particular about the causes of critical thinking. It is rather offering a conception of critical thinking. Missimer may well be right that the cause of particular episodes of critical thinking is "the habit of critical thought" (150)—although that is a tricky thing for her to claim, in view of her contention, just discussed, that that habit can equally be seen as a disposition. In any case, the causes of critical thinking are irrelevant to questions about its proper conceptualization. If episodes of critical thinking were caused by ingesting some chemical concoction, it would remain an open question whether the Skill or the Character View was the more adequate conception. Causal worries are simply irrelevant here.

Missimer contends (personal communication, July 30, 1992) that when proponents of the Character View say, as I do above, that an adequate conception of critical thinking *demands* or *requires* that the critical thinker have the relevant dispositions or character traits, they are implicitly implying a causal connection between those character traits and success at critical thinking; if not, then this language "is, to say the least, misleading." I confess that it never occurred to me to interpret the relevant language as Missimer does; if it had,

I would have tried to explain myself more clearly. But I think that Missimer's interpretation is (to put it gently) unorthodox. Philosophers frequently make claims using this sort of language. When they do, they typically take themselves to be making not causal claims, but *constitutive* ones. Consider:

1. In order to be a physical object, an entity *must* have extension.
2. Democracy *requires* a free press.
3. Justice *demands* treating like cases alike.
4. Critical thinking *requires* the comparing of alternative theories in light of their evidence.

Would anyone interpret the first as implying that having extension *causes* an entity to be a physical object? Or the second as implying that a free press *causes* democracy? Or the third as implying that treating like cases alike *causes* such treatment to be just? I think not. These claims suggest rather that these properties are *necessary* (and sometimes sufficient) *conditions* for the relevant states to be successfully realized. Thus the first asserts that if something fails to have extension, it fails to be a physical object; the second that if some government does not permit a free press, it does not count as democratic; the third that if relevantly like cases are not treated alike, that treatment is not just. What is asserted, that is, is that the property is constitutive of the state: part of what it is to be a physical object is to have extension; part of what it is to be a democracy is to have a free press; part of what it is to treat justly is to treat like cases alike. I am not claiming that these assertions are correct. I am claiming only that this is the most plausible interpretation of these claims.

Apply this interpretation to the fourth case listed, which is actually Missimer's favored interpretation of critical thinking (and which is discussed further below). Is it best interpreted as implying that the comparing of alternative theories in light of their evidence *causes* critical thinking? Perhaps Missimer indeed intends this. But this interpretation faces an obvious and overwhelming difficulty: the comparing is indistinguishable from the thinking, which entails that on this interpretation critical thinking causes itself—hardly a plausible or helpful account of the cause of critical thinking. A more plausible, and charitable, interpretation is rather that Missimer is asserting that comparing alternatives is a necessary condition of, or is constitutive of, critical thinking—so that on her view if thinking does not involve such comparison, it does not qualify as critical thinking. This interpretation does not render the claim unproblematic (see below), but it does render it in a way which is not immediately overcome by the problem facing the causal interpretation just noted. Thus even her own view is best interpreted as constitutive rather than causal.

69

The same goes for the statements of the Character View Missimer interprets as implying causal connections between character and critical thinking. Those statements make not causal, but rather constitutive, claims, concerning what is involved in (is a necessary condition of) being a critical thinker. I do not think that they are misleading in the way Missimer suggests. She is simply misreading them. Conceptions are not causes.[17]

The Character View Commits the Ad Hominem Fallacy

Missimer suggests that the Character View is guilty of the ad hominem fallacy:

> Why should we tear the mantle of critical thinker from a Marx or a Rousseau on the basis of how they lived? To do so is to reason in an *ad hominem* fashion. . . . To insist that their lives have any bearing on the truth of their theories seems quite beside the point. Yet the Character View enjoins this unfortunate entanglement. (149)

This charge is without merit. The Character View in no way suggests that a person's character has any bearing on the truth of her belief. What it suggests, rather, is that the truth—or, rather, the epistemic status[18]—of a person's beliefs is only part of what is relevant to that person's status as a critical thinker. One can deny that that status is determined solely by the quality of the contents of one's beliefs without thereby committing the ad hominem.

The Definition of Critical Thinking

Missimer defines critical thinking as "the consideration of alternative theories in light of their evidence" (145; see also 150; 153 note 16; Missimer [1988]). While her criticism of the Character View does not depend on this definition, a brief comment about it is I hope in order.

The claim that the consideration of alternatives is necessary for critical thinking is—like so many superficially promising philosophical claims—either trivial or false. On a weak reading, it amounts simply to the idea that all evidence for a claim needs to be taken into account, and that that evidence typically includes evidence concerning the merits of alternatives. On this reading, the claim is trivially true. All extant accounts of critical thinking, including my own, endorse it; it adds nothing to those accounts.

On a strong reading, however, the claim is that no theory or argument can be critically evaluated without explicit attention to its alternatives; that such comparison is necessary for argument evaluation to be critical. This is false. One can, for example, critically evaluate an argument, and judge it appropriately, without contemplating any alternatives. Missimer explicitly denies this (153, note 16; [1988]). Thus on this strong reading one cannot critically determine that an argument begs the question, or generalizes on the basis of an overly small sample, without considering alternatives. But this is transparently false: if I am presented with an argument of the form "'A,' therefore 'A'," for example, I can surely judge it to be question-begging without considering any other argument.[19] Similarly for other errors (and strengths) of arguments.[20] As Bailin says, while critical thinking is not wholly a matter of evaluating individual arguments, "critically examining individual arguments is part of the job" (Bailin [1988], p. 404).

Moreover, considering alternatives "in light of their evidence" is too weak, in that it completely ignores relevant standards in accordance with which evidence must be evaluated if such consideration is to count as critical. Suppose I am considering alternative theories in light of their evidence, and I find the evidence for T_1 more compelling than the evidence for T_2, because the former evidence is composed of sentences with even numbers of words, or is advanced by Jews, or because so regarding it will advance my career. Here I am considering alternative theories in light of their evidence, but am hardly doing so critically. Entirely missing from Missimer's account is any acknowledgement of standards or criteria in accordance with which evidence is properly assessed. Given this absence, it is unclear why critical thinking is to be preferred to uncritical thinking.

I have gone on far too long. I am grateful to Missimer for her provocative article, which has prompted me to rethink my conception and defense of the Character View in some detail; my hope is that this chapter both develops the "critical spirit" portion of my view of critical thinking, and defends it from the criticisms Missimer puts forward to challenge it. In any case, for the many reasons given above, I continue to think that the Character View is a more adequate conception of critical thinking than the Skill View. Critical thinking can be adequately conceptualized, but not by skill alone.[21]

71

WHY BE RATIONAL?

Justifying the Commitment to Rationality

Reason, at last, joins all those other abstract monsters such as Obligation, Duty, Morality, Truth and their more concrete predecessors, the Gods, which were once used to intimidate man and restrict his free and happy development: it withers away. . .
—Paul Feyerabend

. . . in some cases it is really more creditable to be carried away by an emotion, however unreasonable, . . . than to be unmoved. [A person] who is always sensible is to be suspected and is of little worth.
—Fyodor Dostoyevsky

chapter 5

CRITICAL THINKERS must be critical about critical thinking itself. The quest for reasons and justification which is central to critical thinking must be respected even when that quest self-reflexively involves reasons for engaging in critical thinking. "Why should I (or anyone) engage in critical thinking?" and "Why should I value critical thinking?" are questions which must be respected, and seen as legitimate, by proponents of critical thinking. Since those proponents conceive of their commitment to critical thinking as itself justified, they are bound to strive to provide reasons which justify that commitment. If they don't, or can't, their commitment to critical thinking is inconsistent with their own ideal of having their commitments accord with reasons which justify them. A fundamental task for the theory of critical thinking, therefore, is to fend off this threatening inconsistency by providing reasons which justify our educational commitment to the ideal of critical thinking.[1]

Because of the close conceptual connection between critical thinking and rationality, the demand for reasons which justify a commitment to critical thinking is tantamount to a demand for reasons which justify a commitment to rationality. Our operative question, then, is "Why should I (or anyone) be rational?," or, alternatively, "Why should I value rationality?"

The problem of justifying rationality is a classic philosophical problem. Many eminent philosophers have dismissed the question as confused or as a pseudo-question which does not need an answer; others have argued that the question is proper but has no satisfactory answer; still others have argued (as the opening mottoes suggest) that we should not be rational or value rationality. If any of these views is correct, however, then the proponent of critical thinking appears to be in trouble, for her commitment to critical thinking will be uncritical and unjustified, and so will be inconsistent with her own ideal.

In what follows I consider the problem of justifying rationality (and its relevance to the theory of critical thinking). I will first consider the major philosophical responses to the problem; then I will offer my own. I will argue that the demand for a justification of rationality (and so critical thinking) is legitimate; and I will offer a justification which I hope and think satisfies the demand.

THE QUESTION IS CONFUSED

Several authors have argued that the demand for a justification of rationality is a bogus demand. The general idea underlying the rejection of the demand is that there is an unremovable circularity in offering reasons for being rational. Being rational involves believing and acting in accordance with reasons; asking for reasons which justify believing and acting in accordance with reasons presupposes the legitimacy of believing and acting in accordance with reasons. Consequently, reasons which offer putative justification for believing and acting that way cannot, in principle, add anything to the reasons we have for believing and acting in particular ways. Any answer to "Why be rational?" will necessarily be circular; since the question cannot, even in principle, be answered in an informative way, it is and must be a defective question. The demand for a justification of rationality, on this view, is simply a bogus demand, which fails to recognize the limit beyond which one cannot meaningfully press the demand for reasons.

Roger Trigg, for example, suggests that

> Any attempt to justify rationality must avoid . . . any suspicion of invoking an arbitrary commitment [to rationality]. The trouble is that any justification . . . must give reasons for rationality which are themselves subject to rational scrutiny. The circularity involved in this latter exercise seems inherent in any justification of rationality. It seems as if it is logically impossible to justify being rational. (Trigg [1973], p. 146)

Anthony O'Hear similarly points to the seeming impossibility of providing a noncircular justification of rationality:

> . . . there is something paradoxical in the very attempt to produce a rea-
> soned defence of reason itself. . . . Rationalism . . . [consists in] a commit-
> ment to critical argument and experience. Any rational defence of a
> position is one that appeals to argument and experience. In the case of
> rationalism itself, then, a rational defence is viciously circular . . . [There is]
> a fatal inconsistency in the very attempt to defend rationalism by rational
> means. . . . any argumentative defence of arguments begs the question.[2]

Neither Trigg nor O'Hear conclude, from the apparent fact that attempts to justify rationality must be question-begging or circular, that rationality itself cannot be rationally justified. They conclude, rather, that the impossibility of providing a noncircular justification of rationality shows that the demand for such a justification is an illegitimate demand; that it is a mistake to suppose that rationality needs to be justified:

> There must . . . be something very odd with the notion of a *justification*
> of rationality, because clearly it is itself a concept from *within* rationality.
> Anyone who wants such a justification wants to stand outside the frame-
> work of rationality while remaining inside, and this is obviously incoher-
> ent. (Trigg [1973], p. 149, emphases in original)

> . . .the natural conclusion to draw from this [the impossibility of provid-
> ing a non-circular or non-question-begging justification of rationality] is
> that the demand for justification of this sort is senseless. [There is no]
> rational standard against which rationality . . . fails to be rational. It fails
> only to satisfy a demand which, for logical reasons, cannot be satisfied,
> and this could hardly be held against it or be taken to show its irra-
> tionality.[3]

> [The rationalist] takes it for granted that one must be able to justify a
> position, but this could clearly only be so if it is logically possible that a
> justification be forthcoming. If it is not, there can be no shame in not
> being able to give one. (Trigg [1973], p. 150)[4]

For both Trigg and O'Hear,[5] then, the question of justifying rationality is misconceived. It is impossible, on their view, rationally to justify a commit-
ment to rationality. If this impossibility were a contingent impossibility, we would be forced to conclude that a commitment to rationality must be a- or irrational. But since it is logically or in principle impossible to justify ratio-

nality, it is a confusion even to raise the question of the rationality of a commitment to rationality. The demand for a justification of rationality is thus a bogus demand.

This rejection of the demand for an answer to the question "Why be rational?" is I think mistaken. For one thing, the rejection hinges on determining that it is not merely contingently impossible noncircularly to answer the question, but rather that it is logically or in principle impossible to do so. But this determination can be made only by considering candidate answers and the characteristics of theoretically possible answers. Thus, on the line Trigg and O'Hear take, the demand for a justification of rationality starts out being legitimate, and becomes illegitimate only after it has been fruitlessly pursued and considered for a time. This appears to make the purported illegitimacy of the demand a rather convenient out for the friend of rationality, rather than a satisfying or satisfactory account of why that friend should not be bothered by her inability to meet the challenge posed by the demand.[6]

Second, it is not clear that there is anything problematic about the stance the rationalist takes towards the demand. Trigg writes, in the passage most recently cited, that "[The rationalist] takes it for granted that one must be able to justify a position, but this could clearly only be so if it is logically possible that a justification be forthcoming." But what is troublesome about the rationalist's taking it for granted that one must be able to justify a position *if one is entitled to regard that position as rationally justified*? Here it seems that the rationalist is perfectly within her rights to take for granted what she does: if it turns out that it is not "logically possible that a justification be forthcoming" for some claim or position, then the rationalist should conclude that that claim, if held, is held a- or irrationally. Trigg provides no reason for thinking that what the rationalist assumes—namely, that for a position to be justified, it must enjoy rational justification—is in any way problematic. If it turns out that it is not logically possible that a justification for some claim be forthcoming, then the rationalist—and anyone else—should conclude not that the demand for justification of the claim is inappropriate or illegitimate, but simply that the claim does not and cannot enjoy rational justification. And this conclusion should apply to the rationalist's embrace of her own position. Showing that it is not possible to justify some position, in short, in no way undermines the rationalist's contention that that position, embraced without justification, is not a rationally embraced or justified position; nor does it undermine her contention that to be justified in embracing a position—even one concerning the possibility and necessity of rational justification itself—there must be reasons (or experience) which warrant or justify that position.

Third, despite the arguments canvassed thus far, the demand for a justification of rationality remains perfectly legitimate. When our critical thinking students ask questions like "Why is a certain form of reasoning, e.g. post hoc reasoning, fallacious?," we are obliged to answer, and we do, by pointing out the inability of that form of reasoning to provide proper warrant for conclusions reached by that argumentative route. (Here we appeal to epistemology to determine the warrant such reasoning provides.) When they ask "Why should we not be moved by fallacious reasoning?," we are obliged to answer, and we do, by pointing out that if they are asking why they should not be *rationally* moved by fallacious reasoning, then they should not be moved by fallacious reasoning because such reasoning fails to warrant the conclusions it reaches. (Here again our appeal is to epistemology, specifically to the epistemology of informal logic.) When they ask "Why should we be governed by such epistemological concerns—why shouldn't we be moved to accept some conclusion, even though it is reached by fallacious reasoning which can't *rationally* move us?," they are asking for reasons for accepting our view of the importance of epistemological constraints on our thinking, believing and acting, and of the importance of rationality more generally. In this case our students are asking why they should be rational. If we cannot answer them, then they will have detected a fundamental inconsistency in our position: we encourage them to think critically, to seek reasons and justifications with which to guide their beliefs and actions, and to believe and act on the basis of reasons; yet for this fundamental lesson, concerning the importance and value of rationality, we can provide no reasons or justification. If they accept our teaching of this lesson, then they should reject it, since the lesson instructs them to embrace only that which can be justified, and this lesson itself cannot be. Any student who took our lesson to heart would soon discover this lacuna at its core, a gap sufficient to undermine the lesson. And it would help us not a bit to learn from Trigg and O'Hear that the gap is logically impossible to fill. In this case we would have to conclude, with our students, that our lesson falls to a fundamental reflexive difficulty: what it urges generally, it cannot satisfy itself. The demand for reasons which warrant a commitment to rationality is as legitimate a demand as is the demand for reasons which warrant any other claim, position or commitment.

If the demand for reasons which justify a commitment to rationality is legitimate, then friends of rationality cannot escape that demand by suggesting, as Trigg and O'Hear suggest, that it is logically impossible to meet it. This result—that the demand is legitimate—leaves the rationalist with the burden of justifying her commitment to rationality. This is the obligation I hope to discharge below. I could not do so if Trigg and O'Hear were correct in thinking that meeting it is logically impossible. Fortunately, they are not. They have not shown that reasons which justify rationality must be viciously circular or question-begging. I shall argue below that there is a sort of justificationist strategy—a self-reflexive strategy—that, if successful, justifies rationality without involving either of these defects.

I conclude, then, that the demand for a justification of rationality is legitimate. Below I will try to meet it. First, let us look at the position defended by Karl Popper, who argues that the demand is legitimate but cannot be met, so that the commitment to rationality cannot be justified and rests instead on an irrational faith in reason.

THE QUESTION IS LEGITIMATE,
BUT CANNOT BE RATIONALLY ANSWERED;
WE MUST HAVE AN "IRRATIONAL FAITH IN REASON"

On Popper's view, "Why be rational?" is a perfectly legitimate question which must be recognized as such by the rationalist. But the question cannot be answered in a way which justifies the rationalist position, for all attempts to justify rationality will in the end be circular or question-begging, and excusing the rationalist position from its self-imposed demand for justification will render the position inconsistent. We must settle, says Popper, for an irrational commitment to rationality:

> Uncritical or comprehensive rationalism can be described as the attitude of the person who says "I am not prepared to accept anything that cannot be defended by means of argument or experience." We can express this also in the form of the principle that any assumption which cannot be supported either by argument or by experience is to be discarded. Now it is easy to see that this principle of an uncritical rationalism is inconsistent; for since it cannot, in its turn, be supported by argument or by experience, it implies that it should itself be discarded. . . .
>
> But this means that whoever adopts the rationalist attitude does so because he has adopted, consciously or unconsciously, some proposal, or decision, or belief, or behaviour; an adoption which may be called "irrational." Whether this adoption is tentative or leads to a settled habit, we may describe it as an irrational *faith in reason*. . . .
>
> Although an uncritical and comprehensive rationalism is logically untenable, and although a comprehensive irrationalism is logically tenable, this is no reason why we should adopt the latter. For there are other tenable attitudes, notably that of critical rationalism which recognizes the fact that the fundamental rationalist attitude results from an (at least tentative) act of faith—from faith in reason. Accordingly, our choice is open. We may choose some form of irrationalism, even some radical or comprehensive form. But we are also free to choose a critical form of rationalism, one which frankly admits its origin in an irrational decision (and which, to that extent, admits a certain priority of irrationalism). (Popper [1962], pp. 230–31, emphasis in original)

Popper here frankly regards the question "Why be rational?" as a legitimate one; he despairs, however, of any attempt to rationally justify a commitment to rationality or the adoption of "the rationalist attitude." At bottom, according to Popper, we must irrationally embrace rationalism. A rational justification of rationality simply cannot be had. As O'Hear summarizes Popper's view: " . . . rationalism, however desirable it may be, is ultimately a matter of irrational faith" (O'Hear [1980], p. 147).

Popper is right, I have already argued, concerning the legitimacy of the question: "Why be rational?" is a question which demands, and deserves, an answer, if our commitment to rationality is itself to be rationally justified. But is Popper correct that there can be no rational justification of rationality?

A preliminary difficulty with Popper's position is that he does offer reasons for adopting critical rationalism, i.e. the view that we should value and commit ourselves to rationality but recognize that doing so rests upon an irrational faith in reason.[7] In arguing for critical rationalism, he offers reasons which in his view are not inconsistent, circular or question-begging. If it is possible rationally to defend critical rationalism, why should it not be possible to defend a comprehensive rationalism which does not admit a "priority of irrationalism," as Popper's more limited critical rationalism does?[8]

The answer, at least for Popper, is that defending comprehensive rationalism (as opposed to a more limited rationalism) must necessarily be inconsistent. Consider again the passage recently cited: ". . . this principle of an uncritical rationalism is inconsistent; for since it cannot, in its turn, be supported by argument or by experience, it implies that it should itself be discarded."

But why can't comprehehensive rationalism itself be supported by rational argument? Presumably, Popper thinks that it can't for the same reasons given earlier by Trigg and O'Hear: such an appeal to rational argument to support comprehensive rationalism, if consistent, would be viciously circular or question-begging:

> The trouble is that any justification . . . must give reasons for rationality which are themselves subject to rational scrutiny. The circularity involved in this latter exercise seems inherent in any justification of rationality. (Trigg)

> Rationalism . . . [consists in] a commitment to critical argument and experience. Any rational defence of a position is one that appeals to argument and experience. In the case of rationalism itself, then, a rational defence is viciously circular . . . [There is] a fatal inconsistency in the very attempt to defend rationalism by rational means. . . . any argumentative defence of arguments begs the question. (O'Hear)

But are these authors correct that any rational defense of rationalism is doomed to inconsistency, vicious circularity, or question-begging? The appearance of the unavoidability of logical difficulties with a rational defense of rationalism is due to the following looming, depressing dialogue:

Rationalist: One should be rational because there are good reasons for being so.

Sceptic: But why should one heed those reasons? Why be rational?

Rationalist: Because there are good reasons for being so.

Sceptic: But again: why should one be moved by such reasons? Why be rational?

As this brief dialogue suggests, the rationalist appears to have to assume rationalism in order to argue the case for it. Since that assumption is the very question at issue, however, such a response will beg the question at issue, or be viciously circular, or, if rationalism is excused from the requirement of justification (as Trigg and O'Hear recommend), be inconsistent with its own precepts. It appears that a rational justification of rationality cannot be had.

But this presumes that the rationalist cannot utilize a certain kind of argumentative strategy—a *self-reflexive* strategy—that promises to supply the wanted justification without the attendant logical difficulties. Below I will offer a self-reflexive justification of rationality; first I want simply to illustrate the strategy and show how it can be used in circumstances in which charges of inconsistency, circularity and question-begging seem to threaten.

Consider first an example concerning explanation. Evolutionary theory can explain not only the evolution of mollusks and molecules, it can also explain the evolution of creatures capable of formulating evolutionary theory itself. It can explain (at least in principle) its own evolution, both in terms of the evolution of creatures who have formulated it, and its own "evolution" (in the sense of a Popperian "evolutionary epistemology') from its earliest formulations to a theory very much more complex and informative than those early formulations. In this sense evolutionary theory can self-reflexively explain its own evolution: the theory contributes to its own explanation. But it does so without being inconsistent or engaging in viciously circular or question-begging reasoning.

Philosophical theories often need to be, and are, self-reflexive in this way. Theories of epistemic justification, to take an example close to our present concerns, need themselves to be justified, and theorists of various epistemological persuasions—foundationalists, coherentists, pragmatists, naturalists, etc.—regularly offer accounts of epistemic justification which they hope will both succeed as accounts of such justification, and also will turn out themselves to be justified in their own terms. Such accounts self-reflexively apply to themselves. But they are not necessarily logically defective for doing so. Indeed, if it were not possible for an account of justification to apply self-reflexively to itself, there could be no theory of epistemic justification which was itself justified. This would constitute an argument, not merely for the irrationality of rationalism, but for wholesale scepticism, since no judgment concerning epistemic justification could be itself justified. The problems facing such versions of scepticism are well known. In any case, epistemologists are quite content to apply their theories of justification self-reflexively: foundationalists hope to show that foundationalism follows appropriately from appropriate foundational beliefs; coherentists hope to show that coherentism most adequately coheres with other relevant beliefs; naturalists hope to show that naturalism is the theory of justification most justified by naturalistic epistemological inquiry; and so on. In all these cases, theories are offered which self-reflexively apply to themselves. If successful, they can be thought of as *self-justifying*: justified by themselves, without need for recourse to self-exception or to other avenues of justification which open the door to problems involving inconsistency, circularity, or question-begging. It is clear, I think, that evolutionary theory can properly be thought of as self-explanatory, and that theories of epistemic justification can properly be thought to be self-reflexively self-justifying, at least in principle. If so, then attempts to justify rationality need not necessarily fall to insuperable logical difficulties; the examples just given serve as counter-examples to the claims of Popper, Trigg and O'Hear to the contrary.

What is needed, then, is a self-reflexive justification of rationality. To this I now turn.[9]

THE QUESTION CAN BE ANSWERED:
RATIONALITY IS SELF-JUSTIFYING

Consider again the brief dialogue reviewed above:

> Rationalist: One should be rational because there are good reasons for being so.
>
> Sceptic: But why should one heed those reasons? Why be rational?
>
> Rationalist: Because there are good reasons for being so.
>
> Sceptic: But again: why should one be moved by such reasons? Why be rational?

This dialogue appears to be a depressing one for the rationalist, for it appears to show that the rationalist cannot adequately answer her opponent without begging the question against her or arguing in a circle. I believe, though, that this appearance is dispelled once one pays more attention to the sceptic's own position, and to the possibility of the rationalist employing a self-reflexive justificatory strategy.

The sceptic is herself asking our question. She is asking "Why be rational?"; that is, she is asking for reasons which justify the rationalist's commitment to rationality. She is suggesting that if reasons cannot be adduced which justify the rationalist's position, then that position fails to be justified and so should be seen by the rationalist as insufficient to command her (i.e. the rationalist's) respect.

In doing so, the sceptic is playing the rationalist's game. Indeed, she is presupposing[10] rationalism, in that she is asking for reasons which justify a position in order to determine whether or not the position is actually justified or is worthy of embrace. Of course in this instance the position in question is that of rationalism itself. But that is irrelevant to the present point, which is that the sceptic is presupposing rationalism in order to call it into question. In presupposing it, she is inadvertently determining the outcome of her inquiry: rationality, and the commitment to it, cannot help but turn out to be themselves rationally justified, because they are presupposed by the very posing of the question concerning their justificatory status.

In asking "Why be rational?," the sceptic is asking for reasons which justify rationality and our commitment to it. In genuinely or seriously asking the question, she is committing herself to take seriously putative reasons for being rational. Consequently, she is acknowledging the potential epistemic force of reasons which purport to answer her question; in so doing, she is presupposing the very rationalism her inquiry calls into question. The very posing of the question "Why be rational?," in short, is possible only if rationalism is assumed. For the serious posing of any question commits its poser to the taking seriously of putative answers to it, and answers just are reasons for settling questions one way or another. Thus the posing of this question presupposes the possible forcefulness of putative answers, and so presupposes the epistemic legitimacy of reasons and the appeal to reasons. And that reasons are legitimate and forceful just is the position of the rationalist. The serious posing of the question assures that the poser is committed to the justifiedness of the rationalist's stance.

Rationality can thus be seen to be self-justifying, in that seriously querying the justificatory status of rationality presupposes that very status. In order seriously to question the value or justificatory status of rationality, one must assume the relevance of considerations which rationally support one or another answer to the question; in so assuming, one is presupposing the rationalist's position. To raise the question is to answer it in favor of rationality. In this sense rationality is self-justifying: one cannot question it except by accepting it, for acceptance is a precondition of the serious posing of the question. To ask

"Why be rational?" is to ask for *reasons* for and against being rational; to enter-
tain the question seriously is to acknowledge the force of reasons in ascertaining the answer. The very raising of the question, in other words, commits
one to a recognition of the epistemic force of reasons. To recognize that force
is to recognize the answer to the question: we should be rational because (for
the reason that) reasons, as the rationalist holds, have force.[11]

Of course one might never ask the question. One who never asks the question, though, does not engage the issue: she raises no sceptical challenge to the
rationalist's position; nor does she challenge our regarding the fostering of critical thinking as a fundamental educational ideal. But once one poses the question, that is, wonders whether or not (or why) one should be rational, one's
wondering insures that one has reasons for being rational.[12]

This proposed solution to the question "Why be rational?" is actually very
much like Nicholas Rescher's (1988) solution. It will I hope prove instructive
to consider briefly Rescher's discussion.

Rescher, like me, is concerned to answer the charge that the "self-justifying" strategy employed above is circular. The worry is that Rescher's "pragmatic"[13] justification of rationality relies upon rationality—one "should be
rational just because that is the rational thing to do" (Rescher [1988], pp.
43)—and, therefore, that this attempted justification is problematically circular. Rescher accepts that his proffered justification is circular, but denies that it
is viciously or problematically so:

83

> It might seem questionable to establish the jurisdiction of reason by
> appeal to the judgement of reason itself. But, in fact, of course, this cir-
> cularity is not really vicious at all. Vicious circularity stultifies by "begging
> the question'; virtuous circularity merely coordinates related elements in
> their mutual interlinkage. The former presupposes what is to be proved,
> the latter simply shows how things are connected together in a well-
> coordinated and mutually supportive interrelationship. The self-reliance
> of rationality merely exemplifies this latter circumstance of an inherent
> coordination among its universe components. (1988, p. 43)

Rescher here argues that a justification of rationality which presumes rationality need not beg the question even though it presupposes exactly what is
to be proved: namely, that reasons can have genuine evidential force, and therefore that one ought to acknowledge, and believe and act in accordance with,
such reasons. But it is not immediately obvious why this is not in fact question begging. Rescher is arguing that one ought to be rational because there
are good reasons for being so. But if the point at issue is whether—and if so
why—we should take "good reasons" seriously, then Rescher's argument does
seem to beg the question, since it presupposes that putative good reasons are

in fact epistemically forceful. That, after all, is why (according to Rescher's argument) we should be rational: we should be rational because there are good reasons for being so. But if the sceptic is asking why we should take good reasons seriously, and endeavor to believe and act in accordance with them, then Rescher's argument does appear to beg the question against the sceptic by presupposing that good reasons actually afford warrant, and so are to be taken seriously.

Rescher acknowledges that his argument appears to beg the question, but denies that it actually does so:

> Admittedly, the reasoning at issue has an *appearance* of vitiating circularity because the force of the argument itself rests on an appeal to rationality.... But this sort of question begging is simply *unavoidable* in the circumstances. It is exactly what we want and need. Where else should we look for a *rational* validation of rationality but to reason itself? The only reasons for being rational that it makes sense to ask for are *rational* reasons ... we have no way of getting at the facts directly, without the epistemic detour of securing grounds and reasons for them. And it is, of course, rationally cogent grounds and reasons that we want and need. The overall justification of rationality *must* be reflexive and self-referential. (1988, p. 43, emphases in original)

84

Rescher here argues that a justification of rationality must rely on reasons if it is to be of any worth; that any such justification must therefore presuppose the potential forcefulness of reasons and in this sense be self-reflexive; and therefore that the circularity involved in his justificatory argument is unproblematic:

> There is accordingly no basis for any rational discontent, no room for any dissatisfaction or complaint regarding a "circular" justification of rationality. We would not (should not) want it otherwise. If we bother to want an answer to the question "Why be rational?" at all, it is clearly a *rational* answer that we require. The only sort of justification of anything—rationality included—that is worth having at all is a rational one. That presupposition of rationality is not vitiating, not viciously circular, but essential—an unavoidable consequence of the self-sufficiency of cognitive reason. There is simply no satisfactory alternative to using reason in its own defence. ... Given the very nature of the justificatory enterprise at issue, one just cannot avoid letting rationality sit in judgement on itself. (What is being asked for, after all, is a rational argument for rational action, a basis for rational conviction, and not persuasion by something probatively irrelevant like threats of *force majeure*.) (1988, pp. 43–4, emphases in original)

Rescher's point here is I think exactly right. A rational justification of rationality needn't be regarded as viciously circular, or as begging the question against the sceptic, because the presumption of the (possible) force of reasons utilized by Rescher in his argument is a presumption made by the sceptic—and indeed by anyone who asks "Why be rational?"—as well. As Rescher argues, asking for a justification of rationality is asking for a *rational* justification of it; the very asking of the question commits the questioner to the presumption of the potential probative force of reasons, for in asking the question she is asking whether there are *reasons* which justify rationality, and in asking it seriously she is committing herself to judging the matter in accordance with the strength of reasons which can be brought in favor of or against being rational. Thus anyone who seriously asks the question "Why be rational?" has, in committing herself to judge the matter in accordance with reasons, already committed herself to the (only *seemingly* problematic or question begging) presumption of the potential epistemic force of reasons.

So Rescher is right: a rational defense of rationality is not question begging or viciously circular; it merely acknowledges, as any serious questioner must, that seriously asking "Why be rational?" presupposes a commitment to rationality, i.e. to deciding the question on the basis of the best available reasons. Thus the presumption of rationality in Rescher's argument does not beg the question against the sceptic, but rather presupposes that which the sceptic, and indeed *any* serious inquiry into the question "Why be rational?," must presuppose: that the question must be settled on the basis of reasons if it is to be properly settled, and therefore that all parties to the debate must presume the potential force of reasons. As Rescher argues, this presupposition is

> not vitiating, not viciously circular, but essential—an unavoidable consequence of the self-sufficiency of cognitive reason.... Rather than indicating the defect of vicious circularity, the self-referential character of a justification of rationality is a precondition of its adequacy! It is *only* a rational legitimation of rationality that we would want: any other sort would avail us nothing. (1988, p. 44, emphasis in original)

As Rescher suggests, the self-referential justification of rationality does not beg the question, nor is it viciously circular. Rather, it is itself probatively forceful—despite the fact that it is the probative force of reason which is at issue. Rescher's argument rests on his insistence (a) that genuine, satisfactory justifications are based on good reasons, and therefore (b) that seeking a justification of rationality—asking "Why be rational?"—involves seeking good reasons for being so, and so acknowledging that reasons can (at least in principle) be good. Since good reasons provide warrant for their targets, anyone seriously asking "Why be rational?" is committed to the potential warranting

85

force of reasons. Consequently, the question is answered in its being seriously asked: one should be rational—i.e. believe and act an accordance with reasons—because reasons have (or at least in principle can have) warranting force. This much is presupposed in the very asking of the question.

This solution to our problem has it that rationality is self-justifying in the same sense that theories of epistemic justification purport to be self-justifying: reasons are epistemically forceful in guiding belief and action, and this is true even in the case when the question before us is the fundamental one of whether (and why) we should believe and act in accordance with reasons— that is, of whether and why we should be rational. Earlier we saw that Popper, Trigg and O'Hear regard the question as one which does not admit of an answer free of logical difficulty. Let us see if the solution proposed here is free of the difficulties adumbrated by those authors.

Popper, we saw, argues that a rational justification of rationality, if it is to avoid question-begging or vicious circularity, must be inconsistent, since the only way to avoid those logical difficulties is to exempt rationality from its own requirement, imposed on every other claim or position, that it itself be justified on the basis of reasons and argument. But on the solution proposed, rationality is not exempted from its own constraints on rational justification. It is itself justified on the basis of the argument given above.

This solution, Popper might claim (as Trigg and O'Hear claim), avoids inconsistency by falling prey either to question-begging or to vicious circularity: I am justifying rationality by appealing to reasons, but such an appeal begs the question against the sceptic who has not already recognized the legitimacy of the appeal to reasons. The solution, however, does not beg the question against the sceptic or argue in a circle. Rather, it points out that the sceptic, in posing her sceptical question, has already committed herself to and recognized the epistemic forcefulness and legitimacy of reasons and the appeal to them. It points out, in short, that the only way the question can meaningfully be posed is one which determines that the question be answered in such a way that rationality turns out to be justified. Thus it is not the case that the rationalist must beg the question against the sceptic or argue in a vicious circle. It is rather the sceptic's own questioning of rationality that secures rationality's epistemic standing for rationalist and sceptic alike; the rationalist needs simply to point this out.

Since the question can be answered this way, the other difficulty that Trigg and O'Hear see—that the demand for a justification of rationality is a bogus demand, since it cannot even in principle be met without introducing overwhelming logical difficulties—is no longer rightly seen as problematic. The question can be answered in a way which avoids question-begging and vicious circularity; consequently there is no reason, even from the Trigg/O'Hear point of view, to regard the demand as a bogus demand. The demand is legitimate, and is met, by appeal to the self-reflexive strategy utilized in the proposed solution. The solution is neither inconsistent, nor question-begging, nor circular.[14]

It remains now only to conclude by spelling out the ramifications of that solution for critical thinking.

CONCLUSION: "WHY BE RATIONAL?" AND CRITICAL THINKING

If we cannot say why we should be rational, then we cannot justify educational efforts aimed at fostering critical thinking. Students who accept our lesson concerning the importance of critical thinking will naturally extend the critical attitude to critically examine our endorsement of critical thinking itself. They will seek reasons for being critical. The demand for reasons for being critical is tantamount to a demand for reasons for being rational. Consequently, our efforts to justify our regarding critical thinking as a fundamental educational ideal hinge on our ability to answer the question with which we began: Why be rational?

Fortunately, we *can* say why we should be rational: our question has been answered above. Consequently our educational efforts on behalf of critical thinking can proceed without fear of falling to this justificational worry. In saying why we should be rational, we provide an underlying rationale and justification for our efforts to foster critical thinking in the schools. In so doing, we add an important dimension to the theory of critical thinking—a dimension of philosophical *and educational* importance.

87

CRITICAL THINKING AND PREJUDICE

The real struggle is not between East and
West, or capitalism and communism, but
between education and propaganda.
            —Martin Buber

chapter 6

SOME MONTHS AGO I was invited by my campus' chapter of the Intervarsity
Christian Fellowship to participate in a debate on the topic "Is Christianity
Rational?" I argued against the proposition, relying on the problem of evil
and on difficulties with the form of the Cosmological Argument favored by
my opponent, Dr. Norman Geisler of Dallas Theological seminary, in order to
make my case. The debate was lively but friendly; it was well-attended, mainly by members of the ICF; and the straw vote taken at the end showed that
Christianity survived quite nicely, at least in the minds of the members of the
audience, despite my arguments.

I was quite surprised, therefore, when several days later I received in the
mail an anonymous message. It was a bright red swastika. Next to it was
scrawled the message: "America is a Christian nation. Jews are neither white
nor Christian. Why don't you go to Israel?"

Attempts to identify my correspondent proved futile. It did and does seem clear that the message was inspired by my participation in the debate. Since I had argued for an atheistic position, not a Jewish one, I was surprised to receive, not an anti-anti-Christian message—which would have been appropriate given the stance I took in the debate—but an anti-Jewish one. Why did my correspondent regard me as a Jew (I was not identified as such at the debate) rather than an atheist or an anti-Christian? If s/he wanted to criticize my anti-Christianity, why focus on my Jewishness? My correspondent, it seemed, harbored a certain anti-Semitic (and racist) prejudice, and I was the target of that prejudice.

How is such prejudice best understood? Was my correspondent in any way thinking badly in harboring it? Was this instance of prejudice, and is prejudice more generally, a function of faulty thinking? Faulty character? Poor argumentation? Is there any way in which anti-Semitic or racist prejudice can profitably be seen as a failure of argumentation, of rationality, or of critical thinking? There is a reason to hope that the last question can be answered affirmatively. For if prejudice can be seen as a violation of the canons of rationality/critical thinking, then effective educational intervention aimed at increasing students" critical thinking abilities might serve to ameliorate our shared circumstance by reducing prejudice.

In what follows, I shall try to provide that affirmative answer. That is, I shall try to spell out the way in which prejudice and prejudicial thinking fail to meet the standards of critical thinking. In doing so, I will presume the view of critical thinking articulated and defended in the preceding chapters. In the next section I address the phenomenon of prejudice and the character of prejudicial thinking. In the following section I address the relationship between prejudice and critical thinking, and try to specify the different ways in which prejudice is rightly seen as a failure of critical thinking. This will pave the way, I hope, to a better understanding of the ways in which education aimed at the promotion of critical thinking can help to reduce prejudice. Finally, in the last section I consider the implications of the position defended for democratic social change.

WHAT IS PREJUDICE?

Prejudice is often thought of in terms of overgeneralization—all blacks are lazy, all Jews are cheap, all women are emotional. If this were a sufficient characterization of prejudice, the job of understanding it from the point of view of critical thinking would be easy: prejudice would involve unjustified, irrational overgeneralization, and our directive would be to spend extra time teaching students about the evils of hasty generalization. Unfortunately, this characterization of prejudice is not sufficient. For prejudice does not always involve overgeneralization, or any generalization. One can be prejudiced toward a single individual, without ascribing to that individual perceived properties of her group.[1] Prejudice can sometimes be simply a failure to treat persons as persons; it can be to give illicit preference to oneself and one's interests. Whether prejudice is of one of these sorts, or involves illicit overgeneralization, we should note the problematic role of *reflection* in the forming and maintaining of specific prejudices.

Bernard Williams nicely brings out this aspect of prejudice. He offers two characterizations of prejudice relevant to the present discussion. A prejudiced belief, he says, can be "any belief one holds only because one has not reflected on it." (Williams [1985], p. 117) In this sense, prejudice is inevitable: our beliefs are too legion for them all to be the object of our reflection. My belief that no one in Miami wears mittens in July has been, up to this very moment, a belief I have held without reflection; it would dilute the notion of prejudice, and lessen its pejorative flavor, to regard beliefs such as this one as prejudiced simply because they have not been reflected upon. Nevertheless, the absence of reflection is an important aspect of prejudice, for genuinely prejudiced belief does require a lack of critical reflection. We need to say something more about the nature of that lack.

Once again Williams shows the way. He notes that "a prejudice of the racist or sexist kind is usually a belief *guarded against reflection* because it suits the interests of the believers that it be held." ([1985], p. 117, emphasis added) There are two important aspects of this account of prejudice that we must note. First, prejudice does not result simply from the absence of reflection. Rather, prejudice is *protected* from reflection—the believer actively protects her prejudiced belief from "the shafts of impartial evidence."[2] If someone showed me a mittened Miamian, I would be surprised but would happily amend my belief. But if my belief is prejudiced in Williams' second sense, then I will actively strive to protect that belief, and deflect contrary evidence—"She's only wearing mittens because you've paid her"; "You must have imagined the mittens you thought you saw, for in a tropical climate like Miami's no one would wear them"—and in this way my prejudice will be illicitly protected from correction or evaluation by way of reflection on relevant evidence.

The second aspect of Williams' characterization to be noted is that according to it it is often in the interests of the prejudiced to maintain their prejudiced beliefs. It is in the interests of nonblacks for blacks to be generally regarded as lazy; it is in the interests of non-Jews for Jews to be regarded as cheap; it is in the interests of men for women to be regarded as nonreflective, practically rather than theoretically inclined, or overly emotional. It is in the interests of white Christians like my correspondent (discussed above) for America to be regarded as a white and Christian nation and for Jews to be regarded as neither white nor Christian. This point about the self-interested nature of prejudice is important, because it helps to explain the fact that prejudice is often protected from, or guarded against, reflection. Why does the prejudiced person guard her prejudiced beliefs against reflection? Because it is in her interests for the world to be generally regarded as the sort of place portrayed by those beliefs. The Klansman is better off if blacks and Jews are held to be troublesome and inferior; men are better off if women are thought to be too dumb or emotional for anything better than "pink collar" work; and so on. Noting the self-interested character of prejudice is important in understanding its guardedness against reflection.

Supposing that Williams' second sense adequately characterizes prejudice, how shall we portray the relationship between prejudice and critical thinking?

IS PREJUDICE A VIOLATION OR FAILURE OF CRITICAL THINKING?

Of course. But if education for critical thinking is to be utilized in the battle against prejudice, it is important that we understand clearly the precise ways in which prejudice repudiates critical thinking or violates its canons of good argumentation.

Prejudice can (and frequently does) violate both components of critical thinking: it is incompatible with proper execution of the skills of reason assessment, and it is incompatible with the attitudes, dispositions, habits of mind and character traits constitutive of the critical spirit. Prejudice is a violation of the "reason assessment" component of critical thinking because it violates the canons of reason assessment: it sometimes illicitly overgeneralizes, it neglects or ignores contrary evidence, indeed it protects itself from contrary evidence. Prejudice is equally a violation of the "critical spirit" component of critical thinking. For the prejudiced believer does not seek out evidence with which to challenge her belief; her belief is not based on a systematic assessment of relevant evidence; her character is not one which abhors and avoids arbitrariness, wishful thinking, or special pleading. The dispositions, habits of mind and character traits associated with the critical spirit all discourage prejudice, for they encourage the monitoring of belief in light of relevant evidence, the disposition to believe only that which is genuinely supported by an impartial evaluation of evidence, and the avoidance of the special protection from evidence which prejudiced beliefs enjoy.

The "guard against reflection," noted by Williams, which prejudiced belief enjoys, similarly illustrates the way in which prejudice violates both dimensions of critical thinking. It violates the reason assessment dimension by refusing to honor contrary evidence or evaluate relevant evidence fairly and honestly. These are exactly what are guarded against in "guarding against reflection." In guarding beliefs against reflection, moreover, one manifests a lack of dispositions to seek out evidence relevant to those beliefs, to utilize reason assessment skills, and to be guided by such skilled evaluation. In manifesting this lack, and the related absence of habits of mind and character traits already discussed, the "guard against reflection" aspect of prejudice is seen to violate the critical spirit dimension, as well as the reason assessment dimension, of critical thinking.

The self-interested nature of prejudice also belies any connection it might have to critical thinking. For critical thinking requires impartial evaluation of evidence; it requires that belief and action follow the path of evidence, even when that path is not the one that it is in one's interest to follow.[3] Thus both aspects of Williams' second characterization of prejudice—its guardedness against reflection, and its self-interestedness—speak against conceiving of prejudice as something sanctioned by critical thinking. And it is important to see that prejudice violates both the reason assessment and the critical spirit components of critical thinking.

HOW CAN EDUCATION FOR CRITICAL THINKING COMBAT PREJUDICE?

Generally speaking, education aimed at the fostering of critical thinking can combat prejudice by fostering both the skills of reason assessment and the dispositions, habits of mind, attitudes and character traits of the critical spirit. For those skills and that spirit are incompatible with prejudice. A critical thinker is able to recognize prejudiced thinking in herself and to work to eradicate it; she is disposed to so eradicate and to have a character which condemns prejudice. The skills of reason assessment are necessary to recognize prejudice as unjustified, while the willingness and tendency to reconsider one's beliefs and to examine their justifiedness—attitudes and dispositions characteristic of the critical spirit—foster and help constitute a mental environment hostile to prejudice. Thus encouraging the development of each of these aspects of critical thinking can contribute to the defeat of prejudice.

A dimension of critical thinking particularly relevant to the battle against prejudice is the relationship between critical thinking and the Kantian ideal of respect for persons.[4] To be unprejudiced towards persons different from oneself is to have a certain moral sensitivity. It is to be able to empathize with such persons and to be able to understand what it feels like for them to be the victims of prejudice. This sensitivity, moreover, is closely connected to Kant's injunction to treat persons as ends, and not as means: that is, to honor the legitimacy of others' wants, desires and needs, and to recognize that their wants and needs are as relevant to the way they are to be treated as one's own wants and needs are to one's own treatment. To be sensitive to the wants and needs of others in this way is (at least to a significant extent) to respect them as persons. To respect others as persons is the fundamental Kantian dictum. To be prejudiced towards others is to fail to treat them with respect, while to so treat them is to avoid being prejudiced toward them. Helping students to be sensitive to the situations of others, and to the relevance of their wants and needs to their treatment, is to help students learn to treat others with respect as persons. It is also to foster critical thinking. The relevance of Kant's ethical injunctions to critical thinking thus sheds further light on critical thinking's ability to combat prejudice.

Consider again the prejudice manifested by my swastika-sending correspondent. In what way might critical thinking combat or mitigate her/his prejudice? One way to see the relevance of critical thinking to that prejudice is to construe my correspondent's message as an argument:[5]

1. America is a Christian nation.
2. Jews are neither white nor Christian.

---

3. Therefore, Jews should not be in America.
   (They should "go to Israel.")

Once this is seen as an argument—or even as a series of assertions—my correspondent's failure to think critically is overwhelmingly apparent. Consider the first premise. Is there any reason to think that America is a Christian nation? Is it true that non-Christians, e.g. Jews, atheists, Muslims, etc., are not properly regarded as Americans? Is there anything in the official self-characterization of the nation—its laws, its Constitution and Bill of Rights, etc.—which supports such a view of America? Is American culture uniformly, or even importantly, supportive of such a view? Once questions such as these are raised, it is easy to see that belief in the first premise requires either ignorance, willful inattention, or profound misunderstanding of the laws, documents and culture which define the nature of that nation. The first premise is both false and unjustified; even minimally competent reason assessment is sufficient to show that one can believe the first premise only by being at odds with the dictates of critical thinking. (I note in passing the problematic identification of America with the U.S.A. How many of the non-U.S.A. sharers of North, Central and South America would sanction this identification?)

The second premise is revealing of an interesting weakness in my correspondent's argumentative powers. The claim that Jews are not white (as well as not Christian) shows a failure to understand the distinction between necessary and sufficient conditions, a distinction competent reason assessors grasp. My correspondent believes, apparently, that to be a "real" American one must be both white and Christian. These then are necessary conditions of being an American. Since they are both necessary, anyone who fails to meet either fails to be an American; failing to be white, and failing to be Christian, are each independently sufficient for failing to be an American (on my correspondent's view). Thus, noting my Jewishness—and hence my non-Christianity—is sufficient to show that on her/his view I am not an American. But my correspondent does not understand this; s/he feels compelled to say that Jews are not white as well as not Christian in order to deny that Jews are American. (A similar difficulty arises for my correspondent in the categorizing of black Christians.) So the second premise demonstrates a failure to grasp the distinction—simple, and basic to proper reason assessment—between necessary and sufficient conditions. (Again, I waive here complicating considerations involving the relationship between Judaism and Christianity, the problem for my correspondent raised by Jews for Jesus, etc., which do not effect the present point.)

Sentence 3, when understood as a conclusion and not simply a statement of prejudice, follows from premises 1 and 2 only if one adds additional, suppressed premises. Of particular note is a suppressed premise of "national purity": the idea that only people of the sort who characterize a nation should be comfortably allowed within its borders. On this view, only white Christians should reside in the U.S.A.; only white atheists in the former Soviet Union; only Muslims in the Arab nations; only blacks in the African nations; etc. Such a view is extremely problematic. It utterly ignores the contributions "outsiders" can make to nations and cultures; it ignores or denies the virtues of international and interracial interaction; it condemns nations to a stultifying stagnation. Even if one truly believed in a white Christian America, such an America would suffer, in ways practical as well as intangible, by the serious enforcement of racial and religious restrictions on residency and citizenship.

The premises and conclusion of my correspondent's argument thus fail to meet even minimal standards of reason assessment. (If taken not as an argument but simply as a string of assertions, they still so fail for the reasons mentioned.) Moreover, my correspondent is not sensitive to the obviously self-serving nature of her/his position, a self-servingness so flagrant that a critical thinker could not help but reconsider the merits of the case because she would be aware of the pitfalls of self-serving thinking and would be disposed to avoid it. Equally flagrant are the weaknesses of the reasons my correspondent offers for her/his conclusion, thus providing evidence of a lack of critical spirit—an unwillingness to subject beliefs to critical scrutiny and to believe and act on the basis of a systematic assessment of reasons. All in all, then, my correspondent demonstrates a rather thorough-going failure to think critically. An education which succeeded in fostering critical thinking would go at least some way toward reducing the frequency of this kind of prejudice.

I am not suggesting that education for critical thinking is a panacea which will eradicate prejudice. Prejudice is a complex phenomenon; it is not entirely a cognitive one. I've said nothing about the importance of getting at the deep-seated experiences and cultural, political and economic influences which cause prejudice. But a full confrontation with prejudice surely requires attention to those deep-seated causes. So critical thinking should not be thought of as a universal corrective for prejudice.

95

But I am suggesting that an education successful at fostering critical thinking can aid significantly in the fight against prejudice. An education which develops skills and abilities of reason assessment, and which imbues students with the critical spirit, cannot help but foster in students a sensitivity to, and an abhorrence of, prejudice and prejudiced thinking. Such students will be able, and disposed, to reject prejudice in others and to root it out of their own thinking. An education which successfully attends to both the reason assessment and the critical spirit components of critical thinking can be a powerful tool in the task of eradicating prejudice.

PREJUDICE, CRITICAL THINKING, AND DEMOCRATIC SOCIAL CHANGE

Prejudice is straightforwardly and dramatically antisocial. A healthy society ought to strive to change itself in ways that eliminate, or at least reduce, such antisociality. Such a society ought therefore to endeavor to eliminate or reduce prejudice. To succeed would be to change society for the better. How should we think about effecting such change?

One prominent suggestion is that social change be *democratic*. What this means is not completely clear, since there are many conceptions and theories of democracy extant in the literature. Ignoring this difficulty, we can perhaps agree that, other things being equal, democratic social change is better than the alternative. But it is important to keep in mind, when considering social change, that others things are often not equal. When they are not, the desirability of democratic social change can be quite problematic.

For example, in many societies, both at present and throughout history, the presence of prejudice is and has been more common than its absence. Consider a society in which the members of the dominant group are uniformly prejudiced against some minority group within it. Suppose that that society democratically decides to change itself in such a way that that group is systematically and lawfully mistreated. This would be a case, I think we should agree, of democratic, but nevertheless undesirable, social change—as would be any democratic social change which reflected or fostered prejudice. The democraticality of social change is thus not sufficient for its desirability. By the same token, the nondemocraticality of social change is compatible with its desirability, as the case of the enlightened monarch shows. In sum, democraticality is neither necessary nor sufficient for the desirability of social change. There are independent criteria—concerning fairness, nonoppression, equality, justice, etc.—which social changes must meet in order to be rightly regarded as good or desirable; and being "democratically arrived at" constitutes neither a sufficient, nor even a necessary, condition of a change's desirability.

However, while these criteria have independent moral and/or epistemic status, there is a crucially important role for democratic discussion in their establishment and legitimation. For any argumentative discussion purporting to establish such criteria is suspect to the extent that some perspectives are silenced or marginalized, while others dominate or exert hegemonic control. Criteria of good thinking and quality argumentation, like criteria of desirable social change, are established theoretically/philosophically; democratic agreement is neither necessary nor sufficient for their legitimation. Nevertheless, our philosophical efforts to establish them as legitimate are best conducted in as democratic and open a way as possible.[6] This is a moral constraint on our efforts; it may well also enhance our chances for philosophical success. Democratic procedures and values are thus centrally, but only indirectly, relevant to the establishment of the desirability of social change. Democracy is not to be valued because the majority is always right, but because morality demands circumstances which permit the full and fair participation of all relevant people, groups, and ideas. Democratic procedures are for this reason desirable. We may hope, in addition, that they will conduce to the establishment of good and desirable outcomes, even though democratic decisions are neither automatically nor necessarily right in virtue of their democraticality.[7]

Finally, I should note that the just-mentioned criteria also function as criteria for the evaluation of social organization and of procedures for the establishment of social and public policy. Many would argue, as would I (Siegel [1988], pp. 60–61), that the form of social organization best supported by those criteria is that of democracy. If so, then there are independent reasons for thinking that democratic social organization is preferable to its alternatives—and so, that social change should also be democratically orchestrated. But again, this is not because social change which is "democratically arrived at" is automatically desirable. Its being arrived at democratically is neither necessary or sufficient for its desirability. Still, if democratic social organization and change can be independently justified, as I think they can, then critical thinking and skilled argumentation will be of fundamental importance for participants engaged in the contemplation and actualization of social change. For they promise to contribute importantly to the quality of democratic discussion of social policy and social change, precisely because critical thinkers can make better—epistemically better—judgments and decisions concerning the desirability of potential social changes. These judgments and decisions will be better precisely because they will be based on fair evaluation of relevant evidence and argument, and in this way reflective of the standards of reason assessment which rightly guide and inform critical thinking. If so, they will be blessedly free from prejudice as well.[8]

DIALOGUE

part two

THE RATIONALITY OF REASONABLENESS

The essence of the liberal outlook lies not in
what opinions are held, but in how they are
held: instead of being held dogmatically, they
are held tentatively, with a consciousness that
new evidence may at any moment lead to
their abandonment.

—Bertrand Russell

chapter 7

MANY PHILOSOPHERS OF EDUCATION and educational theorists recommend
critical thinking as their favored educational ideal. Some of them analyze that
contentious phrase—as I do—in terms of rationality, and argue that it is rationality, and the fostering of rationality in students, that is the desirable educational end referred to by "critical thinking." If rationality is to be regarded as
a fundamental educational ideal, how should that term be understood? In particular, should rationality be understood as a "formal," bloodless notion,
ascribable to computers and calculating machines; or should it be understood
as a "substantive" notion, involving more than the mere reasoning ability of
the student? If the latter, how much more is involved?

In this chapter I argue, as I have in previous chapters, that rationality must
be conceived substantively, and must be understood as involving dispositions,
attitudes, and character traits as well as reasoning ability. That is, I argue that

regarding rationality as a fundamental educational ideal involves explicit recognition of the "critical spirit."

But some writers who favor educational ideals associated with "reason" argue that this ideal must be understood not only substantively, but also contextually. The suggestion here is not only that contextual considerations are highly relevant to determining what, in a given context, it is rational to believe, judge or do—with this I agree—but also that what rationality is, the very substance of this notion, is itself contextually determined, so that rationality itself—as a concept, and, therefore, as an educational ideal—is contextually bound, and alters from context to context.

From this latter version of contextualism I demur; I will argue against it in what follows, paying specific attention to the contextualist position articulated and defended by Nicholas C. Burbules. In doing so I hope to carve a middle path between an overly formalistic conception of rationality, and an overly contextualist conception which faces difficulties at least as severe as that formalistic one. The aim of the exercise is to say something constructive about the sense in which the notion of rationality, when construed as an educational ideal, is best understood "substantively."

AGAINST A FORMALISTIC CONCEPTION OF RATIONALITY

While it is true that "rationality" can be construed as denoting a formal relationship between sentences or propositions, such a formalistic conception of it is both epistemologically and educationally inadequate.

For one thing, the notion of "formal" being utilized here is too narrow and limited to ground or explicate successfully the notion of rationality. "Formal," as used in expressions like "formal logic," refers to structural relationships between certain sorts of items, which relationships involve no reference to the "content" of the items allegedly related. This is the standard sort of relationship treated in "formal" logic, wherein one need not know the sustantive content of a sentence to know that it, for example, is entailed by, or entails, another. Relations such as "is entailed by" and "is a logical consequence of" can be seen to hold (or not) between (sentences and) propositions irrespective of the propositional content of those propositions. For example, in the propositional calculus, 'q' is a logical consequence of 'p' and 'if p, then q,' independently of the propositional content of the sentences for which the letters p and q are taken to stand. Logical validity, entailment, etc. are relations which are *formal* in the sense that their obtaining is a matter strictly of the form, and not the content, of the related propositions, or, strictly speaking, of the formal relations obtaining between symbols standing for such propositions.[1]

This sort of formal relation between sentences or propositions is not sufficient to underwrite a conception of rationality. This is because rationality is fundamentally an epistemological, rather than a logical, notion; to say of two sentences that it is rational to believe one in virtue of the support it receives from another is, typically, to comment on the substantive rather than merely the formal relations that obtain between the two sentences. For example, it is rational to believe "The Philosophy of Education Society is an international organization" in virtue of the support provided that claim by "Some members of The Philosophy of Education Society have non-U.S. mailing addresses, while some have U.S. mailing addresses." But this latter sentence doesn't deductively entail, or stand in any particularly important formal relationship with, the former—it may be, for example, that all those members with non-U.S. mailing addresses have those addresses only temporarily, say because they are currently on sabbatical and away from their permanent homes. This possibility, though farfetched, is sufficient to rule out a formal characterization of the relevant relationship between the two sentences. But the one sentence does provide considerable support for—though it does not formally entail—the other. The relevant relationship between the two sentences is not a formal one; it is rather an *epistemic* one, which involves the contents of the two sentences, and the evidential relations between them. And this point is quite general—rationality generally involves relations of justification, which in turn involve propositional content, rather than (merely) form. A purely formal conception of rationality could not do full justice to the normative, epistemic, evidential dimensions of the term.[2]

So, even from a purely philosophical point of view, and without any regard to education, a formal conception of rationality is inadequate. Once we consider rationality as an educational ideal, the inadequacies of a purely formal account become even more obvious.

If we were stuck with a purely formal conception of rationality, regarding that conception as an educational ideal would be foolish indeed. For one thing, education involves people. Would we be saying that people should stand in formal relations with each other? With sentences or propositions? This idea makes no sense.

Perhaps we could think that regarding rationality as an educational aim or ideal would involve regarding it as a primary educational desideratum that students be brought to a sophisticated understanding of the formal relationships obtaining between sentences or propositions. But why should we regard such understanding as an important educational aim? To do so would be to regard our educational ideal as realized to the extent that students approximate "logic machines." This is not only pyschologically dubious, in view of humans' quite limited computational capacity (Harman [1986], Cherniak [1986]); it is educationally dubious as well. For a student so educated could nevertheless manifest the grossest of educational deficiencies—she might know little, understand less, and have gross deficiencies of character. We could not regard such a student as an educational success, much less as having achieved to any significant degree an important educational ideal.

Moreover, such an educational vision completely ignores the human dimension of education. It takes no account of the sort of *person* we think education should strive to help create; it pays no attention to the personal qualities we value and think it important to foster, or to the moral dimensions of educational interaction. In particular, it pays no attention to the attitudes, dispositions, habits of mind, or character traits which, I have argued in earlier chapters, are fundamental to the educational ideal of rationality, and are emphasized by many exponents of the ideal in their portrayal of it.

For all these reasons, we must reject a formal conception of rationality—both as an epistemic notion, and as an educational ideal.[3] We must, instead, regard rationality as a substantive epistemic notion, involving the substance or contents of sentences rationally related; and, especially, we must regard education for rationality as involving both this sort of substance, and also a substantive treatment of the personal and moral dimensions of education. Let us then turn to the further development of this substantive conception of rationality.

SUBSTANTIVE RATIONALITY, CONTEXTUALISM, AND "REASONABLENESS"

If what I've said so far is correct, then rationality is substantive at least in the sense that it involves epistemic or evidential relations between sentences or propositions, and therefore propositional contents as well as formal relationships. Moreover, in so far as rationality is regarded as an educational ideal, it must be understood as involving properties of persons, in particular their attitudes, dispositions, habits of mind and character traits. Only such a conception as this would be thick enough to allow us plausibly to regard rationality as a fundamental educational ideal.

Nicholas C. Burbules suggests an even thicker conception of rationality—or, as he prefers to call it, "reasonableness." (Burbules [1991], [1991a],[4] [1993], [1995]). While I agree with much of what Burbules says, I believe that he overstates the contextual dimensions of rationality. In what follows I shall try to distinguish between weak and strong versions of that contextuality, and to endorse the first but reject the second—and in doing so, to make clear my reasons for not going all the way with Burbules on the contextuality of rationality.

Burbules offers important criticisms of a formal conception of rationality; with these I mainly agree. He also writes:

> [Siegel's] argument for critical thinking has quite properly tried to go beyond the formal conception, in terms of skills, knowledge of certain principles, and "logicality," to the development of a particular kind of

person. Possessing certain skills or formal knowledge without truly valuing their application—*and the limits of their application*—does not constitute a critical thinker or a rational person. I agree, and would like to suggest that developing the dispositions and character of rationality is in fact the more fundamental and difficult educational goal. (Burbules [1991a], p. 249, emphasis in original.[5]

I agree that valuing the application, and the limits of application, of critical thinking, is basic to being a critical thinker; and that developing the character side of critical thinking (the "critical spirit') is both more fundamental and more difficult an educational project than developing the reason assessment side. With the educational ideal of rationality being substantive in this sense I have no problem. However, Burbules continues:

> This consideration leads to a significant conclusion, in my view: rationality is a substantive achievement; it takes shape in the activities, decisions, and judgments of persons who possess the skills and formal knowledge of rationality, but who apply these in real contexts of belief and action. It involves making choices about how and when to apply these principles, and when to refrain from applying them, as [Siegel] suggest[s] in phrases like "*appropriately* moved by reasons." This argument leads in the same direction as our discussion earlier: while there are some general standards of good reasoning, there is an unavoidable judging component as well, and hence an inherent personal, idiosyncratic, and indeterminate character to what it will mean to be rational (I would say "reasonable") for any particular person in any particular circumstance. (Burbules [1991a], p. 249, emphasis in original.[6]

105

If "takes shape" is to be read as "manifests itself" in the opening sentence, then I see no problem with this passage; but if it is to be read rather as "is constituted by," so that the sentence suggests that what rationality *is* is determined by the actual activities, decisions and judgments which people make, then I see a big problem: namely, there is no room on this view for actual activities, decisions and judgments to fail to be rational, for there is no role for criteria to play in assessing specific activities, decisions and judgments as rational (or not). This "constitutive" view of rationality is strongly contextual, for it implies not only that the rationality of particular judgments, etc. is relative to context— which it surely is, since the evidence one has at one's disposal is context-bound—but also that rationality itself is determined by context, in the sense that what "rationality" means, and whether and why it is to be valued, themselves are determined by context. Burbules suggests this stronger contextualism when he writes:

> Thinking in terms of substantive rationality, or reasonableness, compels us to inquire deeply into *how* we foster such a set of virtues; into the *contexts* that support or encourage them; and into the *barriers* that impede them. These no longer can be seen as merely the instrumental questions of how to achieve a (separately identifiable) ideal, but as *inherent in the identification and justification of the ideal itself.* (Burbules [1991a], p. 250, emphases in original)

As I've already said, there is much I agree with in Burbules" articulation of his ideal of reasonableness. I agree that in some sense "rationality is a substantive achievement"; I also agree that judgment is central to critical thinking, and that judgment is often "indeterminate" in the sense that in a given context alternative, incompatible judgments might be equally rational or reasonable—to see this, one need only consider Buridan's ass. And as suggested earlier, I'm quite in agreement that rationality in its bloodless, "logicality" conception is to be deplored and rejected. Moreover, I agree that it is important to inquire into the means by which we might best foster rational virtues, which contexts help foster them and which barriers impede them, etc.[7] But I don't agree that these instrumental questions concerning the fostering of the virtues and dispositions of reasonableness are "inherent in the identification and justification of the ideal itself."

Part of the difficulty here stems from the way in which Burbules regards "reasonableness" as substantive:

> A substantive conception of rationality, or "reasonableness," begins with the assumption that the purely formal characterization neglects factors that are not purely external to reason, but are part of it. I want to incorporate into the very idea of reason the elements of personal characteristics, context, and social relations that support and motivate reasonable thought and conduct. (Burbules [1991], p. 218; see also Burbules [1991a], p. 252)

Burbules identifies these personal and social factors as involving personal virtues (e.g. of open-mindedness and modesty), the social context in which these virtues are encouraged and fostered, and the social—especially the pedagogical—relations in which potentially reasonable persons are enmeshed.[8] Thus:"*[T]o be reasonable* means to be a certain kind of person, in a certain kind of situation, related to certain kinds of other persons." (Burbules [1991], p. 218, emphasis in original)

I am very sympathetic to the sketch of the reasonable person which Burbules here offers, and equally sympathetic to the idea that contexts, situations and social relations can be said to be reasonable (or not) to the extent that they foster (or impede) the development of the virtues characteristic of the reasonable person. Nevertheless, I think there are four important difficulties with the position Burbules here articulates which need to be addressed.

First, Burbules' account of reasonableness completely excludes epistemic considerations; it says nothing of the way in which beliefs, judgments and actions are reasonable (or not) because of their substantive, contentful relations to putative reasons which support them (or not). However, as suggested above, such epistemic relations are central to reasonableness, in so far as it is substantive rather than merely formal. Any account of reasonableness which includes under that heading *nothing* about the relations between beliefs, judgments and actions, on the one hand, and the reasons which putatively support them, on the other, leaves out the most central feature of that notion. The epistemic dimensions of rationality/reasonableness are primary; without them, it is unclear why what is being offered is a conception *of reasonableness* at all.[9]

Second, how is this conception of reasonableness itself justified or established as reasonable? For brevity, let us consider just one of Burbules' elements: the personal virtues. I completely agree that the virtues Burbules mentions are indeed virtues. But how are they justified? Burbules suggests that they

> are justified . . . not as being instantiations of certain formal rules or standards of reasoned conduct, but as being part and parcel of that sort of person we value, like, and respect as reasonable. (Burbules [1991], p. 219)[10]

107

This justificatory route does not work. Suppose that "we value[d], like[d], and respect[ed] as reasonable" persons with "virtues" radically distinct from and incompatible with the ones Burbules identifies: for example those, like the William Jennings Bryan character in the film "Inherit the Wind," or like Jerry Falwell and other TV preachers today, who have little "tolerance for alternative points of view," are not discernably open-minded, and have little "willingness to admit that one is mistaken" (Burbules [1991], p. 219). Now these putative virtues *are* (or were) "value[d], like[d], and respect[ed] as reasonable" by many. Does that establish that they are genuine virtues, or that they deserve our respect, admiration, and emulation? Obviously not: our "valu[ing], lik[ing], and respect[ing] as reasonable" people with certain characteristics does not begin to justify our regarding those characteristics as virtues, or the people having them as reasonable. (This is one lesson of fallibilism.) Rather, they must be justified by appeal, not to what we like, nor to the fact that they are "instantiations of certain formal rules or standards of reasoned conduct," but to *theory*: in this case to moral, epistemological, and perhaps social theory. Justifying putative virtues of reasonableness by noting that we regard them as such cannot succeed.[11]

Third, Burbules' thesis that instrumental questions concerning the development of the virtues of reasonableness are "inherent in the identification and justification of the ideal itself" (Burbules [1991a], p. 250; [1991], p. 220) is I think deeply problematic. It confuses *causal* questions concerning the fostering/impeding of the virtues of reasonableness with *philosophical* (in this case epistemological and moral) questions concerning the "identification and justification" of the virtues and dispositions to be fostered/impeded in the effort to achieve that worthy educational aim. I want to argue, that is, that *causes* of reasonableness are not *constitutive* of it.

Burbules is quite clear that it is the causal considerations which he thinks are inherent in the ideal. In addition to the passages cited thus far, consider also the following:

> The substantive conception of rationality I have been proposing incorporates factors of individual character and social relations—those that *support and encourage* reasonable conduct—as inherent to our conception of reasonableness. (Burbules [1991a], p. 252, emphasis added)

> I want to incorporate into the very idea of reason the elements of personal characteristics, context, and social relations that *support and motivate* reasonable thought and conduct. (Burbules [1991], p. 218, emphasis added)

> The central question raised by this [i.e. Burbules'] alternative conception of rationality is what personal characteristics, contextual factors, and social relations *actually produce* a situation in which people come to think and act reasonably. . . (Burbules [1991], p. 219, emphasis added)

> Not only are such moral and affective qualities not separate from "reasoning" per se; I think they are the deeper and more important *sources of the very inclination* toward reasonableness . . . (Burbules [1991], p. 220, emphasis added)

> [These virtues] are constitutive of reasonableness because without them the communicative and other social relations that enable us to *be* reasonable are not possible. (Burbules [1991], p. 223, emphasis in original).[12]

In all these passages, the emphasized portions clearly indicate causal concerns. Burbules is out to identify the virtues, contexts and relations which will enable or encourage us actually to be reasonable. This is indeed a crucially important task. But why are these causal concerns rightly thought to be part of the *meaning* of "reasonableness?" Why should they be regarded as constitutive of, or "inherent in the identification and justification of the ideal itself"? It seems to me clear that they should not.

Consider an example: suppose it is true, as we all no doubt suspect, that being involved in a social context or relation which openly encourages and self-consciously practices open-mindedness and intellectual modesty—for example, being a student in a classroom in which the teacher utilizes Scheffler's recommended manner of teaching,[13] or being a child in a home in which parents encourage the questioning of their beliefs, and are always ready to patiently, respectfully, and seriously consider challenges to those beliefs—is causally efficacious in producing persons who act reasonably. We would then be justified, on the basis of this supposed truth, in striving to establish such social contexts and relations—to the extent that we justifiably value reasonable persons, to the extent that no other causal factors are more effective in producing such persons, and to the extent that these contexts and relations meet relevant moral standards and constraints. But these causal factors are not constitutive of the meaning of "reasonableness" itself, or "inherent in the identification and justification of the ideal itself"—any more than child abuse is constitutive of the meaning of "psychological insecurity" because it tends causally to foster that unhappy state. I agree with Burbules that the social contexts and relations which he suggests are causally efficacious in fostering reasonableness are desirable. My point is that understanding why they are requires exactly that we do not regard them as "constitutive of" or "inherent in" the ideal of reasonableness. So understood, their causal efficacy is rendered irrelevant to their justification, as is the warrant they duly enjoy from our moral and epistemological theorizing. Regarding causal factors as "inherent in the ideal" mistakes causal efficacy for epistemic support.

109

My fourth and final critical point involves Burbules' discussion of *judgment*. It might be thought that Burbules' treatment of this key notion supports his strongly contextual view: as we have seen, Burbules suggests that

> while there are some general standards of good reasoning, there is an unavoidable judging component as well, and hence an inherent personal, idiosyncratic, and indeterminate character to what it will mean to be rational (I would say "reasonable") for any particular person in any particular circumstance. (Burbules [1991a], p. 249)

It is a mistake, I believe, to think that the "personal, idiosyncratic, and indeterminate" character of judgment entails that the rationality of judgments is itself personal, idiosyncratic and indeterminate, rather than determined by "general standards of good reasoning." While Burbules is right that "the process of evaluation is judgment through-and-through" ([1991a], p. 239), it doesn't follow from this that there are not standards in accordance with which judgments can be evaluated and their rationality assessed. I agree that the *process* of evaluation is judgment through-and-through. All of our evaluations of judgments are themselves judgments, and all of them are fallible. But accepting that evaluations are themselves judgments does not preclude the existence of standards in accordance with which judgments are to be evaluated. Any particular judgment must admit of criterion-based evaluation, however fallible. Any view which denies this fails as a view of *rational or reasonable* judgment. If the strongly contextual view of reasonableness Burbules espouses precludes the possibility of (fallible) evaluation of judgments on the basis of (equally fallible) standards of rationality, then it fails as a view of *reasonable* judgment, because it will be unable to distinguish reasonable from unreasonable judgment. The problem can be seen in the following passage:

> To be reasonable in social contexts of interaction entails remaining open
> to the influences of other avenues [than that of the force of reasons] of
> mutual exploration, negotiation, and the pursuit of understanding.
> (Burbules [1995], p. 96)

Let us agree that we should remain open to such influences. When should we allow ourselves actually to be influenced by them, and when should we resist such influence? Without recourse to standards which (fallibly) help us to sort out the legitimate from the illegitimate influences—the ones which ought to move us (because they provide good reason to believe, judge or act in a particular way) from the ones whose influence we ought to resist (because they fail to provide such reason)—there is no way to secure the judgment that in a given case our being influenced is/was in fact reasonable. That is, regarding some belief, judgment or action as reasonable requires that we appeal to something other than the process through which that judgment was reached. Consequently, Burbules' remarks concerning the idiosyncratic and indeterminate nature of judgment fail to support the strong contextualism he espouses.

If I am right, these four difficulties undermine the strong contextualism Burbules espouses.[14]

Let me conclude this chapter by noting that the conception of reasonableness Burbules offers, in so far as it is acceptable, will be rationally so. That is, that conception will itself be warranted, and worthy of our embrace, only to the extent that it can be justified by good reasons, established as good by reference to fallible criteria concerning the goodness of reasons. In this sense, it is the sort of substantive, moderately contextual rationality sketched above that will ultimately ground Burbules' ideal of reasonableness. (Hence this chapter's title.) That ideal will be so grounded, I suggest, only to the extent that its contextualism is kept within moderate limits. So while there is very much of value in Burbules' account of reasonableness, and much which I emphatically endorse, the contextualism he favors is I think too strong to be either rationally or reasonably embraced.

THE LIMITS OF A PRIORI PHILOSOPHY

Logic is like the sword—those who appeal to
it shall perish by it.
                                    —Samuel Butler

chapter 8

I AM VERY FORTUNATE to have had two essay-length reviews devoted to both
of my two earlier books (Siegel 1987 and 1988). In the last chapter I discussed
Nicholas Burbules' essay review (Burbules 1991a); in the present chapter I
respond to Mark Weinstein's (1992). I am grateful to Weinstein for his gra-
cious comments concerning my books, for his careful and detailed discussion
of what he takes to be the ramifications of my arguments, and for the impressive development of his own, alternative position. Weinstein's most fundamental points are not directed toward anything I said in either *Relativism
Refuted* or *Educating Reason*, but are aimed rather at a certain type or form of
argument—identified as "a priori" or "foundational" argument—which my
books are said to rely upon. While he has some good things to say about such
arguments, Weinstein argues that they cannot do the job that he thinks I want
them to do. He argues that a different sort of argument is required.

In what follows I shall try to correct Weinstein's impression of my impression of the reach of my arguments. In many cases I agree with Weinstein that my arguments don't settle the issues that he thinks they don't settle. But in these cases I never thought they did. Weinstein's understanding of my philosophical project and ambitions is not my own. This is the subject of the second section below. Moreover, in making his case, he traverses some difficult philosophical terrain with a somewhat unsteady foot; I shall try, in the other sections which follow, to firm up his step a bit. In doing so, I hope that Weinstein will accept my comments as friendly help rather than as carping criticism, for there is much on which we are agreed. My aim is to further clarify my own position, to offer some friendly criticism of Weinstein's, and to strengthen his case in order to further that which is common to both our projects.

THE NATURE OF PHILOSOPHICAL ARGUMENT:
WHAT IS THE TARGET?

Weinstein is critical of a type of argument he finds throughout my books. Of course, in criticizing a certain form or type of argument, it is important to be clear about the sort of argument being criticized. Unfortunately, Weinstein's target is not always as clearly identified as one would like.

Weinstein's target is variously identified as "foundationalist discourse frames" (232);[1] as "deeply foundational arguments within [Siegel's] own philosophical tradition" (232); as "a priori analysis" (233); as argument which uses "extremely abstract and often a priori reasoning" (241); and as argument which is "based on logical truth alone" (249). These are clearly not equivalent expressions: the first item mentioned is not a sort of argument at all; the fourth allows non-a priori reasoning, which the third disallows; the fifth apparently equates a priori reasoning with logical truth; etc. The target of Weinstein's critique needs more careful specification.

This is important, because some of the criticisms made of some of these types of argument are incorrect. Consider, for example, Weinstein's comments on foundationalism. Weinstein writes that "the issue central to contemporary epistemology and education may not be relativism in the sense that [Siegel] reconstructs it, but rather, the priority of foundationalist discourse frames of the sort characteristic of the so called 'Enlightenment'" (232). As a comment on Siegel (1987) this misses the mark, since that book was never intended to speak to the issue Weinstein here mentions. The versions of relativism discussed in that book are not, and are not presumed to be, antifoundationalist in the sense Weinstein specifies. (Whether or not it or any other issue is "*the* issue central to contemporary epistemology and education" I leave to others to judge.) Moreover, the "deeply foundational arguments" I appeal to are foundationalist, according to Weinstein, not in that sense, but rather in the sense that they are basic *within* a particular discourse frame. So Weinstein has two different senses of "foundationalism" in play here.

Furthermore, neither of these senses amount to "foundationalism" as that term is customarily used in epistemology, to refer to a particular solution to the so-called "epistemic regress problem" concerning epistemic justification.[2] Briefly, this problem involves the *structure* of epistemic justification. Suppose I believe that p. How is my belief that p justified? Suppose it is justified by some other belief q. How then is q justified? It is easy to see that we have a problem here: an infinite regress threatens. If it is unavoidable, then scepticism concerning justification threatens as well. (And if justification is necessary for knowledge, then scepticism concerning knowledge threatens too.) "Foundationalism" in epistemology refers to one major sort of attempt to head off the regress. ("Coherentism" is the other.)[3] For this sort of foundationalist, the regress is stopped by beliefs of a certain sort—"foundational" beliefs—which are themselves justified, but not in terms of any other beliefs. Because they are justified, they afford justification to beliefs based upon them. Because they are not justified by any other beliefs, there is no threatening regress. In our earlier example, then, if r is a foundational belief, then it can justify q, which can in turn justify p. If r and q do afford justification in this way, then p's justification is secure, and the threatening regress is avoided.

Of course this sort of foundationalism is not unproblematic. Chief among the many problems it faces are two: First, what sorts of beliefs are these foundational ones? Second, if foundational beliefs are justified, but not by other beliefs, how are they justified? Different foundationalists have answered these questions in different ways: in terms of clarity and distinctness, incorrigibility, indubitability, certainty, evidentness, self-reflexivity, prima facie plausibility or acceptability, the deliverances of sense data, etc. Further discussion of these issues, and of foundationalism's adequacy as a solution to the regress problem and as a theory of epistemic justification (and of knowledge), would take us far afield; I shall not pursue them further. But I feel obliged to point out that both of Weinstein's senses of "foundationalism" are different from the common understanding of that term among epistemologists, according to which "foundational" refers to a sort of belief, not a set of argument-types or a class of discourse frames. One can be a foundationalist in that common sense without thinking either that "Enlightenment discourse frames" somehow have "priority" over alternative frames, or that particular argument forms have pride of place within the discourse frame that Weinstein thinks delimits "[Siegel's] own philosophical tradition." Both of these latter sorts of foundationalism are rather vague, as articulated thus far. To the extent that I understand them, I reject both. (In particular, I reject the idea that any particular discourse frame is in some way "privileged.") In any case, clarity is not served by failing to

113

distinguish them both from each other, and from the sort addressed to the regress problem concerning epistemic justification. It is quite fashionable, in these postmodern days, to trash or dismiss foundationalism; it is regrettable, however, that many criticisms of it are either quite unclear as to what is being criticized, or are aimed at doctrines quite different from foundationalism properly so called. It is unfortunate, I think, that Weinstein's remarks on this subject fall into both of these categories.[4]

Consider next Weinstein's discussion of certainty. He suggests—ironically, as a point in its favor—that a priori reasoning of the sort he is concerned to criticize "yield[s] certainty" (243). But it is unclear that it does, let alone that it must. What is "a priori reasoning" (241)? Is it reasoning which appeals only to premises which can be known a priori, i.e. independently of experience? If so, it needn't yield certainty, since one can begin with such premises, but reason badly, and in so doing reach conclusions which are not even true, let alone certain. Is it reasoning which appeals to such premises, and is also logically valid (244)? Even if understood in this way, it yields certainty only if a priori truths are necessarily certain (and if deduction is certainty- and not just truth-preserving). But the most compelling extant account of the a priori and its relation to certainty and necessity, namely Kripke's (1972), strongly discourages any such link. I doubt that "the certainty of the a priori . . . can be demonstrated" (note 10, p. 258), at least in any nontrivial way, in the face of Kripke's work. In any case, the most telling objection to Weinstein's remarks on certainty is this: even if the notion of a priori truth is clear, that of a priori reasoning, or a priori argument, is not. Consequently, even if it were established that a priori truths are certain—which it is not—it doesn't follow in the least that a priori reasoning, whatever it is (is it reasoning which concludes with an a priori assertion? an a priori truth? which involves at least one premise which is known a priori? which involves only premises which are known a priori?), is certain, or yields only certainties. Weinstein's discussion of the a priori and certainty is insufficient to establish such claims.[5] This is especially clear if we but remember that rival, incompatible positions on philosophical issues are all defended by philosophical argument, i.e. by what Weinstein is calling a priori reasoning. These incompatible alternatives cannot all be true. Philosophical argument/a priori reasoning is therefore insufficient to guarantee even the truth of these alternatives, let alone their certainty. The most that Weinstein can claim, then, is that *correct* a priori reasoning yields certainty. But whether a given piece of such reasoning is correct is almost always controversial, and is never certain.

Weinstein's discussion of the a priori is then problematic. As I will argue below, these problems severely compromise Weinstein's discussion of fallibilism, and of other more straightforwardly philosophical topics. Nevertheless, despite their seriousness, they leave intact his important distinction between correctness (although he calls this "certainty") and applicability. But Weinstein, in utilizing this distinction in order to press his positive case, quite basically misunderstands what he considers to be my agenda. I turn to this point next.

THE REACH OF PHILOSOPHICAL ARGUMENT

I have argued that Weinstein's discussion of a priori reasoning is problematic. Despite those problems, Weinstein makes an important point, by way of his distinction between the certainty and the applicability of such reasoning, concerning the reach of philosophical argument. I agree with Weinstein that philosophical argument, or a priori reasoning, cannot resolve outstanding, largely extra-philosophical problems which are in need of resolution. My question to Weinstein here is simply: who would disagree? Weinstein apparently thinks I would. But here he misunderstands me.

Weinstein is right that philosophical argument, however trenchant, is simply not applicable to many important issues; to try to resolve such issues by resorting to philosophical argument (understood, as Weinstein understands it, as a priori argument) amounts to a misguided "foundationalism" which unduly privileges philosophy as a "discourse frame." Such misguided and undeserved privilege is sheer hubris. Weinstein's criticism of philosophical argument is that it wrongly pretends to an authority which it does not have. Such pretension, Weinstein rightly claims, is wrong. Such argument won't resolve the questions he is most concerned to answer; his own philosophical/educational agenda requires extra-philosophical tools. As I have said, I think Weinstein is right on this point. But further progress here requires that we consider Weinstein's agenda and goals, and their relation to my own.

Weinstein's basic critical thesis is this: my arguments are good, but they are of a type which is incapable of achieving what he takes to be my "greater ends" (232). Those ends—which in fact are his ends, not mine—require non-philosophical, non-a priori means. So what are his ends, and what are mine? At the outset of his discussion, Weinstein cites a passage from *Educating Reason* which provides my own statement: "[Siegel's] aim here is to show that critical thinking is a 'fundamental educational goal, infusing and informing the entire range of educational activities and affairs'" (232, citing Siegel [1988], p. 2). This is correct: my aim in that book (and in the present one as well) was (and is) to establish this philosophical thesis about that particular educational goal. Whether or not my arguments succeed in establishing it, Weinstein offers no reason for thinking that the sort of argument in which I there engaged is in any way inappropriate for the philosophical task specified.

By the bottom of that same page, however, Weinstein has forgotten the cited passage; instead he suggests that the sort of arguments I use are inadequate for quite different goals:

> Despite the effectiveness of his challenge to relativism and his defense of
> critical thinking, Siegel's analysis points away from the paradigm of philo-
> sophical argument that he espouses, indicating rather, the need for greater
> concern with the particulars of extra-philosophical discourse frames and
> a deeper appreciation of the particularities of practices across human
> inquiry. Thus Siegel's methods may confute his greater ends, for abstract
> analysis of the sort he offers, affords little help in resolving the key ques-
> tions towards which his discussion leads: What sort of an educational pro-
> gram is adequate to critical thinking reform, and what is the character of
> an informative and useful epistemology sufficient for its purposes? (232)

The "greater ends" Weinstein here mentions are his, not mine. The aims of
my books are correctly specified in the first clause of the first cited sentence:
to challenge (epistemological) relativism, and to defend critical thinking as an
educational ideal. Since Weinstein regards my arguments to these ends as
"effective," he must regard the type of argument I utilized as appropriate for
the accomplishment of those ends. The "greater ends" he attributes to me,
which concern the practical business of reforming education so as to bring it
in to line with the ideal of critical thinking, are not ends which I addressed
systematically in my books.

Weinstein is right, of course, that to address those greater ends, more than
philosophical argument is required. Although I didn't address those ends in any
detail, I noted in my ([1988], e.g., p. 115) that extra-philosophical considerations
would be required to address them adequately. In so far as I have this sort of
nonphilosophical educational agenda, it of course involves the greater aims
Weinstein mentions.[6] But I distinguish between my philosophical agenda and
other agendas—educational, political, personal—I might have. My books were
intended only to further the first. For that, nothing Weinstein says suggests that
the sort of arguments I utilized were inappropriate. On the contrary, he pays
them the compliment of regarding them as "effective." His complaint, then, is
that philosophical argument—a priori analysis—is inappropriate, or inadequate,
for the pursuit of other, extra-philosophical ends. I agree—who wouldn't? In
other words, Weinstein's complaint about the inadequacies of philosophical
arguments depends on taking them to be addressed to extra-philosophical ends.
Of course they'll be inadequate for that purpose. But they may nevertheless be
perfectly adequate for the purposes to which they are in fact put.

Elsewhere Weinstein attributes to me other aims, and/or complains that
the sort of argument I employ will not help to achieve those aims. For example, he thinks that it is an aim of epistemology to discern how "epistemological commitment is to be evidenced and understood" (245). This seems to me
mainly a sociological/psychological rather than an epistemological problem;

116

in any case it is not an aim addressed in my books. He thinks I aim "to articulate a 'good reasons' approach adequate to the analysis of reasonable judgments in the various disciplinary and educational contexts" (245). This, I
regret to have to say, is not my philosophical aim—though it is clearly
Weinstein's. Take a disciplinary context, e.g. history or physics. In any such
context, the goodness of reasons will depend at least in part on the theoretical and methodological[7] situation within the relevant discipline. That is,
relevant substantive theoretical considerations will contribute to the determination of the goodness of reasons within those contexts. Epistemology's task
is not to decide what in fact is a good reason in history, physics, or indeed any
particular disciplinary context; it is rather to theorize about the nature of reasons, and their goodness, such that a good reason in one context bears the
same relation to that for which it is a reason as a good reason in another context bears to that for which *it* is a reason (Siegel [1980], p. 320; Siegel
[1983a]). This will require theorizing about the nature of justification, the
epistemic regress problem, and the host of difficult problems with which
epistemologists of my ilk regularly occupy themselves. In other words,
Weinstein's project, while perfectly legitimate, far outstrips my own, traditionally conceived, philosophical project. Perhaps he means to be criticizing
that project. But if so, he cannot succeed by showing that it is inadequate to
tasks it declines to set for itself. Weinstein suggests that my project cannot
"bear meaningful fruit" (248) if carried out in abstract, philosophical style.
Here he is correct, but only on the assumption that meaningful fruit is that
which bears on the resolution of Weinstein's extra-philosophical projects. My
contrary assumption is that traditional philosophical projects can also be
advanced, and that when they are the arguments that secure such advance can
equally rightly be said to "bear meaningful fruit." Does Weinstein really disagree?

117

Weinstein says that "our concerns" involve "the development of an objectivist epistemology adequate to ground knowledge claims" (248). But again,
epistemology cannot by itself do this, for the grounding of knowledge claims
requires relevant evidence or reasons, and their adequacy will depend in part
on the theoretical/methodological situation within the context in which they
occur. Epistemology doesn't determine the goodness of reasons in all contexts—doesn't "determine [the] epistemological warrant" of "[m]any real
claims" (243)—though it does aim to tell a generally applicable, and in that
sense context-neutral, story about that goodness. To Weinstein's question,
"What is it to be *appropriately* moved by reasons?" (248), I answer as I answered in *Educating Reason*: it is to believe, judge and act in ways which adequately
reflect the strength of the reasons in question. What Weinstein really wants is
an answer to a different question, namely: For each particular bit of move-

ment on the basis of reasons, is that movement in fact appropriate? But here there is nothing general to say; each case requires consideration of the particulars, and the situatedness, of the case.[8] This is no grand admission of the weakness of philosophical argument. It is rather a simple acknowledgement of the limits of the reach of such argument. Weinstein and I are agreed that that reach is limited. We apparently disagree on two other issues: on the worth and importance of solutions properly obtained within its reach, by its methods; and on the necessity of proposed solutions to philosophical problems to address further questions to which philosophical reflection leads (232). Weinstein suggests that addressing such further questions is required for a proposed solution to a philosophical problem to be adequate. I disagree. Reflection on "Is abortion morally permissible?" will surely lead to further questions, like "How can we most effectively discourage unwanted pregnancies?" and "How can we best protect the conflicting legitimate rights of all involved in the abortion controversy?" On my view, a proposed solution to the first question need say nothing about the other questions to which it leads, and yet can still be a good answer to that first question. Similarly, answers to "What is critical thinking?" and "Is critical thinking an important educational ideal?" may say nothing about effective ways of fostering critical thinking in schools, nor about the strength of particular candidate reasons in the myriad of disciplinary contexts in which reasons play a role, and yet can still be good. Weinstein apparently disagrees—for if not, he will have to explain why it counts against my arguments that they do not resolve further, extra-philosophical questions to which they are not addressed. But if so, he will have to explain why the adequacy of philosophical argument depends, even in part, on its ability to shed light on such extra-philosophical questions.

To repeat: I nowhere claim, nor do I think, that philosophical argument is "foundational" (or that philosophy constitutes a "foundational discourse frame') in the sense that it can resolve outstanding empirical, practical, or extra-philosophical questions. I regard Weinstein's huge project of specifying what counts as a good reason in all disciplinary contexts or discourse frames as perfectly legitimate, albeit enormously ambitious and to a large extent extra-philosophical.[9] I agree with him that my—and indeed any—philosophical arguments will be insufficient to accomplish that enormous task. I wish him well with it, and am even willing to collaborate with him on selected manageable portions of it. I insist only that my own philosophical project is more narrow; that, even so, it is perfectly legitimate; that Weinstein provides no good reason for thinking my (type of) arguments unsatisfactory for, or unsuitable to, that narrower task; and that Weinstein's arguments against my own depend on confusing my smaller project with his larger one. Keep our respective projects straight, and his criticisms of my arguments (and their type) dissolve.[10]

ABSOLUTISM, RELATIVISM, FALLIBILISM, AND JUSTIFICATION

Earlier I suggested that Weinstein's problematic discussion of the a priori and of philosophical argumentation severely compromises his discussion of fallibilism. In this section I want to make good on this suggestion.

Weinstein argues that "the qualified [version of] absolutism that [Siegel] puts forward," which involves a quite general commitment to fallibilism, is subject to the same difficulties that I argue defeat relativism; in particular, the version of absolutism I defend is defeated, according to Weinstein, by "the incoherence of fallibilism in its most general formulation" (238). My arguments against relativism in *Relativism Refuted*, if they are successful, show it to be incoherent, self-defeating, arbitrary, or impotent. Weinstein claims that these same difficulties equally befall my positive view, because of that view's embrace of a general formulation of fallibilism.

How, according to Weinstein, does my absolutistic fallibilism lead to these difficulties? The heart of Weinstein's argument, which is "modeled on Siegel's constructions" (238), is as follows:

> . . . a procedure of continuing evaluation [of claims and their putatively supporting reasons] can either be definite or indefinite. That is, the procedure either ends or remains indefinite as to its extent. If it comes to no definite end, the entire iterated procedure is ungrounded, and hence, accepted as absolute without warrant, whence is dogmatically posited as absolute. . . . If the procedure comes to some definite end, . . . [then e]ither [that end] is accepted according to no reasons, or [it] is accepted in light of the components already included in the construction, accepted in light of the reasons included in it, and nothing else. If the former, [it] is dogmatically posited as absolute, if the latter, [it] is absolute through some principle of self-warrant, hence infallible. (239, note deleted)

The thrust of the argument, clearly enough, is that my version of absolutism—or my defense of it—is either dogmatic or arbitrary. But that version eschews both dogmatism and arbitrariness. Thus it is self-defeating in just the way that relativism is.

There are several problems with this argument. First, the sense of "absolute" utilized in the argument is not my own. For "absolute" in my hands admits of possible error—since my version of absolutism embraces fallibilism—while that notion, as Weinstein uses it here, does not. Second, Weinstein's argument presupposes that epistemic warrant requires infallible "foundations." But this is false—and in any case, it is odd that Weinstein should accept it, given his subsequent argument concerning fallibilism. Let me explain.

Weinstein has posed a trilemma. If a justificatory procedure is "indefinite," then "the entire iterated procedure is ungrounded, and hence, accepted as absolute without warrant, whence is dogmatically posited as absolute." If the procedure "comes to some definite end," then either that end is "accepted according to no reasons," in which case it again is "dogmatically posited as absolute," or it is accepted "through some principle of self-warrant, hence infallible." Ignore for the moment that Weinstein puts all this in terms of the justificatory status of "the entire iterated procedure," rather than the claim which initiates (or ends) it. Consider the first two horns of the trilemma. The problem with them, according to Weinstein, is that a claim "grounded" in either of these two ways is not genuinely grounded at all, because "grounding" requires that the chain of justifying reasons both (1) ends, and (2) ends nonarbitrarily, where an end must be certain to be nonarbitrary. The first horn fails to meet the first requirement; the second the second.

Ignore the fact that Weinstein's requirements amount to the claim that justification must be foundationalist (in the epistemological sense), which claim he rejects elsewhere. Notice rather that he is assuming that justification requires a certain foundation (which he thinks is what you get if you opt for the third horn). Now Weinstein has not argued for either of these two requirements. I shall argue that neither are genuine requirements for justification; that claims can be justified even when neither requirement is met.

Consider the claim: "Siegel's fallibilistic absolutism suffers from the same defects as does relativism." Weinstein believes this. Presumably, he believes that his belief is justified. Suppose it is. Must the chain of reasons which justifies it end? Must it end with a claim that is nonarbitrary because it is certain? To both of these questions, I think the answer is "no." Take the first one: Weinstein has given us an argument which he thinks justifies his claim. I have challenged that argument, and I will add to my challenge below. Does Weinstein's chain end? Surely it hasn't ended yet. It must at least respond to my challenges. And there is no reason to think that more challenges would not result from his attempts to answer the earlier ones. In short, it is in principle possible, and in fact quite likely, that our dialogue concerning the justificatory status of his belief will not end. That it won't is completely compatible with his claim's being justified. If so, then a justificatory chain needn't end at all in order for the claim in question to be justified. (To think otherwise is to be committed to [near-] skepticism concerning epistemic justification, since virtually all our justified beliefs are, as Weinstein agrees, open to challenge.) This view of justification is compatible with the views of both coherence theorists and (some) modest foundationalists. Weinstein's first requirement presupposes without argument a controversial, indeed dubious, epistemological position.

Suppose the justificatory chain does end. Must it end with certainty, if the claim in question is to be justified? A well respected tradition, pioneered by Nelson Goodman, argues not. Rather, Goodman holds, justificatory chains end not with claims which are certain, but rather with claims which are credible, which enjoy what Goodman calls "initial credibility." Such end points are not permanent; one can always challenge them, and in so doing push the justificatory chain back. But absent such challenge, the credibility of one's end point is sufficient, on this view, to warrant or justify the claim in question. If anything like this story is right, then a chain needn't end with a claim which is certain in order for it to end nonarbitrarily.[11] My view of justification is in several respects like Goodman's. Most importantly in the present context, I agree with Goodman (and have argued, e.g. in *Relativism Refuted*) that a reason can afford warrant to a claim even if that reason is not certain. In order to afford warrant, it need not be certain, but only itself justified.[12] But justified beliefs can be false. So they can surely be noncertain. In short, reasons—which are fallible and open to challenge, and so are not certain—can nevertheless both be justified, and can justify or provide warrant for the claims for which they are reasons. When they do, those claims are not "ungrounded," despite their noncertain warrant. Weinstein's second requirement thus collapses. The failure of both of these requirements leaves Weinstein's trilemma in tatters. Justification requires neither "definite" end points, nor certain ones. His argument does not even begin to show that my version of absolutism succumbs to the difficulties which accrue to relativism.

An additional brief point is in order concerning the third horn of Weinstein's trilemma. It suggests that any appeal to "self-warrant" (239), or reflexive "self-grounding" (238), entails that the claim so justified is "infallible" (239), and that any such "self-grounding" must be "some kin to 'vulgar' absolutism of the sort eschewed by Siegel" (238). This is in my view mistaken. On that view, justification can be self-reflexive but fallible. While I recognize that my view is controversial, Weinstein's contrary view—that self-warrant entails infallibility—is equally so. But Weinstein does not argue for his view. I do.[13]

The preceding defense depends in part upon my commitment to a very general form of fallibilism, according to which *all* claims are fallible and open to challenge, and *no* claims are certain. Weinstein argues that this general fallibilism is untenable. If he is right, then my position is seriously challenged. Is he?

Weinstein argues that "[f]allibilism, in general, turns out to be as paradoxical as relativism, and for much of [sic] the same sort of reasons" (240).[14] In what way does Weinstein think that fallibilism is paradoxical or otherwise problematic? His argument depends entirely on Post's (1987, p. 217) "Possible Liar Paradox" (PLP). (Post's argument is provided at Weinstein's p. 240.) I agree with Weinstein that Post's construction is ingenious. What PLP shows, however, is far from obvious.

One plausible response to it is that PLP shows that there is a problem, not with fallibilism, but with the sentence, P, at its core. P is the sentence "This sentence is possibly false." It refers to itself. One might think that PLP shows

121

that there is a problem, not with fallibilism, but with self-reference, i.e. with sentences that refer to themselves. (Here it is possible to draw a close analogy with the classical liar paradox, which does not render the notion of truth paradoxical, but rather identifies the same class of self-referential sentences as problematic, and as requiring for their analysis the tools of the ramified theory of types or some analogous device.) This response then suggests that even if self-referential sentences are not straightforwardly fallible, they are not straightforwardly infallible either. They are distinctive sentences which require special philosophical treatment. But at the most they suggest that a general fallibilism must not be so general as to include them. Fallibilism then amounts to: all sentences are fallible, except the self-referential ones. Notice that (1) this revised version of fallibilism does not hold that the excluded sentences are *in*fallible, and (2) it leaves the doctrine intact with respect to all the sentences we care about, including those of philosophy, science, and everyday life.

This response to PLP seems to me quite plausible, especially when we ask about the status of PLP itself. Does PLP nonfallibly demonstrate that a completely general fallibilism is doomed? I don't see how it could. For PLP takes the form of an argument, after all. Like all philosophical arguments, it is open to challenge and counter-interpretation. Indeed, in the volume in which Post's paper appears, two contributors challenge Post's argument, and argue that, for a variety of reasons, it doesn't show what Post thinks it shows. (Bartley [1987], Radnitzky [1987]) Would Post or Weinstein deny that it is even possible that a flaw, either in the formulation of PLP or in their interpretations of it, could be discovered? I don't see on what basis they could deny that possibility. If they can't, then PLP is itself subject to fallibilism. If so, then Weinstein overstates the case when he claims that "PLP is devastating for an unqualified fallibilism" (258, note 8). How devastating it is is itself a matter of fallible philosophical reflection. For Post's PLP is itself an instance of philosophical reasoning, and, as noted above, whether a given piece of such reasoning is correct is almost always controversial, and is never certain. In any case, PLP forces at most only the very modest qualification on the scope of fallibilism just offered.[15]

JUSTIFICATION, COMMUNITIES OF INQUIRY, AND "EPISTEMOLOGY ACROSS THE DISCIPLINES"

Since "justification" is central to both our discussions, it is important to address briefly some fundamental differences of opinion concerning it. Weinstein writes that

> Any analysis of reason giving, of being appropriately *moved* by reasons, requires some account of the relation of reasoning to individuals and groups, and to the standards in light of which reasons are offered and assessed. For, unless Siegel has some Platonic theory of justification in

> mind, justification independent of reasoning agents, it seems reasonable to assume that justification in terms of reasons is justification for some individual or group of reasoners, that is, typically within actual inquiry, some community of thinkers to whom the reasons are offered, and for whom the reasons serve as objective justification. . . . Reasons, to serve as reasons, must so serve relative to some community who accepts them as warranting. Thus [claims] can only be shown to be reasonably put forward in terms of some community's standards. That is, reasons can only be reasons in respect of some community and in light of some standards. (239, emphasis in original)

There is much amiss in this passage, and in Weinstein's discussion of justification more generally.

First, contemporary epistemologists routinely distinguish between *propositional* justification and *doxastic* justification.[16] The latter sort concerns the justification of a particular belief, in the believer's context (which includes her other beliefs), and requires that justified belief be appropriately related to, or based on, the believer's evidence. The former concerns strictly the relationship between belief and potentially justifying belief, whether or not the former is believed on the basis of the latter. For example, suppose I believe that "The probability of Pat Buchanan winning the U.S. Presidential election in 1996 is less than .10," "The probability of Rush Limbaugh winning the U.S. Presidential election in 1996 is greater than .10," and "Rush Limbaugh has a better chance of winning the U.S. Presidential election in 1996 than Pat Buchanan." My belief in the latter is propositionally justified in virtue of its relation to the former two beliefs.[17] This sort of justification is independent of context, and involves strictly the epistemic status of, and relationships between, the relevant beliefs. Propositional justification (when put in terms of claims or propositions) is exactly "justification independent of reasoning agents." (When put in terms of beliefs, "believing agents" are required, since there can be no beliefs without believers. But the status of any belief as propositionally justified does not depend upon the believer's view of its justificatory status, or of the belief being sanctioned by standards the believer and/or her community accepts.) p can propositionally justify q even if no one thinks it does. I would not pejoratively label this notion of justification "Platonic." Rather, I would call it an objective, and perfectly legitimate, conception of justification—and one, moreover, which is centrally relevant to critical thinking.

Of course doxastic justification is also a perfectly legitimate and important sort of justification, and it is contextualist, in the sense that it requires that beliefs be "based on" their justifiers in particular (and philosophically contentious) ways. Still, it is no more contextualist than propositional justification in the sense of Weinstein's "assum[ption] that justification in terms of reasons is justification for some individual or group of reasoners." Weinstein presumes that "reasons, to serve as reasons, must so serve relative to some community who accepts them as warranting." While this is correct so far as a claim's *serving* as a reason is concerned, it is not correct so far as a claim's *being* a reason is concerned. For a claim can be a good reason for some other, can afford propositional justification, even though no one accepts it as such. Thus Weinstein is I think mistaken in claiming that "reasons can only *be* reasons in respect of some community and in light of some standards" (emphasis added). He is right about the standards, but not about the community (or the contextualism he thinks it implies).[18]

More generally, Weinstein runs together a community's *regarding* or *taking* a claim to be a (good) reason, and that claim's *being* a (good) reason. But this distinction is crucial for any view which seeks, as Weinstein's does, to avoid a pernicious relativism. It is also crucial to any view, including Weinstein's, which seeks to embrace (even his allegedly limited form of) fallibilism. For fallibilism, as Weinstein acknowledges, applies to the judgments of communities of inquirers equally as much as it applies to anything else. But this entails that a community's *taking* a claim to be a good reason must be distinguished from it's *correctly* or *justifiably* so doing, i.e. from the taken claim's actually *being* a good reason. So not only has Weinstein failed to challenge successfully this distinction, he needs it for his own positive story. The "contextualism" he endorses on the basis of the just-cited passage amounts, to the extent that it honors the "is taken to be/is a good reason" distinction, to fallibilism. To the extent it collapses that distinction, it is unworthy of endorsement, even by his own lights.

A similar problem plagues another aspect of Weinstein's discussion of justification. He claims that "an adequate epistemological theory of justificatory reasoning requires moving beyond the level of abstraction characteristic of philosophical discourse, and towards an account that identifies the epistemological role of normative practices across the range of well-constituted disciplines" (244). First, there is the problem noted earlier: is such a theory supposed to be a theory of what epistemic justification *is*, or rather a theory of what specific disciplinary claims are in fact justified? If the latter, then of course abstract philosophical discourse will not suffice; but if the former, it well might. Second, the appeal to practices runs the risk of collapsing the "is taken to be justificatory/is justificatory" distinction which, as just noted, is both legitimate and necessary for Weinstein's overall view. For his view recognizes that such disciplinary practices, though taken to be warrant conferring, may in fact not be. So there is a severe limit to the mileage to be made from an appeal to such practices.

Weinstein offers a challenging argument "for the primacy of communities as the foundation of reasoning" (249):

The alternative to a community based account of reasoning is some version of Platonism. On such a view relations between reasons and claims
subsist independent of judgments. But if so, how are they to be discovered? How are they to be seen as rationally compelling? Even if reasons
relationships are independent of actual judgments, the reasons relationships can only come to light through some process of rational analysis
and assessment. But such procedures need to be identified, implemented
and evaluated if they are to inform us of reasons relationships, and such
procedures, characteristically transpersonal, find their expression in the
active pursuit of inquiry. And so, we are forced back to the consideration
of the procedures that govern such inquiry. Even for the Platonist, God
alone sees the true rational ground for claims, humans are forced to
actively pursue these grounds through the practices that they have adopt-
ed, whether designed ab initio or borrowed from others. The practices of
"well-constituted" discourse communities is all that we have. And so
they must be sufficient, if we are to accomplish the tasks that inquiry
requires. (250)

Applied to our earlier example, this argument points out that even claims
like "'Rush Limbaugh has a better chance of winning the U.S. Presidential
election in 1996 than Pat Buchanan' is propositionally justified in virtue of its
epistemic relationship to the related two claims mentioned earlier" itself
reflects not some Godly perception of justification, but simply the judgments
concerning justification shared by a particular community of inquiry. In this
sense, there is no getting beyond such judgments. All we have are the judgments concerning justification of the reasoning communities we have. Thus
there is no realistic alternative to a community-based account of reasoning
and its justification.

This is a very powerful argument, but it doesn't show what Weinstein
thinks it shows. For one thing, the practices referred to *needn't* "be sufficient";
it might be that we are simply unable "to accomplish the tasks that inquiry
requires." But more fundamentally, the argument fails because it confuses the
process of judgment with the epistemic *status* of judgments arrived at through
that process. All of our judgments, including our epistemic evaluations of
other judgments, are contextual, and all are fallible. But accepting that evaluations are themselves contextual, community-based judgments does not preclude the relevance of (fallible) standards in accordance with which judgments
are to be evaluated. Any particular judgment must admit of criterion-based
evaluation, however fallible—including judgments of the adequacy of such
criteria themselves. Any view which denies this fails as a view of *rational* or
reasonable judgment. In other words, if Weinstein's community-based view of
reasons and reason evaluation precludes the possibility of (fallible) evaluation

125

of judgments on the basis of (equally fallible) standards of epistemic appraisal, then it fails as a view of *rational* judgment, since it will be unable to distinguish rational from irrational judgment.[19]

Weinstein's view appears to avoid this difficulty, because he holds that such contextualist judgment can be legitimately critiqued, from the point of view of criteria upheld by some other community. Thus he claims that "[f]or critique to be possible, there need only be some alternative perspective from which criticism is to be mounted" (247–8). But here we need to be mindful of the distinctions between necessary and sufficient conditions and between possibly and actually successful critique. While Weinstein may be right that the existence of some alternative perspective is sufficient for critique *simpliciter*, it is not sufficient to distinguish epistemically forceful critique from epistemically weak, irrelevant, or inappropriate critique. In order to draw this essential distinction—without which we are left with a deeply problematic relativism—we need to appeal to criteria, not question-beggingly internal to either of the communities in question, with which we can evaluate the merits of the proffered critique. In other words, while the existence of some alternative perspective may be sufficient for possibly successful critique, it is not sufficient for actually successful critique.[20] That is, we need some perspective from which the critique can be fairly evaluated. Here we find the limit of epistemic contextualism. Without some criteria with which, or perspective from which, we can fairly assess the merits of critiques and alternatives, our epistemic judgments will be powerless, arbitrary, or worse. With them, we go beyond an inert epistemic contextualism.[21]

Weinstein is clearly moved by this problem, for he argues that critiques of contextual judgments can be assessed by criteria of descriptive adequacy and pragmatic utility (243 ff.). Here, however, I see two problems. First, it is not clear that either of these criteria can do the work Weinstein wants them to do. Descriptive adequacy will help only if the fact that a community *takes* a reason to be a good one establishes that the reason so taken *is* a good one. But as argued earlier, this "taken/is" distinction is crucial to Weinstein's positive position. Pragmatic utility will serve as a relevant criterion only on the assumption of a generally pragmatist epistemology. While I won't argue the case here, I believe that this sort of epistemology is deeply flawed. Second, to the extent that these two criteria are regarded by Weinstein as relevant to the assessment of community-based judgments and critiques, he is countermanding his own contextualism, which does not permit any such context-neutral criteria to be seen as epistemically forceful. So his argument "for the primacy of communities as the foundation of reasoning" is problematic, both on its own and in the context of the overall position Weinstein wants to defend.

Why, then, do I regard the argument cited as "very powerful"? Not because it establishes a community-based or contextualist epistemology—I have just argued that it does not do this—but because it very well portrays what might be termed[22] "the predicament of fallibilism." We judge community-based and contextual claims, evaluations, and practices, and we strive to do so fairly. In so doing, we strive to judge in accordance with criteria that are neutral with respect to the issue being considered. But those criteria, while neutral in the sense just specified, are not neutral with respect to all controversies or contexts. There is no such completely neutral perspective from which to judge. Our judgments are in *this* sense unavoidably contextual, and, consequently, are forever fallible, forever open to challenge from perspectives and viewpoints both already in view and not yet anticipated. Such challenges can challenge not only our judgments, but our best understanding of judgment and of the criteria relevant to it—that is, even (perhaps especially) our epistemology of judgment itself. Weinstein's argument is powerful precisely because it underscores the unavoidability of this "predicament of fallibilism." But it in no way establishes the stronger contextualism Weinstein here advocates. There is no getting beyond or outside *all* contexts or communities of inquiry, or of judging from a contextless perspective, but, equally, there is no in principle barrier to getting beyond any particular context, or to judging it from a perspective which enjoys critical leverage over both it and its alternatives.[23]

CONCLUSION

Weinstein infers from his arguments against a priori reasoning and a generalized fallibilism that any general epistemological thesis will run into self-defeating self-referential problems, and that therefore we must avoid such general theses, and instead concern ourselves with "limited and particular" systems of propositions, which are "embedded in discourse communities and their practices" (241). I have argued that he has not shown that my own position is defeated by such problems. If I am right, then, a fortiori, the "generalist" approach to epistemology is not in principle doomed. Moreover, I have no objection to Weinstein's "particularist" account of justification, so long as it is clear that it speaks to the "perceived justification" of discourse communities, rather than to the "generalist" epistemological question of the nature and conditions of genuine justification. Weinstein has argued against such a generalist epistemology, but I hope to have shown how problematic his argument is.

Still, he is importantly right about the limits, and even the irrelevance, of that sort of epistemological theorizing for some purposes, including in particular his own. In this concluding section I should like to note the many commonalities and points of agreement in our two projects, and the many strengths of his own. For while I have argued that many of Weinstein's more straightforwardly philosophical arguments concerning the a priori, certainty, fallibilism, foundationalism, absolutism, justification, contextualism and the like are flawed, many of Weinstein's claims are both correct and worth the serious attention of philosophers of education, informal logicians, and critical thinking theorists.

Weinstein is right to insist upon the recognition of the limits of the reach of "a priori" philosophical argument. While some questions of interest to the scholarly communities just mentioned are straightforwardly philosophical, and are properly pursued by traditional philosophical means, some are not. Weinstein does us an important service by reminding us that traditional methods are unable to resolve outstanding questions of serious scholarly or professional interest, and, in particular, that philosophical reasoning is not in general sufficient to determine the goodness of reasons in particular disciplinary contexts[24] or to resolve outstanding extra-philosophical issues.

The last third of Weinstein's paper offers "a positive reconstruction of Siegel's views" (246), in which he highlights our agreements concerning the rejection of relativism, the importance of reason giving in the effort to ground claims and judgments, the rejection of any sort of privileged framework and the importance of pluralism, the possibilities of objective reasons and rational criticism, and the importance of fallibilism (although his attempt to limit it is, as noted, problematic). We are agreed as well that "[g]eneral courses in critical thinking . . . only begin the process" (253) of education for critical thinking. In fact, Weinstein's positive view, his "epistemology across the disciplines," by his own admission "relies essentially on what seems to be the most important contribution that Siegel makes" (248). I am gratified that we agree on so much.[25]

There is much in Weinstein's paper which I have not discussed; this Chapter is far too long as it is. It is a rich and challenging paper, which offers a new perspective on fundamental questions of long-standing concern to the scholarly communities to which it is addressed. While I applaud much of it, I suspect that many of its most important points are just the ones with which I differ. In any case, his insistence that we study the epistemic practices of "well-constituted" communities of inquiry cannot be gainsaid. I would like to end this chapter by encouraging further work on his large project. In the next chapter I continue my conversation with Weinstein, this time on what he regards as the postmodernist elements of his view.[26]

GIMME THAT OLD-TIME ENLIGHTENMENT METANARRATIVE

Radical Pedagogies (and Politics)
Require Old-Fashioned Epistemology (and Moral Theory)

Irrationalism expresses itself in various ways. One of them is...the attitude of looking at once for the unconscious motives and determinants in the social habitat of the thinker, instead of first examining the validity of the argument itself.

—Sir Karl Popper

Arguments are to be avoided. They are always vulgar and often convincing.

—Oscar Wilde

MARK WEINSTEIN'S CHALLENGING (1993) raises issues as profound as any being discussed in contemporary philosophical discussions of education. Indeed, Weinstein's arguments extend beyond the boundaries of philosophy of education; they urge conclusions which are fundamentally epistemological. He argues that certain sorts of cognitive frameworks—"totalizing" or "exclusionary" ones—are epistemologically suspect. They are suspect, he argues, because of their *moral* failings. Weinstein argues, that is, that their *moral* defects constitute *epistemological* defects as well. He urges, further, that this insight resolves the apparently problematic tension between Postmodernism's rejection of metanarrative and its advocacy of progressive social and educational change.

In what follows I will attempt to evaluate these provocative theses.[1] I believe that Weinstein's arguments and conclusions are of the first importance. I accept many of those conclusions. Moreover, there is no denying the clarity and breadth of his analysis, and we should be grateful for both its broad scope and for his singular ability to bring the diverse literatures of analytic philosophy and epistemology, the history of philosophy, Postmodernism, Feminism, Multiculturalism, Critical Theory, the theory and practice of critical thinking, and the theory and practice of pedagogy, into genuine and fruitful communication with each other. I will suggest, nevertheless, that his discussion manifests difficulties which defeat the sort of Postmodernist stance that Weinstein embraces; and that the moral and political imperatives it espouses—which I endorse—require for their justification the sort of Modernist, Enlightenment epistemological (and ethical) presuppositions which Weinstein and other self-described Postmodernists are reluctant to embrace. I will argue, that is, that "radical pedagogy," and radical politics more generally, require old-fashioned Enlightenment epistemology and moral theory.

WEINSTEIN'S POSITION AND ARGUMENTS

Weinstein's aim is to develop "an epistemology adequate to ground educational practice" (Weinstein [1993], p. 25).[2] He criticizes John McPeck's view that rationality is grounded in the disciplines, and Richard Paul's view that it is grounded in natural language: both these grounds, he argues, "invite . . . radical critique," in that "feminists and postmodernists have all challenged the privileged epistemological, cultural and educational positions of such foundationalist heirs to the Enlightenment" (29). Nevertheless, Weinstein finds "strength to McPeck's and Paul's positions, for each affords a basis for rational practice, and it may be provable that some such basis is required" (29). Much to my surprise and delight, he accepts my own arguments as establishing that requirement, in the form of a "framework for objective rationality" (30), and so as providing a basis for rational practice.[3] But he regards that achievement as insufficiently substantial to do justice to Postmodernist intuitions, and his major positive suggestion takes the shape of a Weinsteinian gloss on arguments put forward by Henry Giroux and Stanley Aronowitz, to which the rest of this discussion attends.

There are two questions which the proposed framework for objective rationality raises: (1) does it "accomodate postmodern intuitions" (30)?, and (2) does it provide a satisfactory justification for progressive political and educational change? Weinstein acknowledges

> a dilemma for those who both embrace postmodernism and advocate an emancipatory program of educational reform. Failing the "master narrative" that constituted the core of Enlightenment foundationalism, the possibility of a rational political life is brought into serious question, and with it the hope of supporting progressive educational change in a nonarbitrary manner. (31)

In other words: to the extent that Postmodernists reject "master narratives" which abstract away from individual and cultural differences and regard people as interchangeable participants in social life who are essentially equivalent and only accidentally and nonimportantly different, they run the risk of cutting the ground out from any putative justification for social and educational change they might advocate, leaving their advocacy of emancipatory educational reform looking (epistemologically) arbitrary and without rational justification. On the other hand, to the extent that they forcefully advocate an emancipatory program of educational reform, they appear to undercut their commitment to Postmodernism, since such advocacy appears to require, for its justification, the sort of "master narrative" which Postmodernism resolutely refuses to acknowledge. The question is: can this dilemma somehow be finessed?

Weinstein attempts to finesse it as follows. He reviews Giroux's notion of "border pedagogy," explicated in terms of difference and counter-memory. He notes the connections between Giroux's position and both Postmodernism and Critical Theory. He points out that both for Giroux and for me, "reason giving" is "a fundamental practice" (33). He grants that my argument supports "the necessity of some overarching frame within which one assesses competing claims" (33), and he notes that Giroux agrees. But while Giroux and I can agree on this point, we disagree, Weinstein holds, on the frame itself. Weinstein suggests that my favoured frame is "the familiar epistemological theories that Paul and McPeck build upon" (33),[4] while Giroux's "overarching framework . . . is social transformation towards radical and pluralist democracy" (33). Thus we are agreed on the need for an encompassing framework within which dialogue and reason-giving and -assessing can take place; we differ only on the substance of the frame itself.

But this difference, Weinstein argues, is crucially important. He asks:

> But can Siegel grant what I take Giroux to require: ethical norms of justification in a role heretofore reserved for the purely epistemological? For Giroux the most essential reasons are those that social injustice and marginalization bring to the fore. It is these that constitute the essential framework to understand the failure of putative master narratives, totalizing metanarratives rooted in elite disciplinary practices or in the "ordinary" language of the schools and the educated classes. Giroux sees all of these as subject to critique from the standpoints of those who remain outside and unattended: those Others "seen as a deficit. . . (whose humanity) is either cynically posited as problematic or ruthlessly denied."
>
> This is a profound epistemological move. It requires no less than that the true is to be defined in terms of the good. The basic epistemological thesis is that intuitions of injustice are more dialectically reliable than ordinary discourse or methodologicaly sanctioned inquiries. (33)[5]

Weinstein explains this "profound epistemological move" in terms I find completely compelling. First, he suggests that "[d]iscourse frames . . . are to be judged for their adequacy in terms of their ability to include without prejudice all points of view within their scope" (33). Consequently, "the systematic exclusion of a point of view indicates a structural failing in the discourse frame" (33–4). Taking Feminism as his example, Weinstein suggests that "[i]t is the disregard of women's perspectives despite their apparent availability that marks patriarchal frames as inadequate. It is the injustice that such disregard inspires that privileges the perspective from which the disregard can be seen and analyzed" (34). As Weinstein points out (34), this is not to say that excluded perspectives are necessarily correct. It is to say, rather, that they are "dialectically invaluable," because they afford

> a deep critique of all those views from which they have proved to be unavailable. The resounding question is: How could purported master narratives have failed so abysmally to see what ought to be in common view? The injustice that result[s] from . . . marginalization . . . points to a pathology in discourse frames within which the injustice was invisible. Critique requires the interrogation of such discourse frames and the exposure of those elements that supported . . . the disregard of blatant injustice. (34)

Thus Weinstein's frankly stirring conclusion:

> The excluded must be explained, and the injustices suffered through exclusion indemnified by confronting intellectual blindness and educational error. Right reason does not yield the true, for right reason is corrupted by interest. If my intuition serves me well, the confrontation with social injustice yields the essential epistemological probe for revealing the deep delusions of totalizing conceptual frames, delusions that through their justification of marginalizing and repressive practices, testify to their inadequacy for rational, universal and cosmopolitan inquiry. (34)

I am tempted (though I will resist!) to shout "Hallelujah!" For my Modernist inclinations, no less than Weinstein's Postmodernist ones, are to recoil in outrage from the injustices to which Weinstein so poignantly points. I agree that exclusionary discourse frames are rightly criticized as inadequate because of that exclusion; I agree that the perspectives provided by excluded people and groups often provide insight not only profound but also otherwise unavailable, and for that reason are particularly valuable; I agree that a discourse frame's blindness to injustice, and to what ought to be clearly visible, is a phenomenon crying out for explanation as well as condemnation. But all this gives me pause: if Weinstein (and Giroux) and I can agree on so much, isn't there a problem? How can Modernism and Postmodernism be so close? I want to argue in the remainder of this chapter that Weinstein's important insights are in fact not so radical, and not so Postmodern, as he thinks—and that where they are, they are problematic.

MORAL CRITIQUE OF DISCOURSE FRAMES

As noted, I agree with Weinstein that discourse frames are rightly criticized on moral grounds: a frame in which it is impossible to notice genuine injustice is properly criticized by pointing out that impossibility; the same goes for a frame's *de facto* marginalization of particular groups. Such frames are criticized for their moral failings. This is one criterion for assessing the adequacy of discourse frames. So a frame can be justifiably deemed inadequate if it excludes, silences, marginalizes, or otherwise supports "blatant injustice." This is itself an Enlightenment thesis concerning the adequacy of discourse frames. These are *moral* failings. Are they also *epistemological* failings, as Weinstein claims?

To silence or marginalize is unjustifiably to deprive people from full participation in social life. It is unjustifiably to presume that their perspectives are inferior or without value. It is to sin against them *procedurally*. This immediately brings to mind Habermas' views of ideal communicative situations, which require "equitable access to the dialogue, and equality within it" (29). When frames silence or marginalize, they fail to meet Habermas' criteria; in so failing, they fail to treat potential participants in dialogue justly.

Is this failure a(n epistemologically) *substantive* as well as a procedural one? Not necessarily. A dialogue in which all have full access, and in which all are treated equally, with respect, may nevertheless result in agreement on beliefs which are false or unjustified. On the other hand, a dialogue to which certain people or groups are excluded may nevertheless result in beliefs which are true or justified. So procedural justice is neither a necessary nor a sufficient condition for substantive rationality (or epistemic worthiness more generally).[6] If so, then the moral objections to exclusionary discourse frames which Weinstein so ably articulates do not constitute epistemological objections—i.e. objections which necessarily tarnish the epistemic credentials of the outcomes of dialogue which take place within them—to those frames as well.[7]

The same point can be seen from a different angle. For the moral objection to discourse frames to constitute an epistemological objection to them, one has to reason in something like the following fashion:

1. Inclusionary frames are morally superior to exclusionary ones—dialogue ought morally to be conducted in conditions of full access and equal respect.

2. Therefore, agreements and conclusions reached in dialogue conducted under the auspices of exclusionary frames are epistemologically less worthy—less justified, or less likely to be true—than those reached through inclusionary ones.

This pattern of reasoning is similar to one which has been penetratingly dubbed by Susan Haack as attempting to derive an "is" from an "ought."[8] To recognize this as the structure of the proposed argument is immediately to recognize its inadequacy. No such epistemological (or ontological) conclusion follows from the (true) moral premise.

Of course it could easily be that the moral failure of exclusion could result in epistemological failure: the excluded could have better insight, or more justified beliefs, or less distorted perspectives, than the included. Weinstein is thus correct to insist that "intuitions of injustice" must always be respected[9] in dialogical interaction. Much discussion of the so-called "epistemic privilege of the oppressed" rightly suggests as much.[10] But whether such a failure does so result is a question which must be addressed independently; it can't be read off from the establishment of morally objectionable exclusion itself. It is in this sense that Haack is right that one can't derive an "is" from an "ought'—and that Weinstein is mistaken in thinking that an ethical objection to a frame automatically translates into an epistemological one: "the true" *cannot* "be defined in terms of the good" (33), for epistemological failure is not guaranteed by moral failure.[11]

POSTMODERNIST REJECTION OF "METANARRATIVE"

As Weinstein makes clear, one hallmark of Postmodernist thought is its distrust of "master narratives," i.e. of "totalizing metanarratives" (33) according to which differences among people and groups are rendered invisible or deemed insignificant, and in which all nonprivileged people are evaluated as inferior to those who are privileged, since perhaps the most significant privilege enjoyed by the latter is the power to have their view of reality, their values, and their evaluative criteria imposed upon nonprivileged others.

It is perhaps worth pointing out that the rejection of totalizing metanarratives has a long and honorable place in the history of Western philosophy; its emphasis by Postmodernists is but a special case of Bishop Butler's insistence that "everything is what it is and not another thing."[12] Women, people of color, people of nondominant classes and cultures, nonheterosexuals, and others who have suffered under totalizing efforts to view the world and everything in it in terms of privileged European white men are surely justified in objecting to such dehumanizing and difference-denying treatment. But the epistemological significance of this moral and social/political insight is not what Weinstein takes it to be.

The first point to note is that the key Postmodernist concept of "metanarrative" is ambiguous. It can refer to (1) a story in which all *people* (or groups) are regarded as equivalent, and differences among them ignored or denied. It can also refer to (2) a fully general *philosophical theory*, concerning (e.g.) all knowledge-claims; all justificatory strategies; all moral values, rights, and obligations; all instances of injustice; etc. Weinstein, perhaps like other Postmodernists, I think conflates these, with unhappy consequences. The rejection of metanarrative understood in the first way is more plausible than that rejection understood in the second way, but neither is without difficulty.

The rejection of the first sort of metanarrative is plausible for all the reasons Weinstein mentions. People and groups are not all alike; regarding them as such, and so marginalizing or rendering differences invisible, can easily result in injustice to those who are marginalized or silenced. If so, and if injustice is bad, then surely such injustice-causing metanarratives are to be viewed with suspicion.

But will injustice always so result? Surely scenarios can be imaginatively envisioned—for example, educational scenarios in which the perspectives of young or immature students are denied or devalued; or professional, scholarly, or other scenarios in which the perspectives of the unqualified are denied or devalued—in which no injustice results.[13] If so, such metanarratives cannot be rejected for this reason.

Moreover: is injustice always bad? Is it always morally wrong to exclude, marginalize or silence—independently of the facts of the case, and the people or culture so treated? As a Modernist, my answer is affirmative: injustice and oppression are morally wrong, and for that reason always to be deplored.[14] But this judgment is underwritten by my acceptance of a metanarrative of the second sort concerning morality, according to which some ways of treating people—whoever they are—are wrong. This metanarrative *ignores* difference. It needn't deny it, but it does deem it *irrelevant* to the moral question at issue. It is always wrong to torture or rape, and, if Postmodernists are right, to marginalize, silence, exclude, or oppress—whoever the victim(s) might be. Can the Postmodernist avoid this sort of metanarrative? I don't see how she can, if she continues to harbor "the hope of supporting progressive educational change in a nonarbitrary manner" (31).

Can she avoid a similar metanarrative of the second sort concerning matters epistemological? For Weinstein and Giroux, "the most essential reasons are those that social injustice and marginalization bring to the fore" (33). Any such claim as this is intelligible only as a claim about *all* reasons; to affirm it is to affirm an epistemological perspective as privileged, even with respect to people and groups with incompatible epistemological predilections. That is, it is to regard the claim as justified, independently of the criteria of justification endorsed by others.

135

I am not myself suggesting that such epistemological metanarratives are necessarily problematic.[15] On the contrary, they are the stock in trade of most Modernist epistemologists, who debate the respective merits of the wide variety of proposed metanarratives—i.e., rival theories—concerning reasons (and knowledge, truth, justification, etc.). I am suggesting rather that Weinstein is committed to one such metanarrative, and so cannot simultaneously be committed, in proper Postmodernist spirit, to the rejection of them all.[16]

I conclude that Weinstein has not given up all metanarratives. He can't, if he wants also to continue to stand for nonarbitrarily grounded progressive social and educational change. The tension noted above is not successfully finessed by focussing on the essential nature of certain sorts of reasons, or on totalizing claims concerning the injustice of oppression, exclusion, or marginalization.[17] Moreover, the metanarrative(s) which Weinstein embraces sound(s) very much like those advocated by Modernists like myself.

POSTMODERNISM AND "FRAMES" OF DISCOURSE

The expression "discourse frame" is also ambiguous. For me, a totalizing discourse frame (of the second sort) is composed of sets of *principles, criteria, norms*, and the like, in accordance with which discourse is ideally to be conducted, and the results of discourse assessed. But all such sets are on my view fallible, challengeable, and improvable. There is no single frame which is *the* Modernist, Enlightenment frame. The only candidate for such a frame I can think of is a single metaprinciple: for beliefs, claims, and other outcomes of dialogue to enjoy justificatory status, that status must depend upon, and be determined in accordance with, (fallible) criteria or standards of justification. As we have seen, with respect to this metaprinciple, Weinstein (and Giroux) and I are agreed.

But sometimes Weinstein uses "frame" to denote a set of *practices*. When he disparages the Patriarchal frame for its failure to acknowledge, or even "see," injustices visited by that frame upon women, he is not criticizing some principle or criterion of Patriarchy which forces this blindness. For—at least if the Patriarchal frame is linked to the Enlightment frame, as it usually is—that frame *denies the relevance*, to both moral and epistemic evaluation, of gender difference. That is how it renders women's differences irrelevant and invisible. There is no Enlightment *principle* which forces Patriarchy. It is rather the manifestation of deficient *practice*. On this deficiency Modernists and Postmodernists are, or at least should be, agreed.

Weinstein and I are agreed as well that this sort of blindness cries out for explanation: given the evil of exclusion, and rejection of such evil by their own principles condemning injustice, how could Enlightenment thinkers have missed it? Good question. My point so far has been that the explanation is not, in this case, a matter of deficient principle, since the critics and the criticized are agreed concerning the relevant principles. It is rather a matter of deficient practice: patriarchs ignored relevant evidence, contrary to their own principles of evidence;[18] failed to recognize evidence *as* relevant; misapplied evaluative principles; unjustifiably invoked defective dichotomies and hierarchies; etc. The tasks of explaining frame-inspired blindness, and of eliminating resulting injustice, have to focus as much on deficient practice as on deficient principle.[19]

Moreover, these tasks, according to Postmodernism, can never be finally completed. For frames and perspectives, on that view, are *inevitably* partial and distorting. Consequently, *no* frame, however Postmodernist in aspiration, can completely protect itself from this sort of criticism. It will always take plain hard work—often informed by those harmed by those perspectives—to root out this sort of injustice. The sin here is a sin that is, on the Postmodern view, unavoidable. If so, the Enlightment view takes its lumps—as all frames, including Postmodernist frames, inevitably will—at the hands of specific criticisms. So the project of improving our inevitably defective principles and practices—in part, by listening to and respecting the "intuitions of injustice" of the marginalized and oppressed—is a never-ending one, which we embark upon because of our valuing of truth and justice. Here again, our embrace of these values, and our recognition of a thorough-going fallibilism with respect to our own beliefs, values, principles, and practices—without *all* of which the Postmodernist project makes no sense—is remarkably Modernist. Postmodernism is best seen, then, not as a rejection of Modernism, but as an advanced movement within it: one which accepts basic Modernist, Enlightenment principles and intuitions concerning truth, justification, fallibilism, justice, and respect, and seeks politically and epistemologically more sophisticated understandings of those principles and more realistic explanations for failures to live up to them.[20] Seen otherwise, it is incapable of carrying out and justifying its progressive, emancipatory project.[21] In the end, then, there is rather less to the Postmodern criticism of the Enlightenment than meets the eye.

CONCLUSION

The Postmodernist criticism of a discourse frame, on the grounds that it unjustifiably excludes, is a criticism which Enlightenment Modernists should accept. Exclusion, marginalization, and oppression, by Modern as well as Postmodern lights, are morally wrong; Modernists can and should also accept that these moral failures frequently lead to epistemologically unjustified results. The errors of Patriarchal, classist, racist, heterosexist, and other inadequate frames are errors that Modernism acknowledges, in theory if not always in practice. That Enlightenment thinkers failed to see what is now obvious is a fact that indeed cries out for investigation and explanation as well as condemnation. But this failure cannot condemn Modernism per se, since

Modernism acknowledges the failure, at least in principle. The failure to acknowledge it in practice suggests the partiality and distortion of Modernist vision. But, as Postmodernists proclaim, all frames are subject to partiality and distortion; indeed, all will inevitably succumb to it. If so, then the criticism of those Modernist frames just mentioned constitutes no more of a criticism of Modernism itself—conceived as a particular sort of discourse frame—than it does of Postmodernism, similarly conceived.

In fact, as argued above, the criticisms levelled against Modernist frames are themselves underwritten by Modernist principles. In this respect, Postmodernism is itself best understood as informed by, and committed to, some of the metanarratives of Modernism. Its commitment to emancipatory social and educational change are underwritten both by Modernist moral principles concerning justice, equality, and respect, and by Modernist epistemological principles concerning evidence, reasons, justification, and truth.[22] All of these principles are of course open to challenge and revision, and Postmodernism is perhaps best understood as offering a particular sort of challenge. But that Modernist principles are open to challenge—that they are recognized as fallible and improvable—is itself a thoroughly Modernist (meta)principle.

So: Weinstein's attempt to finesse the dilemma posed by Postmodernism's rejection of metanarratives, together with its advocacy of nonarbitrarily grounded progressive social and educational change, does not succeed. These two positions cannot, despite Weinstein's efforts, be simultaneously endorsed. Weinstein can endorse the second precisely because his attempt to endorse the first fails. One cannot reject all metanarratives—though of course one can reject any particular metanarrative—and simultaneously regard the advocacy of one's favored social/political/educational agenda as nonarbitrarily grounded. The nonarbitrary advocacy of emancipatory social and educational change requires the embrace of both moral and epistemological metanarratives—as does the nonarbitrary condemnation of silencing, exclusion, marginalization, and oppression. Weinstein is right that exclusion and blindness constitute moral defects of discourse frames; he is also right that exclusion can result in epistemic loss in that excluded perspectives can and often do contain important insights and provide the basis for telling criticisms of the excluding frames. But the one sort of defect cannot be regarded as entailing the other; a moral defect does not *eo ipso* constitute an epistemological defect: one cannot derive an "is" from an "ought." Further, Postmodernist criticisms of Modernism must be understood primarily as criticisms of practice rather than of principle, since the criticism of its own principles is itself licenced by Modernist (meta)principle. Postmodernism has made, and no doubt will continue to make, important criticisms of, and expose heretofore undiscovered defects in, our principles, practices, and discourse frames. But if I have understood Modernism correctly, then these criticisms do not undermine Modernism, but rather advance its own project.

So if Weinstein is correct in holding, with Postmodernism, that "[r]ight reason does not yield the true, for right reason is corrupted by interest" (34), this can only be because it is *true* that "'right' reason" so fails because it is so corrupted. And of course it is "right reason" itself which reveals that truth. And therein lies the rub: Postmodernism, or any other perspective which seriously endorses radical or progressive social and educational change, requires an epistemology which endorses truth and justification as viable theoretical notions. That is to say: Postmodern advocacy of radical pedagogies (and politics) requires Old-Fashioned Epistemology (and a good deal of Old-Fashioned Moral Theory as well). Postmodernism's concern with social injustice similarly requires some sort of metanarrative. Weinstein is offering us a frame which he hopes will be adequate "for rational, universal, and cosmopolitan inquiry" (34).[23] This is the very hope of the Enlightenment. If, however, in Postmodern spirit, he rejects the very possibility of such a frame, then he is caught in the arbitrariness he has struggled valiantly to overcome.[24]

"RADICAL" PEDAGOGY REQUIRES "CONSERVATIVE" EPISTEMOLOGY

... to be objective does not require us to be *un*interested, that is, devoid of interests and feelings; it requires us only to acknowledge those interests and feelings, to discount any resulting biases and prejudices, and to do our best to act in a *dis*interested way.

—Stephen Toulmin

QUESTIONS OF ETHICS AND SOCIAL PHILOSOPHY—for example, those concerning fairness, equality, and obligations of various sorts—have long been central to philosophy of education. Because educational institutions are political institutions,[1] philosophers of education have long been interested in the political dimensions of education as well. A particularly popular ethical/social/political position, at least in some philosophy of education circles, is that educational endeavors and institutions ought to value and foster "liberal," "leftist" or "radical"[2] political and moral values. In particular, it is commonly held that education ought to respect all students/persons, regardless of their race, gender, class, sexual orientation, etc.; and moreover that education ought to be particularly, and scrupulously, sensitive to the needs and interests of minority and other "marginalized" students. These needs and interests include (though they are not limited to) protection from the hegemonic domination of the dominant culture. Multiculturalist initiatives in education are generally understood in this light.

I fully endorse this general moral/political perspective. I believe that we are morally obliged to treat students with respect, and that this obligation imposes on us additional obligations with respect to certain (classes of) students, including those just mentioned.

However, this moral/political perspective is often conjoined with a related epistemological perspective. This latter perspective is perhaps best thought of not as a single epistemological position, but rather as a family of related theses: that knowledge is culturally determined and/or relative; that different cultures endorse their own epistemologies, e.g. their own conceptions of truth and views of the nature or criteria of epistemic justification; that the obligation to respect cultural differences extends to respecting those alternative epistemologies as well; etc. This further epistemological perspective will be the focus of my attention in what follows. I will argue not only that that perspective is of dubious epistemic merit, but, additionally, that honoring it has the unfortunate consequence of undermining the moral/political commitment to which it is routinely related. I will argue, in short, that defenders of the moral/political view undermine that view when they embrace the epistemological perspective that they frequently regard as its corollary; and that embrace of the moral/political view requires the rejection of that supposed epistemological corollary. My claim is that liberal, leftist, and/or radical[3] educational views *require* for their satisfactory articulation and defense a traditional, or "conservative,"[4] underlying epistemology, which fully embraces and utilizes traditional conceptions of truth, rationality, justification, and the like.

If I am right, then it is imperative that defenders of radical pedagogy distinguish their embrace of particular moral/political theses from untenable, allegedly related, epistemological ones. They must reject the latter for two reasons: first, the epistemological theses are false or unjustified; second, failure to reject them undermines any argumentative effort to defend the former. In particular, the relativistic thesis that epistemologies are culturally specific—and the related view that respecting members of marginalized cultures requires accepting, or regarding as a legitimate alternative to one's own, their culturally specific alternative epistemologies—must be rejected. The theses that alternative epistemologies are equally legitimate; that respecting marginalized cultures requires regarding their culturally specific epistemologies as equally legitimate to our own; and that a particular one—Western, Modernist, Enlightenment epistemology—is itself implicated in real cases of hegemony, marginalization, and cultural imperialism, and therefore must be rejected as a philosophically inadequate epistemology—are theses which are profoundly mistaken. Much of what follows will be concerned to highlight their deficiencies. First, however, let me briefly articulate the target moral/political views, so as to fix our discussion.

THE MORAL CASE AGAINST MARGINALIZATION

The case against the marginalization or silencing of certain (groups of) students is easily made: it is wrong, morally wrong, to treat students (or anyone else) in ways which harm them; it is wrong to fail to treat students with respect; it is wrong to treat students in such a way that their ideas, and their cultures, are not taken seriously. Treating students in these ways fails to treat them with respect; it obviously has deleterious effects upon them as well. It harms their ability to master the curriculum. It harms their ability to make sense of and understand the social situations in which they find themselves. Perhaps most dramatically, it harms their own images of themselves as persons, which in turn has potentially horrific consequences for virtually all aspects of their lives.

Some, for example Charles Taylor, have put this last forward as the most important reason for favoring multiculturalist initiatives in education. Taylor's argument for multiculturalist education emphasizes the point that one's identity is constructed in part in terms of others' reflected images of oneself, and that incorrect, distorted, or demeaning images of oneself reflected back to oneself by others can have a disastrously negative effect on one's own self-image: as Taylor puts it, " . . . a person or group of people can suffer real damage, real distortion, if the people or society around them mirror back to them a confining or demeaning or contemptible picture of themselves. Nonrecognition or misrecognition can inflict harm, can be a form of oppression, imprisoning someone in a false, distorted, and reduced mode of being" (Taylor [1992], p. 25). As René Arcilla summarizes this aspect of Taylor's view:

143

> Our multiculturalist initiatives in education should be principally concerned with exposing and criticizing images and terms that stunt possibilities for self-definition, particularly for members of cultures that already suffer from a history of discrimination. These initiatives should strive to replace such images and terms with more promising ones that can evoke the potential for growth and achievement in all. Such an education could thus help prevent the seeds of monocultural domination from taking root in our diverse youth. (Arcilla [1995], p. 165)[5]

Is it always morally wrong to exclude, marginalize or silence—independently of the facts of the case, and the people or culture so treated? As indicated in the previous chapter, my answer, like Taylor's, is affirmative: injustice and oppression are morally wrong, and for that reason always to be deplored.

In particular, the injustice and oppression which result from "monocultural domination," which itself often results in defective and harmful self-images and -identities for particular (groups of) students, are always to be rejected. But this judgment is underwritten by my acceptance of basic tenets of traditional "liberal" moral theory, according to which some ways of treating people—whoever they are—are wrong. This theory *ignores* difference. It needn't deny it, but it does deem it *irrelevant* to the moral question at issue. It is always wrong, not only to torture or rape, but also to marginalize, silence, exclude, or oppress—whoever the victim(s) might be.[6]

Thus, accepting education's moral obligation to engage in multicultural initiatives, and regarding as educationally important the obligation to treat marginalized students and their cultures with respect—and in doing so, striving to avoid "monocultural domination"—are straightforward requirements of "liberal" moral and social/political theory. In so far, the obligation to treat marginalized or culturally oppressed students in ways which pay special attention to them and their cultures is underwritten by principles which do not favor (the members of) particular cultures. In this sense, educational multiculturalism is a moral/political view (rather than an epistemological one) which rests on the culture-neutral principles of moral and political theory—principles which apply with equal force to all persons and cultures. Of course, different cultures will call for different treatment, according to those principles, simply because some are dominant or hegemonic and others are marginalized, silenced, or otherwise victimized or oppressed. But the fact remains that the principles which establish that marginalized persons and groups are treated wrongly and deserve better treatment—which establish, that is, that marginalization and oppression are wrong, and that victims of such treatment are entitled to initiatives designed to right such wrongs—are themselves person- and culture-neutral in that they apply with equal force to all persons and cultures.[7]

The moral imperatives of avoiding injustice towards and oppression of members of marginalized cultures seem, to Taylor and to me, to justify fully multiculturalist educational initiatives. That justification rests on standard liberal moral/political principles: respect for persons; avoidance of unnecessary harm; maximization of happiness and potential; etc. Thus the advocacy of "radical pedagogy," multiculturalism, and so on in education is completely in keeping with—and is, indeed, required by—standard "liberal" ethical and social/political theory. In particular, the moral imperative of combatting the oppression which results from foisting upon marginalized others demeaning or distorted images of themselves is, in these standard liberal terms, fully explained and justified.

Thus far, I have been arguing that currently popular educational sentiments which favor marginalized students and groups are grounded, not in moral or political theories which select those students or groups for special favor, but rather in traditional liberal theories which regard them as deserving of exceptional attention in so far as they have been and are being wronged. These theories favor intervention and assistance on behalf of any student or group so wronged. As I argued in Chapter 9, the justification of those sentiments, and the educational initiatives undertaken under their auspices, are dependent upon such liberal, culture- and person-blind, theory.

But does this way of looking at these matters—according to which the justification of educational principles and policies must necessarily rest on neutral principles—do justice to the marginalized students and cultures we think we are obliged to help? In justifying multiculturalism in this way, are we hegemonically imposing on the members of the very minority cultures we are trying to help an alien, unjustifiably dominant, and pernicious epistemology? It is to this question we must now turn.

EPISTEMIC "MONOCULTURAL DOMINATION"?

I want to argue in this section and the next that it is false that the standard "liberal" justification of "radical" educational initiatives rests on a culturally specific and hegemonic epistemology, and that, in so resting, these initiatives marginalize, silence, or otherwise oppress those members of minority cultures who subscribe to equally culturally specific but alternative and incompatible epistemologies. That is, it is false that the epistemology underlying the "liberal" justification of our target educational initiatives is contentious in a morally pernicious way, such that relying on it itself oppresses those the initiatives in question are intended to aid.

What do I mean by "the epistemology underlying the 'liberal' justification of our target educational initiatives"? That justification rests on at least the following: that it is true, or at least that we are rationally justified in believing, that children, students, and persons generally deserve to be treated with respect and in ways that, at a minimum, are not unnecessarily harmful to them; and that it is true, or at least that we are rationally justified in believing, that marginalized students and members of marginalized cultures are not in fact being treated with respect or are in fact being treated in ways which cause them to suffer unnecessary harm. These pieces of the liberal justification of multicultural education are conspicuously "liberal" or "Enlightenment" in their epistemological presuppositions: they presuppose that it is possible for moral principles, and descriptions of factual states of affairs, to have truth values (i.e. to be true or false); they presuppose as well that those same principles and descriptions admit of rational justification. They thus presuppose particular views concerning the applicability to moral and factual matters of the concepts of truth and rational justification—views which may be clearly identified with the epistemological predilections of the dominant, Western, Enlightenment philosophical tradition.[8] Does this fact either discredit the pro-

posed justification of multicultural education, or harm the intended beneficiaries of multicultural educational initiatives by exerting over them an alien,
hegemonic set of epistemological presuppositions? Both questions, I think,
should be answered in the negative. I take them in turn.

First, the fact that the liberal justification of multicultural education presupposes particular, indeed traditional, "conservative" views concerning truth
and rational justification does not discredit that justification, for the straightforward reason that these conceptions are *necessary* ingredients of *any* proposed
justification. If I am to offer a putative justification for some proposed course
of action (e.g., that particular [groups of] students should be treated in some
particular fashion) in terms of some description of a putative state of affairs
(e.g., that such students are being marginalized or otherwise harmed or treated unfairly) and some relevant moral principles (e.g., that it is morally wrong
to marginalize, or harm, or unfairly treat students), that proposed justification
will succeed—i.e. actually serve to justify the proposed course of action—only
if the description of the relevant state of affairs accurately depicts that state of
affairs (e.g., the students in question are in fact being marginalized, harmed, or
unfairly treated), or at least we are justified in believing that it does; *and* if the
moral principles appealed to are themselves true (e.g. that it is in fact wrong
to marginalize, or harm, or treat students unfairly), or, for those who are squea-
mish about attributing truth values to moral principles, at least that we are justified in believing them. If both of these two conditions are not met—that is,
if the relevant facts are not as the description depicts, or if the relevant moral
principles are incorrect (or, more modestly, if we are not justified in believing
the description or the principles)—then the putative justification fails. For
example, if a teacher offers as a justification for the corporal punishment of a
particular student the alleged fact that the student hit a fellow student, when
in fact the student didn't hit her fellow student (or we are not justified in
believing that she did), then the justification fails. It similarly fails if the teacher
denies that students must be treated with respect, or if she accepts that students
should be treated with respect, but holds that corporal punishment is consistent with respectful treatment.[9] That is, for *any* proposed justification of *any*
educational initiative to succeed, the relevant descriptions and principles must
be true and/or rationally justified. If this possibility is denied, then so is the
possibility of justifying educational initiatives. Consequently, the fact that the
"liberal" justification of multicultural education presupposes particular, indeed
traditional, "conservative" views concerning truth and rational justification
does not discredit that justification. To reject those views is to give up the possibility of justifying *any* educational initiatives, whether multicultural or any
other.

Second, and consequently, the intended beneficiaries of multicultural educational initiatives are not harmed by exerting over them an alien, hegemon-

ic set of epistemological presuppositions (concerning truth, rational justification, etc.). For (1) as just argued, these presuppositions are not optional but necessary; they are therefore, in the relevant sense, not alien, but rather apply perfectly well to members of all cultures, despite the fact that Western epistemological traditions may well *seem* alien to the members of particular marginalized cultures, whose epistemological intuitions may be quite distant from them. (I note in passing that it is a problematic conception of education which frowns upon the exposure of students to ideas which are alien to them.) Moreover (2), they can be rejected only at the price either of incoherence or of arbitrariness. For to reject them *justifiably* is to reject them for reasons which satisfy the very conditions concerning rational justification which one wants to reject. To reject them *unjustifiably*, on the other hand, is to reject them for no good reason; it is to reject them in such a way that the rest of us are under no epistemic obligation to respect or honor, or even take seriously, that rejection.[10] Finally (3), how is this alleged harm to be understood? The claim that "'epistemic monocultural domination' harms members of cultures which have alternative epistemologies" presumes a shared, unproblematic understanding of "harm": it presumes universal agreement that, for example, causing people to have demeaning self-images harms them, while causing them to lead long, happy, healthy lives does not. If the claim that "epistemic monocultural domination" is a bad thing rests on a univocal, culturally-neutral conception of harm, the imposition of which is not itself an instance of monocultural domination, then why should a univocal set of epistemic understandings count as objectionably hegemonic? The short answer is that it should not.

This rejection of the "epistemic monocultural domination" charge, while good as far as it goes, does not, alas, go far enough. For the "liberal" justification of multicultural educational initiatives given above presupposes a particular view of justification, according to which particular descriptions, principles and claims admit of nonculturally-bound justification. But why should we accept *it*? I have argued thus far that it *must* be accepted, on pain of incoherence or inability to justify such initiatives. In order to secure this conclusion, more must be said by way of response to the advocates of that charge, some of whom specifically reject both that conclusion and the argument presented for it.

CAN "ENLIGHTENMENT EPISTEMOLOGY" BE REJECTED?

I have argued that "epistemic monocultural domination" is not a serious worry for the advocates of multicultural education or "radical pedagogy," because the key epistemic notions of rationality and rational justification, according to the dominant, Western, "Enlightenment" epistemological tradition, are universally applicable, such that calling the "liberal" justification of multicultural educational initiatives into question presupposes the "liberal" understanding of those very notions—and, therefore, that it is (1) not possible coherently or nonarbitrarily to reject them, and (2) false that relying on them treats unfairly the members of those nondominant cultures which accept alternative epistemologies. I want to consider next three objections to "Enlightenment epistemology" and this type of defense of it.

The Problem of "Metanarratives"

One popular objection to this general epistemic view, pressed by many Postmodern writers, is that any such epistemological "metanarrative" is suspect. Within the broader Postmodern literature, Foucault and Lyotard are famous for their rejection of metanarratives. In the literature of educational theory, Henry Giroux, for example, voices the same objection:

> General abstractions that deny the specificity and particularity of everyday life, that generalize out of existence the particular and the local, that smother difference under the banner of universalizing categories are rejected as totalitarian and terroristic. (Giroux [1988], p. 14; cited in Beyer and Liston [1992], p. 374)

Other educational theorists also press the objection.[11] If it succeeds, then it undercuts the arguments presented above, since those arguments are authorized by just such a metanarrative. Relying on the Enlightenment epistemological metanarrative, then, would not only fail; it would also constitute, in Giroux's words, "totalitarian and terroristic" hegemonic philosophizing, and, once seen in that light, would presumably be rejected by "liberal" philosophers as well as Postmodern ones.

This objection, however, does not succeed. For one thing, the "liberal" justification (and its associated metanarrative) does not "deny the specificity and particularity of everyday life," "generalize out of existence the particular and the local," or "smother difference under the banner of universalizing categories." It can and should acknowledge specificity and particularity, the particular and the local, and difference. It can and should, moreover, accept that difference, particularity, locality, and specificity, are highly relevant to certain questions—for example, in the imagined case above, whether or not the teacher is justified in believing that the student in question in fact hit her fellow student or otherwise mistreated her is a local matter, and can be resolved only by paying close attention to the particular facts of the case, including facts concerning relevant cultural attitudes of those involved concerning the constitution and appropriateness of hitting, etc. However, while the liberal view accepts and acknowledges these particularities and differences—and so does not deny or smother differences, and therefore is innocent of the charges Giroux articulates—it does, as noted above, deem them to be *irrelevant* to certain questions, especially to those concerning the justifiability or correctness of the relevant principles. For example, if it is wrong to marginalize, silence, or otherwise oppress members of minority cultures, then it is wrong to do so—independently of the particularities of the cultures victimized by that oppression. Thus the liberal view acknowledges difference and particularity, but has a nuanced view of the *relevance* of difference: sometimes it is highly relevant; sometimes not. That view rejects the idea that difference is *always* relevant to *everything*. But that rejection escapes Giroux's criticism.

Moreover, the Postmodern rejection of metanarratives—epistemological and other—is notoriously troubled. As many writers have noted, that rejection itself constitutes a metanarrative. To say that all metanarratives are to be rejected, that they are all defective, is to make a universalizing claim of exactly the sort that the person making the claim wants to (universally) reject. But if rejecting metanarratives requires embracing a metanarrative, then there is a logical difficulty inherent in the very idea of rejecting them all. Beyer and Liston ([1992], p. 374, note 8) note the "ironic or self-contradictory" character of Giroux's claim—itself a "universalizing" one—that "general abstractions" characteristic of "modernist" writings are universally deficient and deserving of rejection. I have discussed the same problem in Chapter 9. The bottom line is this: if the rejection of metanarrative requires metanarrative, then metanarrative cannot (coherently) be universally rejected. If not, then the liberal justification of multicultural educational initiatives cannot be tellingly criticized on the grounds that it relies upon a metanarrative.

149

The Problem of "Universal Reason"

A further charge frequently made against the "liberal" view is that it relies upon a hegemonic conception of "universal reason." As we have seen, that view does presuppose a particular conception of reason and rationality, according to which reasons can afford objective warrant for particular claims. This view is "universalistic" in the sense that the goodness—the power and probative force—of reasons is universally applicable: if p is a good reason for q, then anyone who is justified in believing that p, and who believes that q on the basis of p, is equally justified in believing that q. Particularities and differences among the candidate believers or their cultures do not effect the ability of p to warrant q.

I have already argued that universality is not itself a plausible target of criticism, since it is required for its own rejection, and therefore cannot be coherently universally rejected. But many writers suggest that there are special problems here for the universality of reason or rationality in particular. Not only do different cultures and persons evaluate particular reasons differently with respect to their probative force—what you or your culture regard as a good reason for q, I or my culture regard as a bad reason—but a special problem arises with respect to the justification of that conception of reason or rationality itself. For how can I argue for my, or indeed any, universalistic conception of rationality? If I do so on the basis of reasons I offer in its defense, I appear to beg the question against those not already committed to that conception; if I do so on any other basis, my proffered justification fails by my own lights. Thus these two problems threaten, from another angle, any universalistic conception of rationality.

Both of the problems just raised are fundamental epistemological difficulties. I cannot address them at length here, though I have done so elsewhere. Siegel (1987) is aimed at defusing the first, relativistic, difficulty—i.e. that a universalistic conception of rationality is defective because the power and convicting force of reasons appears to differ from person/culture to person/culture. Chapter 5 above attempts to offer a nonquestion-begging, noncircular rational justification of the commitment to rationality. If the efforts undertaken in these works are successful, then these two difficulties with "universal reason," at least, can be met.

I should like here to add to these earlier defenses of "universal reason" by making a further observation: the fact that humans are always located in specific cultural/historical settings does not undermine our collective ability to reach beyond our local settings and speak to broader audiences and arenas of concern. We always judge from the perspective of our own conceptual scheme; there is no way to escape from all schemes and judge from a God's-eye point of view. Since our schemes reflect our cultural/historical circumstances, then these circumstances constitute limits on our judgment; we can't escape them entirely. These premises are I think correct. But some draw from them the conclusion that "universal reason" is impossible; that our judgments cannot, in principle, have any force beyond the bounds of our own scheme. This conclusion is I think mistaken; in any case it does not follow from those premises.

I cannot argue for this claim here; I do so in Chapter 12. But since many of those who argue for the rejection of "universal reason" do so on the basis of the mistaken inference just noted, pointing out the mistake helps, I hope, to establish that the criticisms of "universal reason" just addressed do not succeed.[12]

The Problem of Respect

The final problem to be dealt with here involves the notion of respect. As we have seen, the "liberal" justification of multicultural educational initiatives presupposes the moral principle of respect for persons. We are morally obliged, on this liberal, Enlightenment view, to treat other persons and cultures with respect. What is it to treat others with respect? One possibility is this: to treat another person or culture with respect involves, in part, respecting its epistemological intuitions and predilections. Respecting alternative epistemologies requires regarding them as equally legitimate, equally as good, as one's own. Consequently, any view which presumes that some particular epistemology is always to be preferred to its alternatives fails to treat those alternatives, and the people who hold them, with respect; respecting them requires not regarding one's own epistemology as superior. Therefore favoring liberal or Enlightenment epistemology constitutes a violation of the liberal duty to treat other persons and cultures with respect.[13]

There are several difficulties with this line, the most basic of which is that it requires a kind of epistemic superiority which it cannot allow itself. For in asserting itself as a justified conclusion about what it is to treat alternative cultures, and epistemologies, with respect, it presumes that its own conception of argumentative forcefulness is correct—or at least is superior to alternative conceptions, according to which its conclusion does not follow. But this is exactly to favor its own epistemological perspective in a way which it denounces as disrespectful. Consequently, in advocating its view about epistemic respect, it violates that very view; such advocacy involves a "performative contradiction."

So this way of understanding our obligation to treat alternative epistemologies with respect will not do. A better way to understand it is to regard our own epistemological views as fallible; to acknowledge that alternative epistemologies may be held by others, and may in fact be superior to our own; and to commit ourselves to a fairminded evaluation of ours and its alternatives. Obviously this course favors our own view initially, for we will rely upon it in evaluating all candidates, including our own. As Quine and many others have taught us, we cannot judge from outside our conceptual scheme.[14] Nevertheless, we can treat alternatives with respect by taking them seriously; by recognizing that many people accept them; by seeing what can be said for them; and by allowing them seriously to challenge our own view. In this way we treat them with respect without running afoul of the difficulty noted above. Treating alternative epistemologies with respect does not require automatically regarding them as having as much merit as our own. They may have as much merit—indeed, they may have more—but this needs to be shown by a serious consideration and evaluation of their epistemic credentials. It is simply a mistake to think that the respectful treatment of alternative epistemologies requires, or entails, that we regard all epistemologies (or their associated cultures) as equally good.

I conclude that the several difficulties raised for "Enlightenment epistemology," its conception of "universal reason," and the "liberal" justification of multicultural educational initiatives offered under its auspices, can be met. That justification succeeds.

THE "EPISTEMIC MONOCULTURAL DOMINATION" OBJECTION UNDERMINES THE EDUCATIONAL INITIATIVES IT IS INTENDED TO FOSTER

In the previous sections I argued that the "epistemic monocultural domina-tion" objection, raised against the "liberal" justification of "liberal" or "radical" educational initiatives, especially multiculturalist initiatives, does not success-fully challenge that justification. Here I want to argue that the epistemology underlying that liberal justification is *required* for any putative justification to succeed.

Fortunately, the argument for this point can be briefly made.[15] Suppose that that epistemology is rejected, i.e. that we give up our "conservative" under-standings of truth, warrant, rationality and rational justification, etc. Then we are unable to establish, for example, that apparent victims of marginalization or oppression at the hands of a hegemonic dominant culture are actual vic-tims. Similarly, we are unable to establish that such victimization, even if actu-al, is a bad thing. In order to establish these judgments as true and/or justified, we must have recourse to conceptions of truth, justification, etc., which pro-vide us with the conceptual resources to establish these claims. Without those resources, there is no possibility of acting, in a morally motivated and justified way, so as to end or alleviate the suffering wrought by injustice. As Beyer and Liston (1992, p. 390) put it, in discussing Jonathan Kozol's *Savage Inequalities* (1991), "language must be tied in some sense to an external reality. Moreover, our outrage at the conditions described by the author must be rooted in a moral condemnation of injustice and inequality." That is, Kozol's description of those savage inequalities must be true; moreover, our condemnation of them must be rationally justified. Without the conceptual resources provided by "conservative" epistemology, no concerted and justified moral/political action is possible. But such action is the very raison d'etre of "radical" educa-tional initiatives. Thus the rejection of that epistemology undermines the moral/political perspective the advocates of "radical" educational initiatives most prize. Their moral/political agenda *requires* that epistemology.[16]

CONCLUDING CONSIDERATIONS

I have tried to defend traditional, "conservative," Enlightenment epistemolo-gy from some popular but in my view ill-conceived objections. I have tried also to show that the defenders of multiculturalist and other "radical" educa-tional initiatives require the "liberal" justification of such initiatives under-written by that old-fashioned epistemology.

I should note that the same point applies to the advocacy of other, more "conservative" educational initiatives. For example, to oppose multiculturalist educational initiatives, and to favor politically more conservative alternatives, one must hold that those favored alternatives are justified in terms of true or warranted descriptions and principles. In this sense, my conclusion is politically neutral. As I said earlier, I favor the "liberal" or "radical" political view, and reject the "conservative" one. But I have only indirectly argued for that preference here. To clinch the case, both I and my opponents would have to address the veracity and/or justifiability of the descriptions and principles which are intended to establish as justified those alternative moral/political/educational prescriptions.

Of course, establishing that the justification of educational initiatives requires "conservative" epistemology does not establish the legitimacy of that epistemology. It may be that, while required, that epistemology is nevertheless indefensible. If so, then the possibility of pursuing *justified* educational initiatives disappears. This sort of skeptical position—favored by at least some Postmodern writers, and by some traditional skeptics as well—can be challenged only by the detailed defense of (some version of) traditional epistemological theory, and by criticism of those skeptical (and other) challenges to it. In this chapter, and in some of my other publications, I have tried to provide some of that criticism and defense. But of course, there is always more to be said on such fundamental epistemological issues. I would like to conclude by inviting other defenders of multiculturalist and other "radical" educational intiatives to help me to say it.[17]

153

KNOWLEDGE AND CERTAINTY; FEMINISM, POSTMODERNISM, AND MULTICULTURALISM

I can stand brute force, but brute reason is quite unbearable. There is something unfair about its use. It is hitting below the intellect.

—Oscar Wilde

IN THIS CHAPTER I continue the discussion, begun in the previous four chapters, of the epistemic aspects and ramifications of the several voices in contemporary philosophy of education which challenge more traditional, "Enlightenment" views. I do so by way of reacting to two important recent papers which articulate alternative perspectives on knowledge and education, perspectives which are guided by insights drawn from the literatures of Feminism, Postmodernism, and Multiculturalism.

The provocative essays of Lynda Stone (1995) and René Vincente Arcilla (1995) are challenging on several levels: not only do they question the conventional understandings of the notions of knowledge and certainty as they have been developed in traditional, "Modernist" epistemology; they also interrogate the presuppositions which underlie much of both Modernist epistemological discourse and Modernist philosophy of education.

As both Arcilla and Stone do, I begin by situating myself: I am a white, male, analytically trained philosopher, who writes philosophy and philosophy of education in the no longer dominant (let alone hegemonic) analytic style. My main philosophical preoccupations concern some of the issues long regarded as central to epistemology: issues concerning justification, truth, rationality, and relativism. I believe that these issues are of central importance for philosophy of education; in particular, as the attentive reader of earlier chapters will have noticed, I (along with many others) have advocated rationality as a fundamental educational aim or ideal. Since my understanding of that notion, and my advocacy of it as a fundamental educational ideal, rest squarely on the Modernist epistemological tradition within which I work, the interrogations of that tradition presented in the target essays interest me greatly.

Our mutual task in this exchange is to dialogue across our differences, in a spirit of mutual respect and understanding. I accept these terms. But "conversation" and "dialogue" do not betoken only sweetness and light: in engaging in dialogue with those with whom one has differences, one is not limited to agreements with and compliments of one's partners in the dialogue. To conceive criticism—honest, respectful criticism—as beyond the bounds of dialogue, is to conceive dialogue in so limited a fashion that its point, and its capacity to enhance mutual understanding and respect, are lost.[1] So when, in what follows, my comments are occasionally critical, I hope that it will be possible for the reader, as well as my dialogical partners, to receive them in the spirit in which they are intended: as honest furtherings of the conversation.

LYNDA STONE

Stone's essay insightfully explores the role and relevance of *narrative* for philosophy of education. In this respect the form of her contribution, as well as its substance, reflects her commitment to feminist theorizing. I attempt in what follows to understand and critically consider the implications of her narrative for the epistemological questions she confronts.

Stone's understanding of "knowledge" and "certainty" joins these two notions together; her concern is not with knowledge and certainty but with "certain knowledge." According to Stone, for women only one thing is known with certainty—namely, that their lives are uncertain: "For many women what is certain about their lives is its uncertainty" (175).[2] For women,

> . . . in spite of past successes, of beliefs and convictions, we never know if our actions will be realizable. And, even within the relatively privileged confines of some of our lives, often we are "reminded" of uncertainty and of our lack of control. I further suggest that this standard differs for many if not most

men. Furthermore many of us know that actions we take out of this condition, and those taken by others for us, are not in our own best interests. (177)

The object of knowledge here is *action*, and "action," Stone suggests, has different meanings for men and for women. The "norm of certainty" (176) which on Stone's view characterizes traditional epistemology and theory of action is a *male* or masculinist epistemological norm: for men but not for women, actions have the expectation of realization, of success; action understood as autonomous, freely chosen, and guided by reasons—that is, action as it is characterized in the Western Modernist philosophical tradition—is decisively masculinist in its conception. Moreover, actions performed by males are at least typically in their own best interests. Not so for women, as the most recently cited passage indicates. For women, knowledge and action, as we have seen, are uncertain.

The philosophical importance of this uncertainty involves a rejection of essentialism (the idea that women share "an innate femininity" [181]) and a focus on differences, both of which are central to Stone's conception of philosophical feminism. She deplores an essentialism that "posits something as 'alike' for all persons" (181) and which privileges the experiences and perspectives of "white, middle class women" (181); she applauds contemporary feminism's move "to rename the inquiry itself as 'feminisms'" (182) in order to emphasize the importance of avoiding a theoretically and politically debilitating essentialism. Her discussion of competing strands of feminist theorizing which struggle to formulate an adequate theory which rejects any difference-denying essentialism is both informative and inspiring. Feminists continue to be characterized by uncertainty, but the uncertainty here concerns not action but feminist theory itself.

Stone ends her essay by linking uncertainty with friendship, and proposing that women (and people generally?) adopt the posture of "as if friends":

> Very different persons, even those distanced from one another, act *as if friends* if they exhibit openness to different opinions and perspectives, if they demonstrate humility about their own views, and if they try out trust of the other. This attitude means putting each other in the best light possible within a climate of generosity.
>
> Openness, humility, and trust—to return to the central theme of this essay—all work from an initial position of uncertainty. Here uncertainty does not mean hesitancy in action; in fact it suggests just the opposite. This is to proactively assert the attitude of *as if friends*. Here uncertainty means accepting as natural the tentativeness, ambiguity, fluidity of all of life and particularly of the beliefs and desires, knowledges, and actions of persons. This uncertainty moves from a negative characteristic of women's

> lives to one that is positive. The paradox is that something uncertain
> assumes a certainty—a new kind of knowledge of self and others. (184)

Such friendship, as Stone ably demonstrates, involves receptivity, generosity, trust, humility, and an open acceptance of and commitment to work across differences (184–5). As Stone suggests, it is both theoretically and politically important to recast our philosophical musings so as to reject the traditional desire for certainty and to embrace as something positive—indeed, to accept as "a new ethic" (185)—the uncertainty which characterizes women's lives and actions.

Throughout her essay, Stone enjoins the reader to embrace the ideas that women's knowledge of their actions is uncertain, that it is crucially important to acknowledge differences, and that women who are different ought nevertheless to try and work across their differences, in the spirit of receptivity, generosity, trust, humility, and the hope of friendship. This, I'm sure the reader will agree, is an inspiring vision—for women and equally for men.

Nevertheless, I would like to make some observations concerning Stone's vision, and ask some questions concerning it. Most obviously, I suppose, are these: first, Stone's discussion of knowledge involves knowledge *of the outcomes of purposeful actions*, rather than knowledge in general; in this sense the focus of her discussion is rather more narrow than it may appear at first sight. Second, Stone's failure to distinguish between knowledge and certainty flies in the face of at least the great majority of the ('male') epistemology of this century, which, at least since Peirce, has routinely rejected certainty as a condition of knowledge, and endeavored to develop theories of knowledge according to which knowledge need not be certain. In so rejecting certainty as a condition of knowledge, most contemporary epistemology unproblematically accepts Stone's "feminist" insistence on uncertainty as a characteristic of knowledge.[3]

Third, while Stone rejects essentialism within feminist theory, she seems quite happy to treat "male-stream" epistemology and action theory in essentialist ways, ignoring crucial differences which in fact define the contours of theoretical discussion within the Western philosophical tradition. I applaud Stone's rejection of essentialism, but I wonder why that rejection should not be extended beyond the bounds of feminism. I wonder also if Stone's rejection of essentialism ought to be somewhat more nuanced. Of course genuine differences should not be denied. But aren't differences sometimes properly deemed *irrelevant*, as when, for example, we deplore patriarchal oppression of women generally, whatever differences may obtain among the victims of such oppression?[4]

In rejecting essentialism, Stone insists on acknowledging differences among women. If we acknowledge such differences, then shouldn't we be more cautious about regarding women as being correctly characterized by uncertainty?

Won't some women enjoy more certainty in their lives than others? Moreover, don't most men also lack certainty in their lives? I wonder whether Stone's view is in the end quite essentialistic, despite her sincere rejection of it. Perhaps this is the most defensible position she can take: after all, there are samenesses as well as differences across women, across people, and across theories. But then her discussion ought to take this fact more adequately into account.

A final critical point: like many writers, Stone emphasizes the "situatedness" of knowledge and theory, I think problematically. All theorizing is situated, yes; but the relevance of any theorizing to any particular person, culture, time or place depends on much more than the situation in which it was first theorized. Theories developed and propounded from the vantage point of some particular situation and time are nevertheless often relevant to, and true in, other situations and times as well.[5]

In pointing to the uncertainty, and the unfairness, in Ramatoulaye's life, and in women's lives more generally, Stone teaches us a lesson of profound philosophical importance. Her vision of friendship is an inspiring one; it is a vision to which men (I hope) as well as women can aspire. Her discussion and use of narrative are highly instructive. Stone provides us with a clear, compelling feminist voice; a powerful one within contemporary philosophy of education.

RENÉ ARCILLA

While Stone's essay is couched mainly in the voice of Feminism, Arcilla speaks in the voices of Multiculturalism and Postmodernism. His topic is self-knowledge, and he compellingly argues that recent educational interest in Multiculturalism—in particular, in protecting and fostering cultural diversity—provides us with important new insights concerning the nature both of education and its philosophy. I begin by sketching his argument.

Arcilla's view is developed by way of exposition and commentary on some recent works by Charles Taylor concerning the importance of dialogical interaction across cultures for the Modernist quest for self-knowledge and self-understanding. Taylor's argument for Multiculturalist education emphasizes the point that one's identity is constructed in part in terms of others' reflected images of oneself, and that incorrect, distorted, or demeaning images of oneself reflected back to oneself by others can have a disastrously negative effect on one's own self-image: as Taylor puts it, " . . . a person or group of people can suffer real damage, real distortion, if the people or society around them mirror back to them a confining or demeaning or contemptible picture of themselves. Nonrecognition or misrecognition can inflict harm, can be a form of oppression, imprisoning someone in a false, distorted, and reduced mode of being" (cited in Arcilla [1995], p. 160).[6] Multiculturalist education, on Taylor's view, should have as one of its central tasks the resisting of this form of oppression. Arcilla reviews Taylor's complex analysis of shifting historical conceptions of selfhood, resulting ultimately in Taylor's view that "the quest for self-knowledge has a dialogical character," because of "the crucial role that language learning plays in self-definition" (163). At this point a tension emerges between universalistic and individualistic conceptions of humans and human relations, and between "a democratic politics of recognition that is Multiculturalist and one that is more traditionally liberal and universalist" (165): we must honor the common rights and entitlements of all, while at the same time honoring the unique identities of all, and resisting the temptation to ignore or deny differences. For Taylor, the important question is whether or not the drive for Multiculturalist particularity and recognition of difference can be reconciled with Modernist, universalist liberalism. For Arcilla, the important issue involves the way in which self-knowledge requires dialogical interaction with others. It is this interaction, Arcilla argues, which puts self-knowledge in jeopardy.

Taylor's argument for the necessity of dialogical interaction with others for the emergence of the authentic self concludes, as Arcilla reconstructs it, that "I can define myself only on condition of having learned how to use a language of self-definition from an accomplished language user through a process of dialogue. Our self-understanding depends on dialogue with others who teach us the terms by which that self could be recognized" (164). Because, in the process of dialogue with significant others, those others become internalized parts of my self (164), "[m]y very self-understanding depends on the language I learn and the teachers I incorporate into myself" (165). Arcilla argues that such dialogue is a necessary, and never-ending, condition of self-knowledge. Moreover, the moral imperative, noted earlier, of combatting the oppression which results from foisting upon marginalized others demeaning or distorted images of themselves, is in these terms fully explained and justified:

> Our multiculturalist initiatives in education should be principally concerned with exposing and criticizing images and terms that stunt possibilities for self-definition, particularly for members of cultures that already suffer from a history of discrimination. These initiatives should strive to replace such images and terms with more promising ones that can evoke the potential for growth and achievement in all. Such an education could thus help prevent the seeds of monocultural domination from taking root in our diverse youth. (165)

Here the moral imperatives of avoiding injustice towards and oppression of members of marginalized cultures—imperatives fully endorsed by Modernism—seem, to Taylor and to me, to justify fully "our multiculturalist initiatives in education."

But, Taylor suggests, by endorsing and enacting such initiatives, we pave the

160

way for the emergence for all students of their authentic selves, and in so doing we keep open the possibility of their achieving genuine self-knowledge. Arcilla demures. He appeals here to Derrida and Postmodernism, and suggests that Taylor's argument for the never-ending dialogical nature of self-knowledge misses a key fact about the *language* of such dialogue: the ineliminable possibility that the terms of the dialogue, and those of the mutual recognition which the dialogue fosters, can only be provisionally defined, and so are subject to being recurrently redefined—which keeps the dialogue inconclusive, and the need for it interminable.

The insight that Derrida provides is that of "the thrall of aporia in language" (168). Arcilla's beautifully clear characterization of Derrida's findings concerning the "indefiniteness" (168) of language and linguistic meaning leads him to characterize his own divergence from Taylor in similar terms:

> ... although philosophers continue to spin discourses in order to defer indefiniteness, this indefiniteness, like a force of nature, is bound to come back and haunt terms in the discourse. Once altered and alienated from their context, these now questionable terms stand to provoke new mouths to unweave the old discourse and another generation of pens to declare their independence from its terms. So philosophy perpetuates itself. Yet so too does indefiniteness, which remains the condition for the possibility of calling different thinkers into the conversation that keeps philosophy alive.
>
> I believe that the discourse of self-definition, with which we in large part engage in dialogue with significant others, has this aporetic nature as well. (168–9)

However, the bond between Multiculturalism and self-knowledge which Taylor articulates becomes, in Arcilla's hands, a radical critique of the possibility of self-knowledge. For the indefiniteness, the aporetic nature, of the language of self-knowledge, forces the conclusion (according to Arcilla) that self-knowledge is a will-o'-the-wisp—a goal which can never be attained. The indefiniteness and aporetic quality of language guarantee that our efforts to attain self-knowledge will inevitably fail. And this has a disturbing consequence for Multicultural education: if self-knowledge is impossible, Multiculturalist education cannot contribute to its realization, and so cannot be regarded as important for its contribution to that impossible-to-realize end. In this way, according to Arcilla, Taylor's justification of Multicultural education fails.

But Arcilla offers a different reason for favoring Multiculturalist education—"self-defamiliarization" (160)—and on its basis revives a brand of universalism. Because of the aporetic nature of language and the indefiniteness of

dialogically based meanings, he argues, our self-knowledge is fated to be tragically inconclusive and occasionally disrupted; but, we can fashion a philosophy and politics of education which can serve to prevent this realization from
fomenting political and social tensions. Since the indefiniteness and aporia
which undermine our self-knowledge undermines *everyone's* self-knowledge,
everyone is a member of the community of those whose self-knowledge is
threatened. Consequently, we are joined together in community, and, rather
than embarking on "an epistemological project" "to eliminate or reduce indefiniteness," we can instead "giv[e] thanks for how the return of indefiniteness
reminds us of our awful and awesome, sublime communion with indefinite
Being" (171). Education in a "multiculturalist democracy" (169) can then be
conceived as having a particular task, namely:

> to turn the instability of identity into a supple celebration of what eludes
> identification, to defamiliarize the self. Such an education would aim to
> direct us from a recognition of and respect for the cultural identity of the
> stranger, to a recognition that one's own cultural identity is likewise indef-
> inite and self-estranging, to a recognition that this indefiniteness broach-
> es a shared discourse. In such a discourse, we may learn that we are all
> strangers to ourselves, together cast into an unfamiliar, *unheimlich* home.
> In such a discourse, a politics sensitive to cultural differences would meet
> a politics that finds in these differences the natural limit of our intelligi-
> ble identities; an incongruous mix of cultures would thus yield a common
> sense of strangeness. And so is born hope for a new politics of common-
> ality, one grounded in nature conceived not as an intelligible (to some
> privileged cultural language) cosmos but as the withdrawing source of
> language and linguistic beings, the mysterious X. Such a politics would be
> guided by a discourse of universal rights for a multicultural society. (170)

The vision Arcilla here articulates, albeit an undeniably heady one, raises
some obvious questions. How are we to understand the "indefinite Being?"
Isn't this, too, a culturally bound conception? And is it likely that members of
different cultures, or of any culture, would recognize the philosophical discourse extended by such an education as "sublime?" I worry about the wisdom of a social/educational agenda which rests upon, or has as its aim, the
universal appreciation of a peculiarly *philosophical* understanding, however sublime it may appear to some to be. Moreover, I don't see why the indefiniteness and aporia which (according to Arcilla) undermine the Modernist quest
for self-knowledge don't also impinge upon, and undermine, the positive
social/educational vision that Arcilla recommends—for that recommendation
appears to depend upon the definite establishment of the indefinite (to wit:
"I, Derrida, have definitely and firmly established, in language, that all

language and meaning—and therefore knowledge[7]—is indefinite"). This leads me to some general queries I have concerning Arcilla's discussion of aporia.

First, consider the basic form of Arcilla's argument:

(1) Language is provisional and indefinite.
(2) Therefore, dialogue is interminable.
(3) Therefore, self-knowledge, which depends upon dialogue, is indefinite, inconclusive, and subject to disruption.

The first, fundamental premise is that which expresses Derrida's claim concerning the aporetic nature of language. Should we accept this premise? Not, I don't think, without qualification. Qualification is required because, unqualified, the claim it expresses is subject to a damning difficulty: if language has only provisional meaning, and is indefinite, then the premise expressing that claim is itself only provisional and indefinite. But if so, the claim is at least to some extent undermined, because its grand pronouncement about the nature of language is (to say the least) significantly limited. In other words, if language and meaning are, in general, provisional and indefinite, then so is the language expressing, and meaning of, the Derridean claim itself. But if so, then, first, neither (2) nor (3) above follow from it; and, second, it is incapable of undermining either the possibility of self-knowledge, or Taylor's justification of Multicultural education in terms of the enhanced prospects for genuine self-knowledge of members of marginalized cultures, whose prospects for such knowledge are harmed by the absence of Multicultural education. The fact that Derrida's thesis concerning aporia applies to itself undermines its ability to do the work Arcilla counts on it to do.

163

Second, the self-applicability of Derrida's thesis raises another difficulty. Do we "know" that language is aporetic? How could we, if language is in fact aporetic? This depends, of course, on what we mean by "knowledge." If the thesis is that one understanding of language is as good as any other, then we can't know any claim expressible in language; this of course applies to the thesis itself as well as to everything else. This is a recipe for epistemological skepticism, based on a Derridean linguistic skepticism concerning meaning. I won't pause here to consider the merits of such skepticism. But the thesis needn't be read in this stark way; it is I think more plausibly understood as recommending a form of fallibilism rather than skepticism, to wit: since language is subject to aporia, it is always possible that what we think we know (e.g., to take Arcilla's example, that he is male [169]) we may at some point decide that we don't know. Given the ever-present possibility of new insights, new theorizing, new evidence, and new alignments of meaning, we must always hold open the possibility that putative knowledge-claims, including self-knowledge claims, can be revised. That knowledge is in principle revisable in this sense does not lead to skepticism, but only to fallibilism. In this sense we can know, fallibly, that language is aporetic. (Whether we *do* know this is of course another question.) But this is only possible if we don't hold that one understanding of language is as good as any other; but, rather, that the Derridean understanding of language as aporetic, while in principle open to revision, is the best understanding we currently have. Here knowledge, understandings, and meanings admit of evaluations in terms of better and worse. This sort of fallibilistic but nonskeptical interpretation is the one Derrideans, including Arcilla, require, if their arguments about anything are to rest upon the Derridean premise (1). But if so, then, as I argued above, that premise is actually much weaker than it appears at least at some points in Arcilla's discussion. Indeed, no mention of the premise is required: we are all fallibilists now, and have been since Peirce; Derrida's discussion and thesis, understood fallibilistically, contributes nothing. Understood skeptically, it defeats itself and so also contributes nothing. Either way, then, the Derridean thesis is a lot less impressive than it appears at first blush.

I have been arguing that Arcilla's Derridean aporia entails not skepticism about self-knowledge, but only fallibilism; and that such fallibilism is completely consistent with Taylor's "liberal" reconciliation of the universal and the particular, and his equally liberal justification of Multicultural education. That is, Taylor's justification of Multicultural education succeeds, once the limitations of Derridean aporia are clearly apprehended and appreciated. (I note in passing that if self-knowledge is in this way rescued from Postmodern, skeptical oblivion, then so too is knowledge of others, and other sorts of knowledge as well.)

Despite my unwillingness to embrace fully either the Derridean premise upon which Arcilla's argument rests, or his positive conclusion that the indefiniteness of language dooms self-knowledge to instability, which in turn harbors the possibility of a universal recognition of that instability as a gift which can put us in "sublime communion with indefinite Being," I nevertheless think Arcilla's essay an excellent one. His analysis of Taylor and Derrida is careful, clear, and challenging; his positive resolution of the difficulty he raises for Multicultural education is original, radical, and challenging in the extreme. His essay is a strikingly original and powerful one, which masterfully discusses a variety of complicated philosophical ideas with fluency and flair. While the worries rehearsed above lead me to refrain from embracing Arcilla's vision wholeheartedly, it nevertheless seems to me that he has demonstrated decisively the contributions that Postmodernist and Multiculturalist voices can make to our collective conversation. For that we—that is, all of us, but especially the Modernist laggards among us (among whom I of course include myself)—are in his debt.

CONCLUDING CONVERSATION

In my discussion of both Stone's and Arcilla's essays, I have urged that we sharply distinguish knowledge from certainty. However uncertain these (or any other) times are, there is nevertheless in them all the room we need for (fallible) knowledge. And it is a good thing that there is, if we want to do justice to the important insights of Feminism, Postmodernism, and Multiculturalism which Stone and Arcilla insightfully bring to our attention. While we might argue about exactly what those insights amount to, and about how deeply they challenge important strands of Modernism, I think it clear that the Feminist, Postmodernist and Multiculturalist streams in Stone's and Arcilla's thoughts promise to replenish and energize the too frequently stagnant waters of philosophy of education. This, it is clear, is a major contribution to a field such as ours.

Wendy Kohli, the editor of the collection in which this Chapter originally appeared, poses the question: Who/what counts as a philosopher of education, and why? Stone doesn't answer this question directly; Arcilla regards the answer as necessarily indefinite. My own answer is that a philosopher of education is one who worries about fundamental philosophical questions concerning education—what are the aims of education?; how can such aims be justified?; what moral and intellectual considerations rightly guide and constrain educational activities?; what duties and obligations must educators and educational institutions meet?; how should we understand key educational notions, and key philosophical notions which are intimately related to education, like "teaching," "learning," "knowledge," and so on?; how is the curriculum best understood and designed?; and a host of other such questions—and worries about these questions in a way which is methodologically sophisticated and which is informed by past efforts to come to grips with them. This locates philosophy of education in a tradition, to be sure; and some may wish to reject that tradition. But (1) *informed, credible* rejection requires a nuanced understanding of the tradition being rejected, and a detailed, careful articulation of one's reasons for rejection, which reasons can themselves withstand critical scrutiny; and (2) that tradition, as I have argued in the two previous chapters, itself encourages its own critical self-scrutiny—indeed, it encourages its own rejection, if such rejection is warranted. In so far, the philosophical tradition in which contemporary Western philosophy of education finds itself embedded welcomes the critical initiatives of Feminism, Postmodernism, Multiculturalism, and other challenging new avenues of thinking about the philosophical dimensions of education. That tradition is open to—indeed strives for—growth, correction, and improvement; and advances may be prompted in all sorts of ways. The tradition stands always in need of challenging criticism and insightful guidance from all quarters. It needs the help of these "isms." A panoply of outstanding philosophical questions central to philosophy of education—problems involving knowledge, justification, rationality, essentialism, domination, marginalization, universality, particularity, and many more—equally require that help. So I end by expressing my gratitude for the fact that philosophy of education can conduct the conversation, the dialogue across differences, that involves the many distinct voices that constitute the conversation of contemporary philosophy of education. To see how it turns out: stayed tuned to the conversation. Even better: join in![8]

WHAT PRICE INCLUSION?

Rational thought is interpretation according to a
scheme which we cannot escape.
                    —Friedrich Nietzsche

There is no method of reasoning more common,
and yet none more blamable, than, in philosophical disputes, to endeavor the refutation of any
hypothesis, by a pretense of its dangerous consequence to religion and morality.
                    —David Hume

chapter 12

IN THIS CHAPTER I want to further my treatment of "post-Enlightenment"
themes in recent philosophy and philosophy of education begun in earlier
chapters by focussing on the key ideal of *inclusion*. I argue in what follows that
embracing inclusion as a conversational and theoretical ideal does not require
either the rejection of the universal, or the rejection of scholarly standards.
These are taken up, respectively, in the second and third sections below. I set
the stage for those discussions by first considering the nature of the case for
inclusion.

THE CASE FOR INCLUSION: MORAL, METHODOLOGICAL,
OR EPISTEMIC?

In recent philosophy of education, as in philosophy more generally, it is difficult to find a theme more widely discussed, or universally endorsed, than that

of inclusion. Postmodernists, feminists, critical theorists, discourse ethicists, old-fashioned liberals and many others routinely extol the virtues of inclusionary discourses and theories—discourses which seek out, make room for, and take seriously, and theories which adequately reflect, the voices, views and interests of those who are and have traditionally been excluded from discussion and/or consideration. In the same spirit, discourses and theories which systematically exclude persons, groups and viewpoints are vigorously criticized.[1] Mark Weinstein, for example, argues for the primacy of inclusion as an ideal governing discourse generally:

> Discourse frames. . .are to be judged for their adequacy in terms of their ability to include, without prejudice, all points of view within their scope. . . . [T]he systematic exclusion of a point of view indicates a structural failing in the discourse frame. (Weinstein [1993], p. 33–4)[2]

Lorraine Code argues for the importance of including those attributes and experiences traditionally excluded from theorizing in epistemology and the philosophy of science:

> Feminist critiques of epistemology and philosophy of science/social science have demonstrated that the ideals of the autonomous reasoner—the dislocated, disinterested observer—and the epistemologies they inform are the artifacts of a small, privileged group of educated, usually prosperous, white men. . . . Moreover, the ideals of rationality and objectivity that have guided and inspired theorists of knowledge throughout the history of western philosophy have been constructed through processes of excluding the attributes and experiences commonly associated with femaleness and underclass social status: emotion, connection, practicality, sensitivity, and idiosyncrasy. (Code [1993], p. 21)

Helen Longino argues for the causal efficacy of inclusion in achieving objectivity in science:

> . . . the greater the number of different points of view included in a given community, the more likely it is that its scientific practice will be objective, that is, that it will result in descriptions and explanations of natural processes that are more reliable in the sense of less characterized by idiosyncratic subjective preferences of community members than would otherwise be the case. The smaller the number, the less likely this will be. (Longino [1990], p. 80)

And Henry Giroux criticizes universalizing, difference-denying metanarratives in a passage (cited in part and discussed in Chapter 10) which I have come to love for its characteristic rhetorical excess:

> [A]ll claims to universal reason and impartial competence are rejected [by right-thinking postmodernists] in favor of the partiality and specificity of discourse. General abstractions that deny the specificity and particularity of everyday life, that generalize out of existence the particular and the local, that smother difference under the banner of universalizing categories are rejected as totalitarian and terroristic. (Giroux [1988], p. 14)[3]

As the most recent citation suggests, in the literature the call for inclusion is typically linked with praise of particularity and criticism of "universalizing" discourse and theory. Linda Alcoff and Elizabeth Potter argue the point in the context of epistemology:

> Feminist analyses in philosophy, as in other disciplines, have insisted on the significance and particularity of the context of theory. This has led many feminist epistemologists to skepticism about the possibility of a general or universal account of the nature and limits of knowledge, an account that ignores the social context and status of knowers. (Alcoff and Potter [1993], p. 1)

And in the context of science, Sandra Harding similarly criticizes what she regards as science's pretense to universality, and argues that science must give up that pretense, and "start . . . research from women's lives," paying specific attention to the perspectives and conditions of particular women and other oppressed individuals. (Harding [1991], p. 48).[4] Science will benefit, and the objectivity of science will be enhanced, Harding argues, when excluded others are included and their particularities recognized:

> . . . women scientists can bring certain benefits to the growth of knowledge if they can find ways to use their experience as women, informed by feminist theorizing, to create a critical perspective on the dominant conceptual schemes and how they shape scientific research and practice. ([1991], p. 70)[5]

One of the main complaints made against exclusionary discourse practices and theories, as suggested by the most recent citations, is that they overvalue the universal, and undervalue the particular. Universality and particularity are typically linked to exclusion and inclusion in the following way: universalizing discourse and theory—for example, discourse concerning the traits, interests, or obligations of, and theories which attempt to characterize, *all* people—

ignore the characteristics of particular, especially marginalized, individuals and groups, and in so doing, exclude them and their perspectives. Thus the valorization of inclusion and inclusionary discourse and theory seems to lead naturally to the valorization of particularity, and the consequent devaluing of universality. Indeed, as one defender of universality puts it, "For the challengers [of universality], the universal is an illusion, and the individual has an identity only as a member of some subgroup" (Searle [1993], p. 31). As more and different types of people freely and equally participate in a discourse, are the objects of the discourse, or are the objects of a theory, the possibility of saying anything both true and important about all of them seems to diminish.[6] So, it might seem, we get a less distorted representation of actual states of affairs when we eschew "grand narratives" and "metanarratives," as Postmodernists are fond of putting it,[7] and opt instead for inclusion and particularity: i.e. for discourse which includes many, indeed all, different groups, and which, rather than seeking a "totalizing" story which includes them all, instead seeks to countenance fully the differences which distinguish one from another, i.e. their particularity. Only in this way can we acknowledge, as Nicholas Burbules puts it, that "any attempt to systematize thought inevitably ignores legitimate alternatives and forces disparate groups to account for themselves in terms of monolithic categories that are alien to them" (Burbules [1993a], p. 3).[8]

Philosophy of education is itself a subject about which its practitioners discourse and construct theories; consequently, we can and should ask parallel questions about inclusion, and the virtues of particularity, in our philosophical discourse and theories concerning education. Should philosophers of education value inclusion? If so, should they also value particularity, and devalue universality? Why? Is the relation between inclusion/exclusion, on the one hand, and particularity/universality, on the other, as I have just depicted it? What, if anything, is lost, in our decision to reject universality and embrace particularity and inclusion? Can it be that, as Thomas Nagel suggests, to give up on universality is to give up on philosophy itself?[9]

My aim in what follows is to embrace, and defend, the commitment to inclusion. I share the view that both our discourses and our theories should strive for inclusion. No viewpoint should be systematically excluded from our conversations; no groups or individuals should be rendered invisible or silent by either our practices or our theories.[10] But my reasons for embracing inclusion as a conversational and theoretical ideal are somewhat different from those mentioned above. Moreover, I believe that the epistemological ramifications of regarding inclusion as an ideal are other than those mentioned thusfar. In particular: it is false, I will argue, that embracing the ideal of inclusion forces us to reject either the aim of striving for universalistic theories, e.g. theories concerning what is true of, or best for, all people; or the idea that

170

theorizing is governed by (fallible but) universally applicable standards. My separation of inclusion from the rejection of universalism and of standards is a function of my view that inclusion is to be defended on *moral* rather than epistemic grounds. I embrace inclusion not because universalistic theories necessarily marginalize, silence or oppress, nor because they rest on false or inadequate accounts of knowledge or language.[11] Both of these claims are I think false. Rather, inclusion should be embraced as a conversational ideal because it is morally wrong to exclude people from, or silence them in, conversations in which they have an interest or stake. To so exclude or silence is to fail to treat such people with respect, and is for that reason impermissible.[12] It should be embraced as a theoretical ideal because at least some of our philosophical and other theories concerning people, their aims, and their ideals take as their subject matter *all* people, and thus are defective insofar as they speak only of the features, interests, or properties of some, and insofar as they misrepresent the nature of some people by theorizing about them as if they were otherwise than they in fact are. Why value inclusion, then? In brief: because it is morally wrong to exclude.[13]

Inclusion is not an *epistemic* virtue. By this I mean that inclusive theories are not *in general* more likely than exclusive theories to be true, or justified, and inclusive discourses are not *in general* more likely than exclusive discourses to yield such epistemically worthy theories; there is no *necessary* connection between inclusion and epistemic worthiness, or between exclusion and epistemic defectiveness.[14] On the one hand, inclusionary discourse routinely gives rise to false beliefs and theories. For example, "the Earth is flat" was believed by virtually everyone in medieval Europe. It was believed by royalty, nobles, and serfs; by men and women—that is, it was believed by all. No persons, groups or alternative viewpoints were excluded from conversation concerning it. Nevertheless, it was/is false. It is arguable whether or not this belief was, though false, justified for its Medieval believers, but other such beliefs—concerning, e.g., the existence and properties of local deities, or the causal origins of sneezing—seem clearly to have been unjustified, even then, despite the inclusive character of the relevant discourse. More recent examples include widely shared beliefs in this century concerning the transmission of certain diseases (e.g. via toilet seat or frog). We have then a wide range of counterexamples to the thesis that there is a necessary connection between inclusion and epistemic goodness.

On the other hand, there are equally many counterexamples to the view that exclusion necessarily results in epistemic defect. Exclusionary discourses routinely yield epistemically worthy, i.e. true and/or justified, theories. Here the obvious examples, though not the only ones, are from science. Modern physical and biological theories, as feminist and other recent scholarship shows, developed in discourses from which women and most non-European men were systematically excluded. Nevertheless many of these theories enjoy impressive epistemic credentials—which we all implicitly acknowledge every time we fly in an airplane, communicate electronically, or visit a trained physician.[15]

Since inclusion is routinely conjoined with epistemic weakness, and exclusion with epistemic strength, it seems to me a mistake to regard inclusion as an *epistemic* virtue.[16] Rather, inclusion is a *moral* virtue, and should be valued as such. People and groups deserve inclusion not because of any special epistemic privilege they enjoy, nor because including them necessarily increases the probability of obtaining true or justified theories, but rather because of "the demands of justice" (Bar On [1993], p. 97). This simple view of exclusion as primarily a moral wrong will be developed further as we proceed.

In saying that inclusion is not an epistemic virtue, I do not mean to deny that in some sorts of cases inclusive theories are indeed closer to the truth than exclusive ones, or that inclusive research communities, at least in certain sorts of circumstances, stand a better chance of obtaining worthwhile results than exclusive communities. For example, as Feminist and other scholars have shown, the exclusion of women, blacks, and other "Others" from the social science community has been partly responsible for a variety of misogynist, racist, heterosexist, and just plain silly theories (for example, those concerning brain size and intelligence and racial superiority). We should straightforwardly accept the point, stressed by Harding, Longino, Searle, and many others, that inclusion, by adding previously ignored perspectives to scientific research and debate, can and often does serve to correct and enhance ongoing theorizing. In *this* sense, I happily agree that inclusion can be and often is an epistemic or methodological virtue.[17]

But the sorts of inadequacies illustrated in these examples are not unique to exclusion, obviously; any theory which is inadequate in these ways is to that extent defective. Any theory can be defective in these respects; there is no reason to think that exclusionary theories will inevitably suffer from these defects, and exclusion is only one of many possible sources of them. (Others include lack of information, inadequate sources of evidence, inadequate tools and techniques of gathering and evaluating evidence, etc.) Perfectly inclusionary discourses can also manifest these defects, due to lack of imagination, failure to criticize theoretical presuppositions, etc. In at least many such cases, they can be remedied without enhancing the inclusivity of the discourse, simply by utilizing standard methodological techniques: gathering more data, being more critical of one's presuppositions and one's methodology, etc.[18] Finally, while it is true that increasing inclusivity and alternative perspectives within the relevant scientific discourse might aid in the discovery and eradication of such defects, it is also true that *de*creasing inclusivity might so aid (e.g. by removing "red herrings" from the theoretical environment). The upshot of all this is that the sort of defect we have been considering should not be regarded as having any necessary relation either to inclusion or its opposite. Inclusion is not necessary for good science; exclusion does not guarantee bad science.

Moreover, the attention to particularity which, as we have seen, is often regarded as the hallmark of inclusion, is in some cases simply *irrelevant* to the theoretical issue being considered. This is especially the case in ethical matters, but is found throughout the realm of philosophical theorizing. For example, if, as philosophical consultant to Amnesty International, I am engaged in the project of constructing a theory accounting for the immorality of torture, false imprisonment, "disappearances," and other noxious political activities, my theory need not and should not concern itself with the particularities of the victims of these benighted deeds. There is no factual flaw here; the theory which explains the wrongness of such acts will not deny the real differences which exist among the victims. Rather, their particularity, while genuine, and no doubt important in other contexts, will be simply *irrelevant* to the moral wrongness of the deeds.[19]

I have been trying in the last several paragraphs to defend the view that inclusion is better seen as a moral than as an epistemic virtue; that is, that the case for inclusion is fundamentally a moral rather than an epistemic one. Having done so, I am now in position to treat the real subjects of this chapter. In what follows I consider certain epistemological ramifications of recent discussions of inclusion, exclusion, particularity, and universality. First, I will challenge the idea that embracing inclusion as an ideal of discourse and theory requires us to give up on the possibility of universal "metanarratives" or theories concerning all people. Here I will argue that the parallels drawn above, between inclusion and particularity and between exclusion and universality, are mistaken. I will try to show that universality and particularity are not in fact mutually exclusive, and that any theory (or "metanarrative') worthy of the name—and of our assent—will be both particular *and* universal. If so, then the embrace of inclusion and the valorization of the particular do not force the rejection of the universal. Consequently, the rejection or devaluation of the universal is not a price we must pay for our desire to be inclusive in our discourse and in our theories.

Second, I will argue that embracing inclusion as an ideal governing our philosophical discourse about education (or anything else) need not discredit our maintenance of scholarly standards of argumentative quality. I will argue, that is, that maintaining scholarly standards, while guaranteeing a certain sort of exclusivity, need not worry us, for the sorts of discourse/theory excluded are *properly* excluded, and therefore that *this* sort of exclusion is not in violation of our commitment to inclusion.

I turn first to the universality/particularity dichotomy.

RECONCILING UNIVERSALITY AND PARTICULARITY

> I have always supposed that the universal and the
> particular are compatible, that grounding in a par-
> ticular historical and cultural matrix is inevitable
> and could not conceivably be in conflict with uni-
> versal principles. (Scheffler [1995], p. 14)

I begin by noting a simple and obvious difficulty facing anyone who wishes,
for whatever reason, to renounce universality and accept only particularity.
Consider some articulations of this position, e.g.

(1) There are no universal truths; truths are always particular, or
(2) There is no universal "human nature"; there are no proper-
    ties shared by all humans.

(1), which purports to reject universality and universal truths, is *itself* universal: (1) speaks of *all* (and *no*) truths; it says that all truths are of particular objects
(or contents), and that none of them are true of universal classes of objects.
Similarly, (2), in denying any universal human nature, declares this denial in
universal form: no property had by any human will be had by every other; all
properties which some humans possess will fail to be possessed by others. In
denying the universal, it appears, one embraces it; one can't escape the universal by denying it. Thinkers like Lyotard, who try to reject the universal as
illegitimate, routinely run into this problem.[20]

This simple difficulty is surprisingly difficult to overcome for the theorist
who attempts systematically to reject universality. But I do not want to rest
only on it. I want rather to focus on the idea that the universal and the particular are mutually exclusive, so that a commitment to embrace and not marginalize particularity entails that one strive to avoid universalistic theorizing.
That entailment is illusory, I will argue; a focus on particularity, as the motto
from Scheffler at the head of this section suggests, in no way precludes universality. If not, then a commitment to particularity, and inclusion, does not
force, or even suggest, a rejection of the universal.

The idea that particularity and universality are mutually exclusive and
exhaustive, i.e. the idea that we must opt for one or the other, is clearly
defended in the work of Richard Rorty. Rorty contrasts "objectivity"—the
view that as philosophical inquirers we must "step outside our community
long enough to examine it in the light of something which transcends it,
namely, that which it has in common with every other actual and possible
human community," perhaps "an ahistorical human nature" (Rorty [1989],
p. 36)—with "solidarity," according to which people locate themselves with

174

reference to some community, and which conceives inquiry and inquirers as fundamentally "ethnocentric" (37). Rorty embraces solidarity: "we must, in practice, privilege our own group, even though there can be no noncircular justification for doing so"; in doing so, he embraces "[t]his lonely provincialism, this admission that we are just the historical moment that we are" (44). He argues that striving after objectivity is but "an attempt to avoid facing up to contingency" (46).

I don't want here to offer any sort of systematic criticism of Rorty, though I believe that his general view suffers from overwhelming difficulties.[21] I want instead to emphasize that, in embracing solidarity over objectivity, Rorty is rejecting the sort of universalistic, transhistorical perspective he identifies the latter tradition as striving to articulate and embrace.[22] He holds that this sort of universality is philosophically untenable, and that the only alternative is to settle for solidarity with nonuniversalistic particularity (e.g. [1989a], pp. 190–192). That is, he holds that the objectivity/solidarity dichotomy, and consequently the universality/particularity dichotomy, is exclusive and exhaustive; that, while one must embrace either particularity or universality, one cannot embrace both.[23] Is this correct?

Ernest Sosa argues that it is not: "the dichotomy of objectivity or solidarity is false. We want *both* inquiry *and* community, and often we want each in part for the sake of the other" (1987, p. 726, emphases in original). Similarly, Jay F. Rosenberg argues not only that the dichotomy is problematic, but that the universal or objective is needed to intelligibly conceive the practical, local correctives that Rorty's liberal needs (1993, p. 207). But I want to address the issue directly, without further reference to Rorty. I will next present an argument intended to establish the compatibility of the universal and the particular.[24]

My argument is simple. The fact that humans are always located in specific cultural/historical settings does not undermine our collective ability to reach beyond our local settings and speak to broader audiences and arenas of concern. We always judge from the perspective of our own conceptual scheme; there is no way to escape from all schemes and judge from a God's-eye point of view. Since our schemes reflect our cultural/historical circumstances, then these circumstances constitute limits on our judgment; we can't escape them entirely. With these premises I agree. But some draw from them the conclusion that universality, or a perspective unencumbered by our particular situation, is impossible; that our judgments cannot, in principle, have any force beyond the bounds of our own location or scheme. From this conclusion I dissent.[25]

I will not dally over the obvious logical difficulty that anyone who presses that conclusion on the basis of those (or any other) premises presumes the legitimacy of the very sort of universality she is out to reject, since she thinks that the conclusion follows—for everyone, judging from whatever conceptual/

cultural/historical scheme—from those premises. Instead, I want simply to argue that the argument is a non sequitur, and that its conclusion is false. If all of our judgments are made from the perspective of whatever scheme we happen to employ—which they are—then, according to that argument, none of them have any such legitimacy. But counter-examples to this thesis abound. Many of my arithmetical/mathematical judgments, for example, though made from my scheme, surely have legitimacy, and are correct, even though small children, and members of certain other cultures, do not share either my scheme or my judgments—for example, the ancient Greeks before the invention/discovery of irrational numbers; nineteenth-century mathematicians before Cantor's discoveries concerning the sizes of infinite sets; nineteenth-century geometers before the discovery of non-Euclidean geometries; bettors and merchants of the middle ages before the development of the modern probability calculus; etc. Important scientific theories and theses similarly have application, and validity, beyond the scheme of those who invented them and their cultural mates—smoking causes cancer, particular biological traits are determined and transmitted genetically, space "curves," and mass is convertible with energy, for example, even for those whose schemes do not sanction these judgments.[26]

Counterexamples to the thesis under discussion—that the epistemic legitimacy of judgments is bounded by the perspective of the scheme from which the judgments are made—are not restricted to the mathematical and scientific domains. Moral and social/political judgments also aspire to, and sometimes achieve, extra-scheme legitimacy: for example, our judgment that oppression and marginalization are wrong, though made from the perspective of our own scheme, is thought (by us) to have legitimacy beyond the sharers of that scheme. Similarly, even though racist, patriarchal, and heterosexist schemes approve of their associated forms of marginalization and oppression, we have no difficulty in criticizing such schemes, or the judgments made within them, as inadequate or unjust. Indeed, to advocate inclusion is to insist upon the scheme-independent[27] legitimacy of such criticism. If our pro-inclusionary stance does not permit this, on what basis can we advocate and try to ensure that others endorse and practice inclusion as well?[28]

The central point is this: though we judge from the perspectives of our own schemes, our judgments and their legitimacy regularly extend beyond the bounds of those schemes. Thomas McCarthy, in discussing the conception of truth as ideal rational acceptability advocated by Hilary Putnam (1981), and utilizing Putnam's[29] "immanent/transcendent" distinction, articulates the point well:

> . . . any adequate account of truth as rational acceptability will have to
> capture not only its immanence—i.e., its socially situated character—but
> its transcendence as well. While we may have no idea of standards of

176

rationality wholly independent of historically concrete languages and practices, it remains that reason serves as an ideal with reference to which we can criticize the standards we inherit. Though never divorced from social practices of justification, the idea of reason can never be reduced to any particular set of such practices. Correspondingly, the notion of truth, while essentially related to warranted assertibility by the standards or warrants of this or that culture, cannot be reduced to any particular set of standards or warrants. To put this another way, we can, and typically do, make historically situated and fallible claims to universal validity. (McCarthy [1988], p. 82)

As Putnam puts it:

If reason is both transcendent and immanent, then philosophy, as culture-bound reflection and argument about eternal questions, is both in time and eternity. We don't have an Archimedean point; we always speak the language of a time and place; but the rightness and wrongness of what we say is not *just* for a time and a place. (Putnam [1982], p. 21, emphasis in original)

Immanence does not preclude transcendence: as both Putnam and McCarthy suggest, our judgments, while immanent, strive also for transcendence. There is no difficulty in thinking that occasionally they attain that transcendence; nor is there any reason to think that it is impossible in principle that they might. Consequently, the fact that our judgments are immanent does not entail their nontranscendence. Thus, the argument that immanence and transcendence are mutually exclusive and exhaustive, and that, since we can't escape immanence, we must reject transcendence, fails.[30]

Just as immanence does not entail the denial of transcendence, particularity does not entail the denial of universality. Our judgments inevitably reflect particularity: they are made by particular people, in particular historical and cultural circumstances. But this fact in no way undermines the universality of some of our judgments. Any statement, of universal principle or of anything else, will be situated and located, and will reflect the particularities of that locale; but this does not force the conclusion that such statements are not universal, either in their applicability or in their legitimacy. The particular and the universal are not mutually exclusive; at least some of our judgments are both. If so, then in embracing inclusion and the particular, we needn't give up the universal.[31]

If the preceding discussion is cogent, then it is a mistake to think that valuing inclusion, and the particularity of the included, requires devaluing the universal—just as it is a mistake to think that opting for "solidarity" requires rejecting "objectivity," or that championing "immanence" precludes our striv-

177

ing for "transcendence." When we include others in our discourses and as objects of our theories, we include also their particularity. When our theorizing concerns that particularity, but fails to see it, our theories are straightforwardly defective on factual grounds. When our theories are not in this way defective because they take due account of that particularity, or when they ignore particularity because they correctly note its irrelevance to the question at hand, they are not precluded from waxing universal. More generally, there is no contradiction, or even tension, between acknowledging particularity and at the same time constructing universalistic theories. Ideals, and theoretical claims about them, can be both particular and universal. Consequently, embracing particularity does nothing to undercut the universal.[32] Philosophical theories, as Nagel suggests—including philosophical theories concerning education—are inevitably concerned with universal claims, concerning (in the latter class of theories) all students, all teaching, all learning, all educational ideals, institutions and practices, all particularities, or whatever. Such claims, to be cogent, must not ignore particularity (except in cases in which it can be shown to be irrelevant to the issue being addressed). But they can fully account for, and respect, that particularity, without compromising their universality. If so, then we can have inclusion, in our conversations and our theories, without paying the price of limiting ourselves to particularities and giving up on the universal. The mutually-exclusive-and-exhaustive understanding of the universal/particular dichotomy is one that advocates of inclusion should reject.[33]

178

INCLUSION AND STANDARDS: CAN WE HAVE BOTH?

As we have seen, there is, in the present philosophy and philosophy of education environments, much talk of the virtues of inclusion, multiple voices and perspectives, etc. Mainstream (white, privileged, "malestream") philosophy of education is often criticized on the grounds that it mistakenly and immorally excludes the voices and perspectives of the marginalized, silenced, oppressed and unprivileged others. How might mainstream philosophy of education accomplish this silencing and oppression? It is sometimes suggested that it does so by relying upon disciplinary "standards," standards which are portrayed as unbiased, neutral determiners of quality—standards of argumentative rigor, for example—which in fact tip the playing field in favor of the dominant, hegemonic group of mainstream practitioners of the craft.[34] This suggests, in turn, that rejecting this sort of oppression requires the rejection of all such standards, since these standards are in the end what is responsible for the silencing and exclusion of nontraditional views and perspectives. If so, then it appears that we can't have both inclusion and standards: if we have standards, certain voices will be excluded; if we have inclusion, we will have to give up our standards. How is this argument to be evaluated? Can the apparent tension between inclusion and standards be resolved?

The objection that extant standards are themselves exclusionary and so must be rejected by defenders of inclusion has been developed most impressively by Feminist writers, whose discussions focus on the exclusionary character of allegedly *rational* standards, and I will focus on that version of the objection in what follows. Many Feminist philosophers, e.g. Susan Bordo, Genevieve Lloyd, Evelyn Fox Keller, Sandra Harding, and Hilary Rose, among numerous others, have argued that "reason" is problematically "male."[35] The central contention is clearly articulated by Louise M. Antony and Charlotte Witt:

> Feminist challenges have, indeed, reached into the "'hard core' of abstract reasoning" itself, with charges that the most fundamental elements of the Western philosophical tradition—the ideals of reason and objectivity—are so deeply corrupted by patriarchy that they must be greatly transformed (if not utterly abandoned) by any philosopher committed to the development of conceptions of knowledge and reality adequate to the transformative goals of feminism. (Antony and Witt [1993], p. xiii. The embedded citation is from Harding and Hintikka [1983], p. ix.)

and by Sally Haslanger:

> ... a rational stance is itself a stance of oppression or domination, and accepted ideals of reason both reflect and reinforce power relations that advantage white privileged men. (Haslanger (1993), p. 85)

179

and, in a critical discussion of Catharine MacKinnon, by Elizabeth Rapaport:

> For MacKinnon, rationality is an enemy to be unmasked and destroyed (Rapaport [1993], p. 129).

As MacKinnon develops the point:

> The *kind* of analysis that such a feminism is, and, specifically, *the standard by which it is accepted as valid*, is largely a matter of the criteria one adopts for adequacy in a theory. If feminism is a critique of the objective standpoint as male, then we also disavow standard scientific norms as the adequacy criteria for our theory, because the objective standpoint we criticize is the posture of science. In other words, our critique of the objective standpoint as male is a critique of science as a specifically male approach to knowledge. With it, we reject *male criteria* for verification. (MacKinnon [1987, p. 54, last two emphases added)[36]

What follows from the rejection of "male criteria"? There are only two possibilities: either that there are *no* criteria in terms of which theories can be evaluated, or that there are *different* criteria which should be appealed to in theory evaluation. The first of these is deeply problematic. If there are no criteria in terms of which we can legitimately evaluate theories, then the very possibility of evaluation is rejected. But this option is self-defeating: if evaluation in general is rejected, then we are unable to evaluate, or rationally prefer, the suggestions that male criteria should be rejected or that evaluation itself should likewise be rejected. But then we have no reason to accept these suggestions. Normative evaluation cannot be entirely given up; to attempt to do so is, as Putnam suggests, to attempt "mental suicide."[37]

On the other hand, the rejection of male criteria of theory evaluation in favor of other, incompatible, "female criteria," must itself—if the preference for the latter is to be itself defensible and nonarbitrary—rely upon (meta)criteria in accordance with which these two rival sets of criteria can themselves be fairly evaluated. Standards and criteria are in this way *required* for the conducting of any sort of serious scholarly endeavor, including that of arguing for the ideal of inclusion (or for feminism). In short, one cannot coherently embrace the ideal of inclusion and at the same time reject standards entirely.[38] And with respect to MacKinnon's rejection of the standards of science, and so science itself, as male, it is difficult not to see this as a classic instance of cutting off one's nose to spite one's face. Consider in this regard the comment of (lesbian philosopher of science) Noretta Koertge:

> If it really could be shown that patriarchal thinking not only played a crucial role in the Scientific Revolution but is also necessary for carrying out scientific inquiry as we know it, that would constitute the strongest argument for patriarchy I can think of! I continue to believe that science—even white, upperclass, male-dominated science—is one of the most important allies of oppressed people. (Koertge [1981], p. 354)[39]

Martha Nussbaum similarly suggests that feminist philosophers err if they reject reason and objectivity in their endeavor to combat patriarchy:

> Convention and habit are women's enemies here, and reason their ally. Habit decrees that what seems strange is impossible and "unnatural"; reason looks head on at the strange, refusing to assume that the current status quo is either immutable or in any normative sense "natural." The appeal to reason and objectivity amounts to a request that the observer refuse to be intimidated by habit, and look for cogent arguments based on evidence that has been carefully sifted for bias. (Nussbaum [1994], p. 59)

Of course, to say that standards are required for the rational defense of the ideal of inclusion, or that rational standards are required for any sort of serious intellectual work whatever, is not to say that particular standards, or particular understandings of them, are themselves beyond critical challenge. On the contrary, one major sort of intellectual advance is precisely the sort which allows us to realize that our standards, or our interpretations of them, have in one way or another been defective and stand in need of criticism and improvement.[40] Indeed, one of the main contributions of feminist scholarship (since we have lately been considering feminist scholarship) has been precisely to establish that particular standards, or particular applications of them, have been problematically biased against women. Nevertheless, it is not possible coherently to reject particular standards as biased, and simultaneously to reject standards of evaluation generally.[41] For in doing the latter, one gives up the very possibility of evaluation, in which case the rejection of the rejected standard is unwarranted. Moreover, one cannot reject all standards and evaluation, and at the same time embrace particular standards. In particular, one cannot reject all standards, and the very possibility of evaluation, and at the same time embrace the importance of inclusion as an ideal or as a standard of evaluation of discourses and/or theories.

Consequently, if we value inclusion—as we should—we must have, and value, standards as well. Not only is there no fundamental incompatibility between inclusion and standards; the former *requires* the latter. The apparent tension between inclusion and standards with which this section began is not a genuine one. We can debate the merits of particular standards and criteria, and particular understandings, interpretations, and applications of them, of course. But we cannot reject standards and criteria altogether—not, at least, if we wish to uphold the value of inclusion.[42]

I have been arguing that there is no general incompatibility between inclusion and standards. But that is not to say that accepting particular standards does not result in exclusion. Of course it does: if we embrace standards governing our scholarly endeavors, then we will exclude all work which fails to meet those standards. Similarly, there *is* a genuine tension between inclusion and one common standard, namely that of *qualifications* or *expertise*. For some discourses, not everyone is qualified or competent to participate. The most obvious case is that concerning conversations among specialists on arcane matters. My grandmother, for example, is best left out of a conversation among postmodernist theorists concerning the philosophical or other merits of the latest wave of postmodernist theorizing (and so, for that matter, am I), just as my grandfather has no rightful place in a conversation concerning the prospects for the development of a grand unified "theory of everything" in physics or the methodological details of an attempt to detect solar neutrinos. Participants in such conversations can typically[43] distinguish between those who clearly can, and those who clearly cannot, meaningfully contribute to their conversations,

181

and are surely within their rights to prefer, and limit entry to, the former. Of course, that is not to suggest that someone who feels wrongly excluded cannot protest, or try to show how their exclusion is in some way or other unjust or otherwise mistaken. In particular, such a person can protest her exclusion by arguing that she is in fact qualified and sufficiently expert to be entitled to participate. Nevertheless, for conversations to be maximally functional, or maximally interesting, informative, or communicative for their participants, some potential participants may well be best left out.

There is then a point to be noted, which is often not noted by advocates of inclusion, about the qualifications of participants in the discourse. For many, perhaps most discourses, everyone is qualified. This is especially true of discourses concerning social and political values and practices, the outcomes of which affect everyone. But for some discourses—including this one?—that is simply not so. Of course the conversation can always be expanded: we can ask, for example, not just how to get my software to accomplish some recondite goal, but why to try to achieve that goal in the first place. Here many more voices will be qualified. It is also frequently possible for persons excluded on the basis of lack of expertise to *acquire* expertise, and in that way come to merit inclusion.[44] The point remains nevertheless that for some conversations, exclusion is perfectly legitimate on the basis of (lack of) appropriate expertise. This sort of *justified* exclusion is not unlike laws which prohibit minors from voting, or untrained drivers from obtaining licenses and driving on public roads (a serious problem here in Miami).

I trust it is clear that this sort of exclusion, on the basis of lack of qualification or expertise, is completely compatible with the ideal of inclusion articulated and defended above. For exclusion based upon either lack of qualifications or expertise, or failure to meet appropriate standards of disciplinary adequacy or those governing scholarly exchange, involves no moral failing. It does not fail to treat the excluded with respect. But as argued above, it is the latter failing which forces the rejection of exclusion and the embrace of inclusion. Consequently, *this* sort of exclusion constitutes no problem for advocates of inclusion.[45]

CONCLUSION

If my arguments are sound, then accepting inclusion as a conversational and theoretical ideal does not require that we give up either universalistic theories, or scholarly standards. There is no significant moral or epistemological price to pay for embracing that ideal. The price of inclusion is low; its value exceedingly high. I realize that many contemporary advocates of inclusion will not be enthused about having me on their side, given the sort of philosophy I do and the interests I am thereby seen to represent.[46] Nevertheless, I have suggested that the ideal of inclusion is best understood in moral terms, and justified on moral rather than epistemic grounds; and have tried to show that embracing the moral and political value of inclusion does not require that we pay the price of abandoning either the philosophical quest for the universal or the commitment to standards of scholarly excellence. In so doing, I have tried to contribute, however modestly, to philosophical efforts to justify the valuing of inclusionary theories and discourses; to criticize theories and discourses which are in fact exclusionary in a morally or politically noxious way; to show that not all exclusions are of that noxious or oppressive sort, and to make clear that, in certain contexts at least, it is quite justifiable—and completely in keeping with the ideal of inclusion—to practice exclusion on the basis of lack of relevant qualifications or expertise, or failure to meet relevant standards; and to show that embracing inclusion as a moral and political ideal governing our discourses and our philosophical theories is compatible both with the possibility of "universalistic" theories which do not limit themselves to the particular, and with the embrace of disciplinary standards. Since neither of these are compatible with many contemporary understandings of Postmodernism, I conclude by pointing out that inclusion is not the intellectual property of Postmodernists alone: one can, and in my view should, embrace the ideal of inclusion and retain both the aim articulated by Nagel, of striving for universal theories in philosophy, and the aim of having our theories conform to the highest standards of disciplinary adequacy it is in our power to achieve.[47]

183

WHY CARE (ABOUT EPISTEMOLOGY, JUSTIFICATION, RATIONALITY, ETC.)?

A Brief Metaphilosophical Excursus

In matters controversial,
My perception's rather fine.
I always see both points of view,
The one that's wrong and mine.
                    —Anonymous

AS WE HAVE SEEN in the chapters in Part Two, many philosophers and philosophers of education today accept the argument that these scholarly fields have in fact been practiced in an exclusionary way, that such exclusion is bad, and therefore that these areas of scholarship ought to open themselves up to hitherto excluded voices. Many of these same philosophers, it seems—especially those who embrace Postmodernism and/or proclaim "the end of philosophy'—deny that that view stands in need of (or enjoys) rational justification. (See, e.g., various essays in Cohen and Dascal [1989] and Baynes, Bohman, and McCarthy [1987].)

   Such a stance—let us call it, for the moment, the "irrelevance of epistemology" view—has always struck me as unacceptable. To hold a position seriously, and yet deny the need to ground it with reasons which justify one's holding it, is I think problematic, since to hold it seriously involves the (perhaps implicit) beliefs both that it is in principle possible for it to be justified by reasons, and that the position does in fact enjoy such justification. Thus, as I argued in Chapter 12, seriously to endorse (for example) inclusion, yet to deny that it enjoys or need enjoy rational justification, is to involve oneself in a logical contradiction. More weakly, it is to involve oneself in a performative contradiction of the sort discussed at length in the work of Habermas, Apel, Benhabib, and others working in the domains of critical theory and discourse ethics. Consequently, if one seriously endorses inclusion—or indeed anything else—one has perforce to be concerned with issues of justification—concerning both the justification of inclusion in particular, and the nature and possibility of epistemic justification more generally.

But this sort of transcendental[1] argument will be of little interest to those not already disposed to worry about rational justification and related epistemological matters. And many simply are not so disposed. Such worries are often seen these days as relics of a discredited Enlightenment project, which is exclusionary, sexist, racist, heterosexist, and thoroughly undeserving of our respect. In rejecting this project, these thinkers also reject the philosophical importance of epistemological ("Enlightenment") questions concerning rationality and rational justification. What can be said to this? Why should philosophers and philosophers of education today care about these issues?

My friend and colleague Nick Burbules, in advising me about Chapter 12, recommended that I resist the temptation to offer "yet another transcendental argument," and instead try to teach such critics of the Enlightenment project why they should care about "my" issues. I don't think that I am able actually to do that. But I'm grateful to Burbules for his suggestion; I would dearly love to do what he recommends. So I hope that I will be forgiven the following brief attempt to address this question. Why should we care about epistemology? About the epistemic force of transcendental arguments? About rational justification? About whether or not our commitments to inclusionary discourses and theories, and to social justice more broadly, themselves enjoy some measure of rational justification; whether or not they fit into a broad, credible view of philosophy, knowledge, persons, and justice?[2]

There is a clear *practical* answer to this question. If one is concerned to bring it about that excluded voices are included, one will have to persuade the agents and institutions of exclusion both that exclusion is taking place, and that inclusion is preferable to it. While such persuasion needn't be rational—it could, for example, involve force—rational persuasion *might* at least be the least costly and most effective sort of persuasion available. If so, then worrying about issues of justification will contribute to the practical task of bringing about more inclusionary scholarly and social environments. Here we have a practical, instrumental reason for taking epistemology seriously.

There is also a good *philosophical* answer to the question, part of which has been sketched in the chapters above. One should care about these epistemo-logical issues because resolving them is relevant to the establishment of the philosophical case for inclusion, and for advocates of inclusion as a philosoph-ical (rather than as a *merely* practical or political) ideal, such resolution is important.

I myself favor the philosophical reason. But I am here trying to address those who reject it outright as a manifestation of a bankrupt and corrupt Enlightenment project. For such persons, the practical answer—whatever its limitations—may be the most persuasive reason for caring about epistemolo-gy I can give.

I suspect that, in the end, this disagreement concerns alternative visions of philosophy. On my (admittedly traditional) view, philosophy is fundamentally concerned with reasons, arguments, and, with Socrates, is committed to fol-lowing the argument wherever it leads—i.e. to basing belief, action and judg-ment on epistemically forceful reasons. The aim of the exercise is the discovery of philosophical truths. While those truths may concern matters of social jus-tice, the philosophical enterprise does not have as its goal the bringing about of social justice or social transformation, Marx's thesis on Feuerbach to the contrary notwithstanding. But a rival view of philosophy—well captured by Marx's thesis that "[t]he philosophers have only *interpreted* the world, in vari-ous ways; the point, however, is to *change* it" (Marx, in Feuer [1959], p. 245, emphases in original)—takes the aim of the enterprise to be not the securing of truth or rational justification, but the achievement of social transformation. On such a view, concern for epistemology might well seem politically regres-sive. Can anything be said here? How is one or the other view of philosophy to be defended?

Alas, I am unable to follow Burbules' sage advice; I cannot resist the temp-tation to wax transcendental. All I can do is argue, in my old-fashioned way, that once the issue is seen in terms of a conflict between rival conceptions of phi-losophy, all we can do is ask "Which conception is more defensible?" Answering this question sets us off on the traditional project of seeking and evaluating rea-sons, and so with taking seriously the epistemological issues that the advocates of the alternative vision of philosophy reject. So I am unable to teach anyone who is not already persuaded that they should care about these issues why they should. All I can say is: if you don't, then whatever you are doing/worrying about, it's not (on my view) philosophy. Why care? Because philosophy requires that you do. If we can agree to debate the merits of these rival conceptions of philosophy, then my transcendental argument—this time, it takes the form: if it is possible genuinely to debate the relative merits of these alternative concep-tions of philosophy, then it is necessary that we seek reasons for our respective views and base our judgments upon such reasons, and so, that we accept that reasons can have epistemic force and in this way recognize the legitimacy of epistemology—kicks in, and you should be persuaded. Of course, you may deny that it is possible to so debate, or be uninterested in engaging in the attempt to ascertain the respective merits of these rival visions. In this case my transcendental argument has no force against you. Here I can only console myself that, since you deny that your vision of philosophy enjoys rational support which mine doesn't, or are uninterested in establishing that it does, you have not joined the issue or provided any reason for thinking that my conception is inadequate. To join the issue, there is no alternative but to take epistemology seriously. That, in the end, is all that my argument can show. But it is, I think, quite enough. The answer to the question, then, is: you should care about epistemology, if you care about philosophy, or inclusion, or justice, at all.

Will this answer succeed in persuading my philosophical opponents of the correctness of my view? I am not so naive as to think that it will. But I hope that it will provoke responses, and in this way further the dialogue between friends and foes of "Modernist" philosophy and philosophy of education. To the extent that these many voices continue to discuss the many issues addressed in the preceding chapters, and the merits and defects of the various arguments advanced therein, I will be heartened, for, to that extent, in one important sense at least—the communicative sense of "reasonableness" advocated by Burbules—rationality will have been redeemed. If it is redeemed in this sense, then the stage will be set for a general consideration of the adequacy of the arguments of the preceding chapters. If those arguments prove to be adequate, then the more substantive, epistemic sense of rationality I have tried to defend, and its status as a fundamental educational ideal, will indeed have been redeemed.

NOTES

INTRODUCTION

1. For more developed statements, see Siegel (1988, 1989, 1992, or 1995).

   While I do not pursue the point here, I believe that this ideal is by far the one most widely advocated in the history of philosophy of education, from Plato to Dewey and beyond. For brief remarks concerning the ideal's place in the history of the discipline, see Siegel (1992, pp. 107–109).

2. The subject-neutral/subject-specific dichotomy is discussed further in Chapter 2 below.

3. For further discussion and defense of the "critical spirit" component of critical thinking, see Chapter 4.

4. For more on the probative force/normative impact distinction and its relevance to critical thinking, see Chapter 3.

5. For further articulation of the "epistemic" view of argumentation I favor, see Biro and Siegel (1992) and Siegel and Biro (1995).

6. *Educating Reason* also contains systematic discussions of ideology, indoctrination, curriculum (in terms of science education), and educational policy and practice (in terms of minimum competency testing). These topics are not addressed in the present volume.

7. As Nicholas Burbules has put it, contemporary philosophy of education is "radically pluralist" in orientation. This description is exactly right, I think; the chapters in Part Two attempt to address this radical pluralism.

8. For a good recent effort to construct such a "critical conversation," see Kohli (1995).

CHAPTER ONE

1. Being able to evaluate reasons is not the whole of critical thinking; skills of reason assessment constitute necessary but not sufficient conditions for a person's being a critical thinker. For discussion of other dimensions, see Siegel (1988).

2. This admittedly hokey example is here for illustrative purposes only; it goes without saying that it is not intended as a serious contribution to the debate concerning the morality of abortion.

3. Or *acceptable*; cf. Blair and Johnson (1987).

   One might be tempted to think that the appropriate criterion here is not justification or acceptability, but *truth*: aspirin's putative ability to lower the probability of stroke does not constitute a reason to ingest aspirin unless it actually has that ability, i.e. unless it is true that ingesting aspirin lowers the probability of stroke. Nevertheless, there are good reasons (canvassed in Blair and Johnson, op. cit.) for resisting this formulation of the criterion. For my having a reason for ingesting aspirin depends not on the truth of my belief that it has the ability to lower the probability of stroke, but on my justifiably believing that it does. If I have good reason to believe that aspirin lowers the probability of stroke, then I have good reason for ingesting aspirin, even if it turns out that aspirin does not lower that probability. On the other hand, if aspirin does have that ability, but I don't have any reason to believe that it does, then I have no reason to ingest it. So it is justification, not truth, which is the appropriate criterion for something's being a good reason. The relationship between justification and truth will be considered further below.

4. Since this chapter was first published several years ago, this example now is somewhat dated. I invite the reader to substitute her own favorite politician.

5. Of course it is always legitimate to question judgments concerning the truth values of reasons. If one disagreed with my claim that *s* is false, then we would seek reasons for thinking that *s* is either true or false. Again, the examples are illustrative only, and do not affect the legitimacy of the more substantive points I am trying to make.

6. This topic is the subject of the next chapter.

7. This case is examined more fully in my (1987), Chapter 2.

8. One can also be a relativist concerning *truth*. For discussion of this sort of relativism, and of the relationship between relativism concerning truth and relativism concerning reasons and justification, see my (1987), Chapter 1.

9. In the following I am assuming that the arguments in Siegel (1987) settle the epistemological question, and am concerned only with the pedagogical issues raised by students' embracing of relativism, both for critical thinking and in general. For further disputation concerning the epistemological question—viz., Do the arguments in that book really refute relativism? Is relativism really indefensible?—I must beg the reader's pardon for pleading constraints of space and topic, and for referring her to that book.

10. Regarding these dispositions and character traits, see Siegel (1988), Chapter 2. For a very different analysis of "student relativism" which also advocates modelling critical thinking, see Satris (1986).

11. Thus, as Scheffler (1965, p. 54) says, "Our job is not to judge the truth infallibly but to estimate the truth responsibly."

12. For further discussion of the absoluteness of truth, see Scheffler (1965), Chapter 2.

13. A further epistemological question, suggested by the above, involves the justification of rationality. Why should we value rationality and strive to make our beliefs and actions conform to its canons? This is a basic epistemological question, and one which is unavoidable once we recognize the obligation to be critical about critical thinking itself. For discussion of its importance to the theory of critical thinking, and an attempt at an answer, see Chapter 5 below.

14. In acknowledging that critical thinking courses often concern themselves with fallacies, I do not mean to be simply assuming that this is automatically a good thing. For criticism of the "fallacies approach" to argumentation and critical thinking and its instruction, see Finocchiaro (1981); for defense, see Govier (1987), Chapter 10. For an excellent text which eschews the approach, see Feldman (1993).

15. Earlier talks on the matters here discussed were given at the Fourth and Fifth International Conferences on Critical Thinking and Educational Reform at Sonoma State University (1986 and 1987) and at the 1987 American Philosophical Association Pacific Division meeting. I am grateful to my audiences at those presentations for their helpful suggestions and criticisms, and to Linda Bomstad and Perry Weddle for their kind invitation to publish the paper on which this chapter is based in *Argumentation*.

CHAPTER 2

1. I am presuming, here and in what follows, the discussion of these issues and the first three authors offered in my Siegel (1988). Matthew Lipman also acknowledges these two aspects of critical thinking; see, e.g., Lipman (1988).

2. I am grateful to Ralph Johnson for helping me see the importance of this distinction between generality and generalizability.

3. Ennis (1989), p. 7, citing McPeck (1981), p. 22. See also Siegel (1988).

4. Ennis (1989), p. 8. Unlike McPeck, however, Ennis does not infer from this variation that critical thinking instruction should be of the "immersion" approach only.

5. For further discussion of alternative criteria of proof in mathematics and the modification of such criteria, see Kitcher (1983).

6. Ennis notes (Ennis 1989, p. 8) the existence and importance of "interfield commonalities." He rightly calls for research concerning the extent of such critical thinking commonalities.

7. I leave aside here the obvious self-reflexive difficulty this position faces: by what criteria can this claim be established, and to what "field" would such criteria belong?

8. Although even here we must be careful, for claims—if understood as propositions—can be variously described, and in ways which make alternative sorts of considerations relevant to their establishment. That is, what evidence is relevant to the establishment of a claim is at least sometimes dependent on how the claim is individuated.

9. For discussion of a telling example of this sort of mistake, concerning the gambler's fallacy, see Siegel (1992a). For further discussion of the need for a unitary epistemology underlying field-specific criteria of reason assessment, see Siegel (1988), pp. 36–37.

10. This point concerning "rubber stamp epistemology" is developed more fully in Siegel (1984), esp. pp. 668–9.

11. David Moshman argues persuasively, from the perspective of developmental psychology, that rational thinking requires both general reasoning ability and subject specific skills, criteria, and content knowledge. See Moshman (1990), esp. pp. 351–353. Matthew Lipman agrees that both sides of this dispute might be importantly right, and that insofar the debate between the generalist and the specifist has been misconceived. See Lipman (1988), p. 37.

12. I should note here that there are a variety of ways of understanding "epistemological subject specificity" (e.s.s.). *Strong* e.s.s. holds that it is *logically necessary* that different fields have their own criteria for the constitution and evaluation of reasons. This version of e.s.s., which is very close to what Ennis calls *conceptual* subject specificity and which is apparently endorsed by Toulmin and at least in some passages by McPeck, is false; it falls both to Ennis' arguments against conceptual subject specificity and to those made above. *Medium* e.s.s. holds that it is *contingently* true that fields have their own criteria for the constitution and evaluation of reasons. Though less strong than strong e.s.s., this version of e.s.s. is also false, and falls to the arguments offered above. *Weak* e.s.s. holds that, as a contingent matter, *some* criteria of reason assessment are unique to fields. This

version of e.s.s. is true, and is acknowledged above; it is, however, a weak enough version of e.s.s. that it creates no difficulty for the generalist.

13. All this is addressed at more length in Chapter 1.

14. See Siegel (1988) and Chapter 1 above.

15. My view of the relationship between epistemology and critical thinking appears to be close to that of Matthew Lipman. See his (1988), pp. 82–3; 150. For some disagreement between us on this score, however, see Siegel (1988a).

16. See Siegel (1988), Chapter 1, for documentation of this claim with respect to Ennis, Paul, and McPeck; see Lipman (1988), p. 63 and elsewhere, for documentation of the claim with respect to Lipman. For consideration of Missimer's contrary view, that the critical spirit is *not* rightly regarded as central to critical thinking, see Chapter 4 below.

17. As before, this characterization of the critical spirit is overly brief. For further discussion, see Siegel (1988), Chapter 2.

18. The "field" of philosophy provides endless examples; so do fields as diverse as art criticism, sociology, economics, biology, chemistry, and physics.

CHAPTER 3

1. Although there are alternative accounts of the character of Ivan's atheism. See, e.g., the account presented in Sutherland (1977).

2. For a systematic treatment of recent discussion concerning the problem of evil, see Peterson (1983). For an enlightening consideration of Ivan's rejection of god, which the author calls "probably the most forceful presentation of the problem of evil ever written" (p. 166), and of *The Brothers Karamazov* as a whole, see Ross (1969), Chapter 10. I am grateful to Bruce B. Suttle for suggesting both of these sources.

3. For another particularly brutal depiction, see ibid., pp. 282–3.

4. Ibid., Translator's Introduction, p. xxii.

5. See, e.g., pp. 78–9; 759; 771; 820–1.

6. E.g., ibid., p. 257.

7. Ibid., Translator's Introduction, p. xviii.

8. Ibid., p. xxv.

9. Cited in Fremantle (1956), p. x.

10. Dostoyevsky appears to be committed to a sharp reason/emotion dichotomy, e.g. p. 397. Such a split is problematic, however; see Siegel (1988), Chapter 2. Sutherland (1977) argues that fully grasping Ivan's atheism requires paying attention to the role of his emotions in his argument.

11. After all, can Ivan *decide*, or *choose*, to believe? This issue, under the label "doxastic (in)voluntarism," is much discussed in recent epistemology.

12. Further criticism of the idea that teachers should be thought of as the performers of behaviors may be found in Scheffler (1973), pp. 2–3 and 90–93; and in Scheffler (1960), Chapter 4, esp. pp. 67–8.

13. See ibid.; also Scheffler (1985).

14. This is a persistent theme of Scheffler (1973), e.g., pp. 2–3, 61, 86–88, and 92–93. As always, my discussion here is heavily indebted to Scheffler's.

    Jane Roland Martin (1982) has argued that the conception of teaching offered here is untenable in that it is drawn from "male experience" and reflects a "male cognitive perspective." I respond to these criticisms in Siegel (1983), esp. pp. 109–111.

15. See here also Scheffler (1965), pp. 11–12. Regarding the deep connection between teaching and rationality, see ibid., pp. 106–107; also Green (1971).

16. The topic may be pursued by investigating the references made in the last few notes.

17. For discussion of this point see Chapter 1.

18. This discussion concerning being moved by reasons suggests a breakdown of the reason/emotion distinction, but that is as it should be. See Siegel (1988), Chapter 2.

19. I hasten to note that portraying characters being moved by reasons is only one way, albeit the most obvious way, in which novels can utilize felt reasons in order to sensitize students to the moving force of reasons. Characters needn't be portrayed as models of rational agency. An author can sensitize students to reasons and their moving force by portraying characters who are not moved by reasons when they should be as well. Thus I am not attributing a didactic, moralistic function to literature. Presumably there are many ways in which felt reasons can be utilized by the skillful novelist. I am considering only one such way in the text. I am grateful to Sharon Bailin for suggestions concerning this point. Furthermore, it would be a mistake to reify the "characters" of a novel. The novel's effects on the reader are in the first instance a result of *language*. It is through the charged use of language, and of rhetorical devices like irony (e.g., the first long passage from Dostoyevsky's text cited above) that characters are portrayed and readers taught. Here I am indebted to Barbara Woshinsky.

20. The present discussion only concerns being *moved* by reasons. To be *appropriately* moved, we need recourse not to the "felt" quality of felt reasons but rather to relevant criteria of reason assessment. Here too, as argued above, felt reasons can make an important educational contribution.

21. It is interesting to note that this example usefully exemplifies the philosopher's distinction between task and achievement senses of "teach." Ivan succeeds in teaching Alyosha; Alyosha learns and takes to heart Ivan's lesson concerning suffering (although he manages to reconcile the lesson with his faith). Alyosha does not succeed in teaching Ivan; Ivan never learns the lesson. Alyosha nevertheless teaches in the sense that he tries to get Ivan to learn.

22. I am grateful to Ed Mooney for reminding me that many teachers ply their trade outside the classroom, and that there is no harm in employing a wide sense of "teacher."

23. In calling this a "pedagogical device" I do not mean to attribute to authors an explicit intention to teach. Here again I am grateful to Sharon Bailin.

24. This is of course not meant to disparage the insights to be gleaned from ordinary teaching; nor to suggest that teachers are incapable of conveying to students the moving force of reasons. Teachers *can* (and should) make clear, by their teaching, attitudes, and behavior, that reasons matter. I am not suggesting that the philosophical novel is the *only* way to convey this lesson. My claim is rather that the philosophical novel, in its skillful utilization of felt reasons, is particularly well suited to the task. Here again I am indebted to Ed Mooney.

25. Of course the novel does more than teach us. It moves us; it brings us pleasure and despair; it captures and exercises our imaginations; it stimulates us in countless ways. My focus has been on the way that *The Brothers Karamazov* teaches us, but it obviously does more than that. For reminding me to place the novel's teaching in the context of its other accomplishments, I am grateful to Sophie Haroutunian-Gordon and Philip Jackson.

26. Dostoevsky also teaches us a lesson about the *dialectical* nature of reasoning: positions develop in interplay with alternatives, e.g. Alyosha's in dynamic opposition to Ivan's. Alyosha feels the force of Ivan's reasons, and responds to it in formulating his own view. Thus, dialectic is illuminated by noting that interlocutors in dialectic interchange must be moved appropriately by the considerations raised by fellow interlocutors. Moreover, in a novel like Dostoevsky's, *we* enter into dialectical interchange with the characters and their reasons, and are ourselves moved to develop our own positions in response to our estimation of the probative force of the considerations they raise. Many have noted the centrality of dialectical exchange to rational/critical thinking; see, e.g., Paul (1982) and Blair and Johnson (1987). Here again I am grateful to Ed Mooney.

27. Thanks are once again due to Ed Mooney for suggesting this point.

28. As the reader may have guessed, I have long treasured *The Brothers Karamazov*. But writing about such topics as these is very much new to me. I am grateful to Philip Jackson and Sophie Haroutunian-Gordon for providing me with the opportunity to write about this wonderful work, and to Haroutunian-Gordon, Jackson, Sharon Bailin, Carol Crowley, Ed Mooney, Madhu Suri Prakash, Bruce B. Suttle, and Barbara Woshinsky for extremely useful and beneficial comments on earlier drafts.

CHAPTER 4

1. Unless otherwise noted, parenthetical page references in this chapter are to Missimer (1990).

2. Except the disposition to think critically, which Missimer claims can as readily be characterized as a habit. For discussion of this exception, see below.

3. In what follows I rely on my own version of the Character View. I apologize in advance to proponents of other versions of that view who might think I am

wrongly representing their views. I here speak only for myself—though I hope (and believe) that what I say is acceptable to Paul, Scheffler, and other proponents of the Character View mentioned by Missimer. Missimer declines to count Ennis as a proponent of the Character View (152, note 2), but Ennis insists that he be so counted (personal communication, September 8, 1992).

4. Missimer writes as if the skills relevant to critical thinking are clearly specified and universally agreed upon. But one has but to notice that her (quite general and nonspecific) characterization of those skills differs from McPeck's, which differs from Ennis', which differs from Paul's, etc., to see that these differences in no way challenge the thesis that reasoning skills are a necessary ingredient of an adequate conception of critical thinking. The case is the same for the heterogeneity of the specifications of the character traits emphasized by the Character View.

5. Missimer is aware of this, as her note 5 (153) cites Scheffler as insisting on the legitimacy of both the feeling of revulsion and the experiencing of surprise and delight. But she continues nonetheless to suggest, incorrectly, that the Character View cannot acknowledge them both.

6. I note here in passing that Missimer's citation of the character traits I have argued are central to critical thinking (145, citing Siegel [1988], p. 41) is erroneous. The features of the critical spirit I emphasize—a disposition to engage in reason assessment; a willingness to conform judgment and action to principle; an inclination to seek, and to base judgment and action upon, reasons; a tendency to challenge currently held beliefs, and to demand justification for candidate beliefs; etc. (Siegel [1988], p. 39)—are not mentioned by Missimer. Instead, the character traits she attributes to me (145) are mentioned by me not as character traits, but as aspects of the *psychology* of the critical thinker (Siegel [1988], p. 41). While Missimer runs these together, in my view they are quite distinct.

7. For this reason the Character View does not hold that having some specific set of character traits to some specific degree is a necessary condition for being a critical thinker. The only relevant *necessary* condition here is that of having, to at least *some* degree, *some* of the relevant traits. So the Character View does not rule that great thinkers who lack to some degree some of the relevant traits therefore fail to qualify as critical thinkers—though it does hold that the more such thinkers manifest the relevant traits, the more secure is their claim to so qualify.

8. Of course to the extent that critical thinking is seen as an ideal, it is general, and applies to everything, including those character traits just dismissed as only indecisively relevant: ideally, a critical thinker is a completely rational, completely moral person. But this is an ideal. These thinkers' character flaws and moral failings count against their being ideal critical thinkers, but their intellectual achievements argue for their status as (to some significant degree) critical thinkers, despite those flaws and failings. The flaws and failings don't disqualify them

as critical thinkers *simpliciter*, though they do disqualify them as *ideal* critical thinkers.

9. It may be that Freud's did not. If so, then his status as a critical thinker is perhaps less clear than that of Missimer's other examples.

10. All the literature on the discovery/justification distinction—including my (1980)—is relevant here.

11. This confusion of process and product is well criticized in Bailin (1988), p. 404, which is a response to Missimer (1988).

12. In addition to the citations just noted, Missimer could also have cited the papers on which Chapters 1 and 5 of the present volume are based, all of which emphasize the importance for critical thinking theory of the fact that our conceptions of critical thinking—including their moral dimensions—must themselves be open to critical scrutiny. Indeed, this is a pervasive theme of my (1988) as well. The parallel point—that conceptions and theories of rationality must themselves be open to rational criticism and defense—is also a staple of my more narrowly epistemological work on naturalism and rationality.

13. See also my (1988), note 23, pp. 156–7, in which I emphasize the further scrutinizability of the moral dimensions of the Character View.

14. Of course proponents of the Character View may well think, as I do, that the moral position in question is the one most able to withstand critical scrutiny, and which emerges as the most adequately justified from the rigors of critical reflection. The point here is just that there is (on the Character View) nothing automatic, necessary, or "beyond scrutiny" about this thesis, despite Missimer's suggestion to the contrary.

15. Actually, the great mathematician Ramanujan might be a counter-example, if by "doing mathematics" Missimer means attempting to *prove* mathematical theorems. I leave this as a curiosity to ponder.

16. Several of my papers on naturalized epistemology (1980, 1984, 1989a, 1990a, 1992c, 1995a, 1995b) argue against the view Missimer here adopts.

17. Missimer suggests (ibid.) that there is "no pedagogical upshot to [my] conception of the critical spirit." But there is: if the Character View is right that that spirit is constitutive of the critical thinker (and that critical thinking is an important educational ideal), then we are obliged to try to foster that spirit. That is an important pedagogical upshot of the Character View's conception of critical thinking. (How we best do that is a question which is largely independent of the different question which Missimer is pressing: is the Character View in fact correct that the critical spirit is constitutive of critical thinking? See the discussion of this point above.)

18. See Chapter 1 for discussion of the relationships among truth, justification, and critical thinking.

19. Missimer demurs ([1988], p. 401, note 7), but her point here is just that it is

"much likelier" that such arguments are evaluated in comparison with alternatives, not that adequate evaluation *requires* such comparison.

20. My point here thus does not rest on examples of arguments which beg the question or involve vicious circularity. For a provocative defense of *some* such arguments, see Sorensen (1991). The present point goes through even if Sorensen's analysis is correct.

21. Missimer offers an extended reply to the original publication of this chapter in her (1995). I refrain from considering it in detail here, however, because I believe that in all essential respects it fails seriously either to challenge the arguments for the Character View presented above or to defend her alternative Skill View. In particular, her more recent paper continues to conflate particular *acts* or *products* of critical thinking with critical thinking as an appropriate description of *persons*; and it continues to misunderstand the notion of *cause* and its place in philosophical argumentation. Nevertheless, I am happy to recommend it to the reader's consideration, who is urged not to take my word for it, but to assess Missimer's arguments for herself.

An earlier version of this paper was presented at a meeting of the Association for Informal Logic and Critical Thinking (AILACT) during the Pacific Division Meeting of the American Philosophical Association in Portland, Oregon on March 26, 1992. I am grateful to my respondent, Mark Battersby, and to the members of the audience for their good discussion on that occasion. I am especially grateful to Connie Missimer for helpful and insightful criticisms and suggestions.

CHAPTER 5

1. This Chapter is an attempt to enlarge the very brief discussions of the problem of justifying the commitment to rationality/critical thinking—a commitment the justification of which is basic to regarding critical thinking as a fundamental educational ideal—which appear in Siegel (1988), p. 132, and (1987), pp. 167–9.

2. O'Hear (1980), p. 147–9. In what follows I follow O'Hear (and Popper) in using "rationalism" to refer, not to the doctrines of the Continental Rationalists, but rather to the view that we ought, ideally, to believe and act rationally, i.e. in accordance with reasons which justify our beliefs and actions.

Throughout this Chapter I write, following Trigg and (sometimes) O'Hear, as if justification were strictly a matter of reasons, and not of experience; and also as if *being* justified requires *showing* (or at least being able to show) that one is. But as the most recent citation suggests, the claim that rationalism cannot be justified is interpreted by its makers such that neither reasons *nor* experience can justify rationalism. So I am not problematically assuming in what follows that only reasons, and not experience, can justify; I am not taking sides on this contentious issue which divides foundationalists and coherentists. Nor am I assuming that in order to *be* justified, a believer must (be able to) *show* that she is—although several of the authors to be considered do appear to assume this. These issues, which are hotly debated in contemporary epistemology, will not be pursued here; the worry about the justification of rationality which is the subject of this Chapter is independent of these other worries concerning justification.

3. O'Hear (1980), p. 150. See also p. 151.

4. O'Hear suggests that the difficulty here is that what is wanted, but cannot be had, is a nonargumentative justification of rationality:

> The mere fact that there is no non-argumentative demonstration of the rationality of the practices of rationality, especially the use of argument, is hardly surprising, given that a justification of a practice demonstrating the value of that practice can take place only within an argumentative context. (op. cit., p. 150)

This is a mistaken formulation of the problem, however. What is wanted is an argumentative justification of rationality, one which takes place "within an argumentative context" but which avoids charges of inconsistency, circularity, and question-begging. O'Hear thinks, with Trigg and Popper, that if the justification proceeds from within an argumentative context, it cannot avoid these logical difficulties (and that if it proceeds outside of such a context, it fails to constitute a justification at all). Below I offer a putative justification from within an argumentative context, which I claim nevertheless avoids these logical pitfalls.

5. This view is also endorsed by Stephen Toulmin (1950). Toulmin regards our question (actually, the parallel question in ethics, i.e. "Why be moral?") as a "limiting" question, for which there is no "logical space" for a literal answer. See pp. 161–5; 202–25. Toulmin's (as well as Trigg's and O'Hear's) arguments for the "logical oddness" of "Why be rational?," and for the logical impossibility of providing a general answer to the question—and so, of providing a justification for a commitment to rationality—are heavily influenced by the later Wittgenstein.

6. It also depends rather heavily on a sharp contingent/in principle distinction, which many philosophers find problematic.

7. Popper's argument for critical rationalism focusses on the moral ramifications of opting for rationalism rather than irrationalism. See Popper (1962), pp. 232 ff.

8. At this point it would be instructive to treat the literature surrounding W. W. Bartley's "comprehensively critical rationalism"; I regret that I cannot do so here. See Bartley (1984). My own solution renders rationality comprehensive, as does Bartley's; but it acknowledges the possibility of positive justification, and so is less focussed on criticism and falsification than his.

9. I ignore here the possible response noted in the introduction, that "Why be rational?" is a legitimate question but that it cannot be answered affirmatively

because we should *not* be rational. Although many thinkers have argued against rationality (see for instance the opening citations from Feyerabend and Dostoyevsky, the works of Nietzsche and Kierkegaard, etc.), for present purposes their arguments can be ignored, since in *arguing* against rationality they are in fact embracing it rather than rejecting it. A fuller study would show this by examining the details of arguments urging the rejection of rationality.

10. Joaquin Medin points out that I need to clarify the sort of presupposition at work here: logical, semantic, or pragmatic. I believe that rationality is presupposed in all three senses, although it would take more space than I have here to make the case. I am grateful to Medin for his suggestion.

11. See Siegel (1988), p. 132, on which this paragraph builds, and also the references cited there.

12. For further comment on the position of one who does not pose the question, see the Epilogue.

13. For critical discussion of the "pragmatic" character of Rescher's analysis, see Siegel (1992b).

14. Indeed, Trigg seems to realize as much in the course of arguing that the demand is illegitimate:

> Anyone who asks "why be rational?," by asking for reasons, assumes that there are reasons, and that rationality is in principle possible. . . .he is asking for reasons and thus has already involved himself in the whole process of rationality. (op. cit, p. 149)

Part of the difficulty with this aspect of the Popper/Trigg/O'Hear position is its failure to distinguish between deductive and transcendental justifications. These terms can co-refer, but needn't do; in any case it is clear that my self-reflexive solution is, in the relevant sense, transcendental, while the logical difficulties worried about by our three authors are more germane to deductive justifications. For more on transcendental justification, see Chapter 12 and the Epilogue below. I am grateful to Donald Hatcher for his suggestions concerning this point.

CHAPTER 6

1. I should note in passing that prejudice needn't be directed against persons; we often are prejudiced against beliefs, theses or doctrines as well. Some of my students' irrational and unjustified hostility to "communismo" qualifies as prejudice, I think, though it is not in the first instance directed at any person.

2. The phrase is Bertrand Russell's. See his (1957), p. vii.

3. Brief further remarks concerning critical thinking's rejection of self-interest, and the place of that rejection in a fuller conception of the critical spirit, may be found in Siegel (1988), Chapter 2.

4. This relationship is further examined in Siegel (1988), Chapter 3.

5. For the idea of viewing this message as an argument I am indebted to Barbara Woshinsky.

6. Burbules and Rice (1991) offers a very insightful and useful discussion of several points I have only barely alluded to here concerning postmodernism, marginalization, dialogue, etc.

7. For further discussion of the moral, methodological, and epistemic epistemic virtues of (democratic) inclusion, see Chapter 12.

8. I am grateful to the Anti-Defamation League for its invitation to participate in a working conference on critical thinking and prejudice, for which an ancestor of this paper was written.

   I must also thank my anonymous correspondent for providing me with a running example of prejudice to utilize in my discussion. Here we have an unexpected virtue of the use of swastikas—though doubtless it is not a virtue of which my correspondent would approve.

CHAPTER 7

1. The attentive reader will have noticed my uncareful sliding between "sentence" and "proposition." I don't think anything of note turns on this carelessness in the present context.

2. Nor could a purely causal conception. For more on both these points, see Kim (1988). For a quite different argument to a very similar conclusion concerning the need for a nonformalistic conception of rationality, see Kekes (1989). (While I reject Kekes' pragmatic justification of logic, I concur with much of his discussion concerning the nonformal character of rationality. For the just-noted rejection, see my [1992a].) Several of the essays in this volume are relevant to the present discussion.

3. There are also important *political* objections to formalistic conceptions of rationality, which I endorse, which are well noted in Burbules (1991) and (1995).

4. Burbules' (1991a) is a remarkable document: a critical review of my books (Siegel [1987] and [1988]), written in the form of a dialogue between Burbules and me, with my part consisting entirely of passages taken from the books. I will always be grateful to Burbules for this creative and labor-intensive effort.

5. It is unclear what Burbules has in mind here by "formal knowledge." He speaks both of "formal knowledge" and "formal rationality" (e.g. [1991], p. 220); occasionally he suggests that formality is a matter of being expressible in the form of a rule (e.g. [1995], p. 86). It may be that the formalistic conceptions of rationality we each reject are not entirely equivalent. It may even be that the substantive, epistemic relations between the contents of sentences or propositions, which I argued above are fundamental to rationality but cannot be understood as formal, Burbules regards and rejects as formal (see, e.g., [1995], pp. 83, 85–6). If so, then Burbules' rejection of formalistic conceptions of rationality amounts to a rejection of the idea that the rationality of a belief (or action or judgment)

has anything whatsoever to do with the reasons which support it. Below I criticize any such nonepistemic view of rationality.

6. Note that here too the meaning of "formal knowledge" is unclear. I address Burbules' discussion of *judgment* below.

7. I also agree, despite Burbules' indirect suggestion to the contrary (1995, p. 85), that being rational is a matter of degree, not an all-or-nothing affair; that is, that beliefs, judgments, actions, persons, institutions, and social arrangements can be more or less rational (or reasonable), and that we are not confined to an overly blunt rational/irrational dichotomy. I believe and hope that this point is clear from the discussion in the chapters above; it is also made, under the name of "gradualism," in Siegel (1988b), pp. 271–2.

8. Burbules has more recently proposed objectivity, fallibilism, pragmatism, and judiciousness as virtues that are central to reasonableness ([1995], pp. 89–96).

9. This point is well made, in terms of the "immanence and transcendence of reason" and the importance of maintaining "the distinction between epistemology and sociology," in Robertson (1995), pp. 119–121; it is also trenchantly articulated in Kohli (1993), p. 353. It is discussed further in Chapter 12 below.

10. Burbules takes pains here to point out the moral and affective dimensions of these virtues; I agree.

11. We might well ask who the "we" is in Burbules' sentence. He interestingly addresses this question at (1995), pp. 97–8.

   Nor is it fair, at least in my own case, to suggest that these virtues are justified, on the view Burbules opposes, as "instantiations of certain formalized rules or standards of reasoned conduct." As just noted, on my view they are justified by appeal to the content of relevant theory, not to matters of form. Here is one point at which the unclarity of Burbules' use of "formal," noted earlier, is problematic.

12. In his more recent (1995), Burbules develops further his view that whatever social and contextual factors cause people to be reasonable are also constitutive of that educational ideal (pp. 98–9 and *passim*).

13. See the discussion of Scheffler's account of teaching in Chapter 3 above.

14. See also the insightful and informative discussion of Burbules (1995) in Robertson (1995), and Robertson's excellent (1991).

   I should make one further point here. One may question—as Burbules ([1991a], p. 242) does—the appropriateness of the label "absolutism" for the fallibilist, pluralist position I endorse. My defense of its appropriateness depends on regarding "absolutism" and "relativism" as not merely contraries but as contradictories. If they are so regarded, then any nonrelativist position is absolutist. As these terms are generally used in epistemology, they are so regarded. Hence the appropriateness of the label for my nonrelativist position. But the important thing is not the label, but the substantive view. I'd be happy to give up the label, so long as the pair are not understood as contradictories. My commitment is not to the label, but rather to the substantive fallibilist, pluralist, objectivist, rational-ist (in the sense of "good reasons") epistemological position sketched in my books and papers.

CHAPTER 8

1. Unless otherwise noted, all simple page references to Weinstein in the text are to his (1992).
2. See Audi (1988), pp. 80 ff., for a fairly standard introductory discussion. Most introductory texts in epistemology discuss the epistemic regress problem in detail.
3. For an important recent discussion which attempts to combine the strengths of these two theories of epistemic justification while avoiding their difficulties, under the name of "foundherentism," see Haack (1993).
4. Criticisms of foundationalism which miss the mark in one or the other of the ways just mentioned in the text are legion in general philosophy. In the philos-ophy of education literature, two recent discussions come to mind. In his (1990), Kenneth A. Strike firmly rejects "foundationalist epistemologies." But his dis-cussion (a) slides between a rejection of that, and a rejection of "foundationalist *moral* epistemology" (my emphasis), leaving unclear his attitude toward epistemic foundationalism *simpliciter* (358–9); and (b) suggests that foundationalism requires, necessitates, or presupposes "some indubitable base from which rea-soning can proceed" (358), thereby ignoring important forms of so called "mod-est" foundationalism, which explicitly disavow any such requirement. (See Alston [1989], Audi [1988], Moser [1985], and several of the papers in Moser [1986] for a sampling of current discussion of modest foundationalism. A pow-erful version of modest foundationalism is developed in my Miami colleague Alan H. Goldman's [1988]. Goldman offers important arguments for founda-tionalism, while insisting that foundational beliefs need not be certain or infal-lible.) Strike's otherwise excellent treatment of individualism, and of the difficulties which accrue to views which do not duly recognize the social char-acter of knowledge, is marred by these two problems. (For a recent defense of the sort of strong foundationalism which Strike here rejects, see McGrew [1995].)

James Giarelli (1990) also rejects foundationalism. The foundationalism rejected is not epistemic foundationalism, but rather the idea that philosophy is a "foundational discipline" which "deliver[s] a grounding" (pp. 35–6) to educa-tional theory and practice. This challenge, like Weinstein's challenge to philoso-phy as a foundational discourse frame, is quite distinct from and independent of a challenge to epistemic foundationalism, i.e. to foundationalism as a solution to the epistemic regress problem. But Giarelli is not careful to distinguish these (and still other) different senses of "foundationalism." He characterizes his foun-dationalist, "professional" opponent, for example, as "assum[ing] that reason gives us a certain foundation for belief" (p. 40), an assumption Giarelli rejects. Note (a) that this assumption is independent of the "foundational" status of philosophy as a discipline, and (b) that epistemic foundationalists needn't assume any such thing about the certainty of foundational beliefs (or reasons). He later (pp. 41–3) identifies foundationalism with "mental monism" (which phrase is borrowed from Young-Bruehl) and a variety of unsavory social and political beliefs and practices. But epistemic foundationalists needn't accept "mental monism"; still less are they committed to the variety of anti-feminist views which Giarelli rightly rejects but wrongly saddles them with. I agree with Giarelli that philosophy is not correctly viewed as a "foundational discipline" as he characterizes that notion. Nevertheless, it must be noted that "foundationalism" is used by Giarelli to refer to a very wide and divergent range of positions and subject matters, and his argument against it is marred by the slipperiness of this reference. Further difficulties with that argument are well noted in Pratte (1990). Giarelli offers further criticism of foundationalism in Giarelli and Chambliss (1991).

5. I am grateful here to conversation with my Miami colleagues Ed Erwin and Susan Haack.

6. At least the first one. I'm not sure what is meant by "epistemology" in the second one, since as I understand that term "usefulness" as Weinstein discusses it has nothing to do with it.

7. Weinstein emphasizes the role of methodology in grounding disciplinary knowledge claims. I agree, although I think it crucial to note that it is theory which provides the backing for any such methodological grounding. In a case in which there is no theoretical rationale for a given methodological practice, that practice provides no warrant for claims arrived at through its exercise.

8. Which is not to say that particular questions are never resolved on the basis of general principles or considerations. Sometimes they are. See Chapter 2 above.

9. Weinstein discusses his project in more detail in his (1990).

10. Weinstein acknowledges that philosophical arguments can be "cognitively binding, within the scope of their application" (258, note 6). That is all I need for the defense of my own project. (Weinstein appeals in this note to Rescher [1988]; for discussion of Rescher, see Siegel [1992b] and Chapter 5 above.)

I must acknowledge, however, that my position depends on a distinction (to which Weinstein is also committed) between philosophical and extra-philosophical issues. This is a contentious distinction. Philosophers who deny it often couch that denial in the context of advocating the "naturalizing of epistemology." I argue against naturalized epistemology in my (1980), (1984), (1989a), (1990a), (1992c), (1995a), and (1995b). It is one of the foci of my ongoing research.

11. The position is first laid out in Goodman (1952). For discussion and further references, see Siegel (1992a). It is widely accepted in a variety of philosophical contexts. For an example from philosophy of science, see Shapere (1984).

12. Here my view diverges in a crucial way from Goodman's. See Siegel (1992a) for extended discussion.

13. In Chapter 5 above. For further discussion, see the earlier references to Alston, Audi, Goldman, and Moser. Contrary to Weinstein (256–7, note 4), the self-justifying relationship some claims bear to themselves is not simply logical, but is rather epistemic, and involves the contents, and not just the form, of those claims.

14. I note in passing that relativism is not "paradoxical"; rather, it is either false or incoherent.

15. Weinstein rejects the completely general version of fallibilism, because it runs afoul of PLP. But before leaving this topic, I should note that his positive, qualified version of fallibilism seems equally to run afoul of it. Consider: "Fallibilism: Again, whatever else, it requires that all claims be open to reasons that indicate their possible inadequacy" (249). This is indistinguishable from the completely general version Weinstein rejects. So is "Any community is a potential critic of any other" (246), whether or not "this can not be reflexively predicated of the plurality as a whole" (246). So is "We have every reason to suspect that any actual claim should be seen as fallible, including any actual claim made in the foreseeable future" (241). So is "Any claim may be false," even if such a statement of fallibilism is "seen as a summary of past experience and as a useful guide to further inquiry" (252).

16. See Moser (1986), pp. 4 ff., for an introductory discussion. Moser (1985) contains extensive discussion of these different sorts of justification, in the context of several main theories of justification. See also Alston (1989).

17. Assuming, of course, that the former two beliefs are themselves (propositionally) justified. Whether that belief is doxastically justified depends upon its being appropriately "based on" those former beliefs. If I believe all three, but believe the latter not because of its epistemic relationship to the former two, but rather because of an irrational antipathy toward Buchanan, then my believing the latter is propositionally, but not doxastically, justified.

18. For criticism of epistemic contextualism, see Moser (1985), Chapter 2; Haack (1993), Chapter 9.

19. The attentive reader will have noticed that this paragraph is taken, with some changes, from Chapter 7 above; there it is presented in the context of my consideration of Burbules' discussion of judgment. Burbules' and Weinstein's views on this crucial notion overlap in important ways; the similarities (and differences) in their views are well worth more extended consideration than I can give them here.

20. Weinstein acknowledges this point in his (1993), in which he accepts that criticisms of a perspective made from an alternative perspective needn't be correct. This paper is discussed in Chapter 9 below.

205

21. The view concerning justification and standards just stated is developed further in subsequent chapters.

22. With apologies to Rescher, who treats "the predicament of reason" at length in his (1988). For discussion see Siegel (1992b).

23. For further discussion, see Siegel (1987), Chapter 2; and Chapter 12 below.

24. I hasten to add that such reasoning is not irrelevant to such determination, either, and that some criteria of reason assessment are indeed discipline-independent. See Chapter 2 above.

25. One further point on which we do not concerns truth. He suggests that I think that correspondence is "a criterion of truth" (235). This is wrong, and is moreover confused. Correspondence cannot be a *criterion* of truth, for we have no independent access to an independent reality and so cannot tell when or whether the criterion is met. Rather, we utilize *justification* as our (fallible) criterion, and regard truth as the *upshot* of the fact that claims and beliefs are well supported. Reasons and evidence give us good reason to believe claims; such good reason just is reason for thinking them to be true. (See Siegel [1983b], and the references to Scheffler therein, for further discussion.)

26. I urge the reader to consult Weinstein's (1992a), which responds to many of the critical points made in this chapter. Given the length of the latter, I will not attempt to reply to his paper here; instead I will simply acknowledge that while I am not persuaded of the correctness of his criticisms, Weinstein makes some helpful criticisms of my discussion, and insightfully furthers our dialogue by clarifying further the dialectical situation in which our dialogue is taking place and the crucial epistemological issues which continue to divide us. Several of his points are addressed, directly or indirectly, in the following and subsequent chapters.

CHAPTER 9

1. In this chapter I am responding to Weinstein's discussion of Postmodernism, not to Postmodernism per se; the latter comprises a much wider range of theses and authors than that considered here. I leave it to the reader to judge the degree to which my remarks are applicable to other Postmodernist thinkers and theories.

2. Unless otherwise noted, all page references to Weinstein's work in this Chapter are to his (1993).

3. Although Weinstein interprets that framework as "furnish[ing] a limit beyond which critique can not go" (30). This is a mistake; my thoroughgoingly fallibilistic view acknowledges no such limit. I believe that the mistake arises from Weinstein's uncritical use of "foundationalism": while in some senses my view is foundationalist, in other important senses it is not; and Weinstein does not distinguish among them. In the paper under discussion he regards my view as foundationalist only because it rejects relativism and insists upon "the necessity of some overarching frame within which one assesses competing claims," i.e. "the necessity for some governing norms if justification is possible" (33), but he

accepts this thesis himself. So if I'm a foundationalist in this sense, so is he. For more extended discussion of foundationalism, see Chapter 8 above, and the papers by Weinstein discussed and referred to therein.

4. Weinstein's claim that "Reason, in some sense akin to both Paul's and McPeck's, is at the center of the educational enterprise for Siegel" (33) is mistaken. My view of rationality is not grounded in either the disciplines or in natural language, as Weinstein should be well aware. He is also mistaken in thinking that on my view truth "stand[s] as a criterion of judgment" (30); on this point see Chapter 8, note 25.

5. In another version of Weinstein's (1993), published in *Inquiry: Critical Thinking Across the Disciplines* (vol. 11, #3, April 1993, pp. 1, 16–22), he inserts "at least in part" into the penultimate cited sentence, so that it reads: "It requires no less than that the true is to be defined, at least in part, in terms of the good" (20). The insertion somewhat softens his claim here, but not sufficiently to avoid the criticism of it developed below.

6. I am grateful to Karl Hostetler for correspondence concerning Habermas and the procedural/substantive rationality distinction just drawn. I do not want to suggest that Hostetler would agree with me on these matters.

7. It is worth asking what Weinstein means by "epistemological'; this may well be a major source of our apparent disagreement. As I am using the term, epistemology is centrally concerned with justificatory status or probative force; an "epistemological objection" to a discourse frame is an objection that, if successful, lowers that status (e.g., such that claims made from the perspective of that frame are less justified, or less likely to be true, than they would be if the frame weren't successfully challenged by the objection). My claim in the text is that the moral objections to discourse frames Weinstein discusses do not constitute epistemological objections in *this* sense. Perhaps they do constitute such objections, if "epistemological" is understood in some other sense. Weinstein reports that he "understands[s] epistemology exactly as Siegel does, except I do not accept the same framework for discussion" (Weinstein [1994], p. 30). I leave it to the reader to determine whether Weinstein's discussion here successfully challenges my argument on this point.

8. My claim is that this pattern of reasoning fails because moral evaluations do not imply epistemic ones. Haack points out that the fact that it would be morally desirable if some proposition p were the case does not constitute evidence that p *is* the case. Both of the criticized patterns attempt to derive "is's" from "oughts." Haack's discussion appears in her (1993a, p. 35). My thanks to Haack for her help in clarifying this point, and for her criticism of an earlier version of this chapter.

9. But notice that to *respect* such intuitions is not automatically to regard them as correct. People sometimes *mistakenly* believe that they have been treated unjustly.

Here again I am indebted to Haack. As noted above, Weinstein makes this point himself (34).

10. Although it is problematic in other respects. As Haack (op. cit.) suggests, for example, the oppressed are in some respects epistemically *un*privileged—e.g., in their lack of access to various sorts of information, which lack serves to maintain that oppression.

11. Weinstein has I think granted this criticism, in his (1994), pp. 28, 30–1, although he tries to minimize the impact of granting the point on his overall view by giving a series of examples in which "an awareness of social justice issues impacts on purely epistemological theories" (1994, p. 31). But that there are such examples I have already granted in the text. They in no way challenge the substantive criticisms of Weinstein's view made in this chapter.

12. Indeed, the history of Western philosophy can instructively be viewed as a struggle between the "totalizing" imposition of Ockham's Razor and the difference-preserving effect of Butler's slogan.

13. This claim is defended further in Chapter 12.

14. But it will sometimes be unclear whether a purported instance of the devaluation of perspectives—like the sort of educational or professional case imagined just above— is rightly regarded as an instance of silencing, marginalization, or exclusion—and so of injustice.

15. Although I do not assent to the one offered by Weinstein, for its key term, "most essential reasons," is unclear. If it means "most epistemically forceful reasons," then it is I think false. While in some cases the reasons that "injustice and marginalization bring to the fore" will be of great weight and epistemic significance, in other cases they will not. Indeed, Weinstein's earlier work emphasizes (with McPeck) the point that the forcefulness of a reason will frequently depend on disciplinary considerations. In his present endorsement of Giroux, he is apparently giving up some of that earlier work, since the thesis that the epistemic forcefulness of a reason is dependent on disciplinary considerations is quite at odds with the thesis that the epistemic forcefulness of a reason is dependent on considerations of social justice. (Weinstein denies that he is; see his [1994, p. 31, note 2] for discussion.)

16. When Weinstein grants that my arguments support "the necessity of some overarching frame within which one assesses competing claims" (33), he is similarly committing himself at least to that "totalizing" metaepistemological thesis.

17. Indeed, as has frequently been noted, the principled rejection of all metanarratives itself constitutes a metanarrative (of the second sort), and is for that reason self-referentially incoherent.

18. Carnap's "total evidence condition" is surely Enlightenment in spirit.

19. In his reply, Weinstein denies the distinction: "A corollary of the central insight of postmodernism is that principles can not be construed as having only abstract propositional content, for principles are only meaningful when interpreted and

put into use" (1994, p. 29). This reply faces two major difficulties. First, every interpretation/use of a Modernist principle will be different from every other, rendering it impossible to identify such principles in order to target them for Postmodernist critique. Second, and more fundamental, this understanding of principles renders it impossible in principle for a principle to be misunderstood or misapplied. This second difficulty seems to me so severe that it constitutes a reductio of Weinstein's denial of the distinction.

20. This point is clearly and persuasively made in Bailin (1992).

21. Here I am indebted to conversation with and recent publications of Nicholas Burbules, from whose distinction between Post- and Antimodernism, and his defense of the former and criticism of the latter, I have learned much. Of course I do not mean to suggest that Burbules endorses the lessons I claim to have learned from him.

22. Notice that none of these principles, as we have seen, require reference to differences among persons; but that all of them are compatible with the acknowledgement of such difference.

23. One final comment: Weinstein's last line contains an important equivocation. "Delusions" cannot (and so do not) *justify*, though of course they can and do "justify" in the sense that they *erroneously* portray unjustified claims and practices as justified. For further discussion of this equivocation, see my (1988), note 12, p. 159.

24. To see this, just ask: How does Weinstein's Postmodernist insistence on the embeddedness of discourse—epistemological and other—affect his own arguments? Do they have validity or probative value beyond the range of practices in which he works? An affirmative answer to the latter question requires the giving up of that insistence; a negative answer reintroduces the very arbitrariness he is endeavoring to overcome.

I have tried to respond (in part) to Weinstein's reply to this Chapter (Weinstein 1994) in the text and notes above, but I strongly encourage the interested reader to consult Weinstein's own discussion.

I am grateful to the audiences who heard and reacted to my presentations of this Chapter (noted in the Preface), and to Nick Burbules, Susan Haack, Karl Hostetler, and Mark Weinstein, for incisive criticisms of and helpful suggestions concerning the presented and earlier versions.

CHAPTER TEN

1. I hasten to add: they are political only in a quite specific sense. I criticize the view that educational ideals are problematically political or ideological in Siegel (1988), Chapter 4. I am grateful to Susan Haack for discussion concerning the senses in which educational institutions are and are not political.

2. I am not drawing distinctions between these three, in many respects different, positions, because I am concerned here with what they hold in common.

3. I am here using the word "radical" to refer to a particular set of educational theorists, who stress cultural phenomena, identity politics, "difference," and especially cultural hegemony in their work. It is this group which typically identifies itself and is identified as "radical" in the current scholarly environment; and it is this group whose epistemological ideas and commitments I endeavor to criticize in what follows. However, I should note that there are other groups of educational theorists who also identify themselves as "radical" and who are equally (if not more) entitled to the label. These theorists include those working in Feminist and Race studies, who emphasize the political imperative of equality, especially of opportunity; and those working in history, sociology, economics, and philosophy of education, often from a Marxist perspective, whose work manifests a "radical" political stance in a more self-consciously scientific way. Such theorists generally do not advocate the sort of epistemological views I criticize below. The views to be discussed there, while advocated by highly visible scholars, represent only one trend in current "radical" educational theory; I in no way want to suggest that those who advocate the views discussed here are the only, or the most important—though they are the most visible—"radical" educational theorists around. I am indebted to Nicholas Burbules for enlightening correspondence on these matters.

4. In using this word I do not mean to suggest that epistemological views are rightly criticizable on political grounds: on the contrary. I use it only to acknowledge the particular criticisms of traditional epistemology to which it is my aim to respond in what follows. I am grateful here to comments made by Susan Haack.

5. A detailed discussion of Arcilla's (1995) analysis and critique of Taylor is presented in Chapter 11.

6. In Chapter 12 I argue that there are some circumstances in which exclusion does not constitute this sort of moral wrong, and therefore can be justified.

7. As both Bruce B. Suttle and Ed Erwin remind me, these "liberal" principles are nearly formal and nearly empty of content: no one seriously disagrees with principles like "one ought not treat others unjustly" or "one ought always to treat others with respect." The difficult philosophical work comes in figuring out what constitutes violations of such principles, for we often do disagree on that. (For example, is it a failure to treat non-English speaking immigrant children in Miami with respect when the school system attempts to instruct them in their native tongues? Does such instruction constitute oppression or marginalization? Would instructing them in English constitute a failure to treat them with respect, or marginalization, or oppression?) I think Erwin and Suttle are right about this: it is very difficult plausibly to challenge these principles themselves. But the upshot of this point is: if such principles are benign or uncontroversial, then woe to those positions, including those discussed below, which

do try to challenge them; any position which denies the obvious is hopeless. My thanks to Suttle and Erwin for their good criticisms here.

8. Eamonn Callan has forcefully reminded me that liberal moral theorists have notoriously differed among themselves with respect to their moral epistemology. Callan is surely right about this; I do not mean to suggest that such theorists constitute a united front with respect to moral epistemology. These particular disputes concerning that epistemology notwithstanding, however, such theorists do I think share the minimal epistemological precepts I attribute to them in the text. But there is clearly much more to be said on this point than I have said here; I am grateful to Callan for his comments regarding it.

9. Corporal punishment is here used for illustrative purposes only. I recognize that its moral (il)legitimacy is a matter on which not all are agreed. I hope, despite the controversiality of the example, that the point made in the text is clear: that for a putative justification to succeed, certain conditions must be satisfied, and that that satisfaction and success depend upon traditional or "conservative" conceptions of, and theories concerning, truth and rational justification.

10. A much more detailed discussion of this point may be found in Siegel (1989b).

11. For general discussion, see Beyer and Liston (1992) and Weinstein (1993). Beyer and Liston offer what appear to me to be compelling criticisms of Giroux, as does Misgeld (1992)—but see Giroux's rather remarkable reply (1992). (I am grateful to Siebren Meidema for supplying me with the latter two references.) For critical discussion of Weinstein (1993), see the previous chapter.

12. I have at this point deleted several paragraphs from the originally published version of this chapter. Those paragraphs are presented, and developed further, in Chapter 12. Naturally, I refer the reader who is doubtful of the claim just made to the discussion of it in that chapter.

13. Feyerabend's liberal, Millian defense of relativism advocates something like this view of what is involved in respecting alternative epistemologies. For critical discussion see Siegel (1989b).

14. Although the lesson concerning this limitation upon our ability to judge is not as simple or straightforward as it is sometimes taken to be. See Siegel (1987, Chapter 2; 1995b) for discussion.

15. I have made it at greater length in the previous chapter. See also the excellent discussions in Misgeld (1992, esp. pp. 137–8) and Yates (1992, esp. pp. 443–5, 448).

16. Of course it is possible that the *misuse* of that epistemology has exercised undue hegemonic control, and that "Modernist" moral/social/political theorists, under the sway of Modernist epistemology, have tried to justify unjustifiable social/political/educational practices—practices which in fact marginalize(d), silence(d), and oppress(ed) innocent victims. Indeed, it is absolutely clear, as Weinstein (1993) shows, that this has indeed occurred and continues to occur; one of the most important contributions made by Postmodernist writers has

211

been to make such oppression visible. But, as I argued in Chapter 9, this criticism in the end targets deficient Modernist *practice*—not deficient (epistemic) *principle*.

17. An earlier version of this Chapter was presented at an annual meeting of the Philosophy of Education Society of Great Britain in 1994; I am grateful to the audience on that ocasion, especially Eamonn Callan, for helpful criticism. I would also like to thank Nicholas Burbules, Edward Erwin, Susan Haack, Wilna Meijer, Bruce B. Suttle, and Mark Weinstein for their excellent critical comments on an earlier version.

CHAPTER ELEVEN

1. This point is well made in Burbules (1993a).
2. All citations to Stone in this chapter are to her (1995).
3. For further discussion see Siegel (1987).
4. As argued in Chapters 9, 10 and 12.
5. This point is developed further in Chapter 12.
6. All citations to Arcilla in this chapter are to his (1995).
7. The relation between language and meaning, on the one hand, and knowledge, on the other, is less clear than Arcilla acknowledges. Does "language and meaning are provisional" entail "knowledge is provisional and indefinite"? Not obviously. It is not even clear what the latter claim comes to—does it assert fallibilism, or skepticism? I regret that I can't pursue this point systematically below, although it is addressed briefly in what follows.
8. I am grateful to Wendy Kohli for helpful suggestions and advice.

CHAPTER TWELVE

1. For a general discussion of the importance of inclusion in education, see Burbules (1993a). I have learned much from Burbules' insightful discussions, both in print and in a variety of less formal media.

    While I cite several advocates of inclusion below, I should acknowledge the fact that there are other important advocates, e.g. Habermas and Benhabib, whose discussions deserve explicit treatment but to which constraints of space forbid attention here.

2. By way of illustration of the general thesis concerning the value of inclusion, Weinstein argues compellingly that it is the exclusion of "women's perspectives" "that marks patriarchal frames as inadequate" (1993, p. 34). For a systematic evaluation of Weinstein's forceful analysis, see Chapter 9 above. For Weinstein's rejoinder, which is responded to in part in that chapter, see Weinstein (1994). I am indebted to Weinstein for teaching me much of what little I know about Postmodernist critiques of "Modernist" philosophy of education.

3. I should note that Lyotard also uses "terror" in this way—see, e.g., his selection in Baynes, Bohman, and McCarthy (1987), pp. 89–90; and that Giroux (1988,

pp. 14 ff.) acknowledges difficulties with this Lyotardian view of "theoretical terrorism" and with postmodernism more generally. For critical discussion of the cited passage, see Chapter 10 above.

4. I should point out that while in some passages (like this one) Harding criticizes science's pretense to universality and urges its abandonment, in other passages she harshly criticizes scientific institutions for failing to live up to their proclaimed commitment to the ideal of universality, according to which "the social identity of its members is irrelevant to achievement" ([1991], p. 32), thus embracing that very ideal. This suggests that Harding is not opposing universality as such, but rather a "false universality" in which the particular and peculiar experience of dominant groups is represented as if it were universal, when in fact it fails to capture the experience of subjugated groups. I am grateful here to the excellent suggestion of Barbara LeClerc.

5. Harding emphasizes the importance of inclusion throughout her work, e.g. Harding [1991], p. 170; Harding [1989], p. 196.

6. For example, a generalization concerning a particular group, such as "philosophers regard philosophical argumentation as if it were a form of armed combat, in which the arms are words and the purpose of the discourse is to defeat the opponent" (for discussion see Moulton [1983]), may be plausible when the philosophers under consideration are in key respects alike (e.g., white, middle-class males, trained in "prestigious" North American analytically-oriented graduate departments), but less plausible when other philosophers (Feminist, African, Native American, Asian, Indian, those trained in Continental and other traditions, etc.) are included. More broadly, traditional accounts of human nature which emphasize rationality, and conceive of rationality as something wholly distinct from emotion, might be thought (and are thought by many feminist writers) to exclude women from the broad class of humans.

7. The *locus classicus* here is of course Lyotard (1984).

8. I hasten to point out that Burbules takes himself here to be describing a central theme of Postmodernism, but not wholeheartedly endorsing it. As his discussion makes clear, he is sympathetic towards some aspects of Postmodernism, but not all.

9. "Philosophy cannot take refuge in reduced ambitions. It is after eternal and nonlocal truth, even though we know that is not what we are going to get" (Nagel [1986], p. 10).

10. Except, in some contexts, on the basis of lack of relevant qualifications or expertise. This exception is discussed below.

11. For criticism of the latter claim, especially with respect to Derrida, see Chapter 11. For general discussion of the epistemological presuppositions and ramifications of Postmodernism, radical politics and pedagogy, and inclusion, and for arguments against the view that these moral matters should be understood in epistemic terms, see Chapters 9 and 10, in which I have argued that one needs

to distinguish moral from epistemic virtue in order to argue the case for the moral desirability of inclusion.

12. Treating people with respect does not of course entail that we regard all beliefs or viewpoints as equally good. Treating a person with respect is compatible with regarding her views as unjustified or false.

13. There is also sometimes a further benefit which accrues to inclusion: as just noted, it is a mistake to attribute to particular people properties they do not in fact have, and striving for inclusion can sometimes help to avoid this mistake. This virtue is discussed further below.

14. I am grateful here to Nick Burbules, whose penetrating criticism made me see the need to clarify what I mean by "epistemic virtue." Roy Mash has pointed out that the formulation in the text, which denies a *necessary* connection between inclusion and epistemic worthiness, allows for a *contingent* one. I agree that there may be such a contingent connection, and explore its character below. Thanks to Mash for his insightful criticism.

15. This is not to say that modern science is unproblematically wonderful—far from it. Recent scholarship has amply demonstrated the many ways in which contemporary theory and research suffers from biases, blindspots, and much else. These genuine defects do not, however, tarnish the positive epistemic credentials which our best theories enjoy.

16. Although I agree with Longino (cited above) that inclusion can have a salutary *causal* effect in helping to avoid idiosyncrasy and in that way increasing the chances of attaining objectivity in our theoretical endeavors, and I agree that in *this* sense inclusion can be seen as an epistemic virtue. A related point is made by Searle (1993, p. 46).

17. Distinguish between (1) rules governing the *conduct* of inquiry, and (2) criteria for evaluating the *products* of inquiry. I have been arguing that inclusion may be an epistemic or methodological virtue in the first sense, but not the second. For the distinction, see Haack (1993), pp. 203–5.

18. In this respect the Kohlberg/Gilligan case is instructive. The fact of the matter, apparently, is that it took Gilligan to point out that Kohlberg's theory rested on a nonrepresentative sample, and to explore the theoretical implications of that bias. But the importance of fair sampling was (or should have been) well understood by Kohlberg and his male (and female) associates. How likely it is that the inclusion of "other" voices and perspectives will be causally efficacious in exposing bias and increasing objectivity is an open question; I am inclined to think, with Longino, Harding, Searle, and others, that in many cases the likelihood is reasonably high. I have been endeavoring to challenge only the idea that such inclusion will inevitably or necessarily so result. Thanks to Denis Phillips for suggesting that I consider this case.

19. For further discussion, see Chapters 9 and 10.

20. See the selection from Lyotard (1984) reprinted in Baynes, Bohman, and

McCarthy (1987), pp. 73–94, and also the editors' introduction to that selection. This difficulty is related to that of attempting to reject all metanarratives; on this point see Chapters 9 and 10 above, and Fraser and Nicholson (1989, p. 289).

21. In particular, it is unclear why we should accept Rorty's claim that the impossibility of objectivity or universality follows from or is entailed by contingency—especially in light of the fact that the very notion of entailment on which this argument depends is itself only understandable in universalistic terms, i.e. such that the premises entail the conclusion, whoever is considering the argument. (Of course Rorty wants sometimes to reject the very idea that he is *arguing* (Rorty [1989a], p. 44), despite the fact that his writing is full of arguments, and would be unintelligible without the assumption that he is in fact engaging in argumentation.) The argument—language, self and community are contingent; therefore, universality is impossible or unachievable—is simply a non sequitur.

    Two powerful criticisms of Rorty are Sosa's (1987) and Rosenberg's hilarious and hard-hitting (1993).

22. Rorty also embraces "solidarity" in quite another sense: that which is *public*, and contrasts with the private and the ideal of self-creation. (Of course he embraces self-creation as well as this sort of solidarity, so the public/private dichotomy, unlike the solidarity/objectivity dichotomy, is in Rorty's hands not mutually exclusive; one can embrace both public solidarity and private self-creation, even though the two are "forever incommensurable.") (1989a, p. xv) I note this only to make clear that there are (at least) two notions of "solidarity" in play in Rorty's discussion; the two are not always distinguished.

23. Of course Rorty is not alone here. In fact, in the introduction to their (1987), Baynes, Bohman, and McCarthy characterize many recent challenges to philosophy in terms of critics' rejection of the presumed universality of philosophy in favor of a view of philosophy (and key notions such as truth, reason, the person, human nature, etc.) as necessarily contingent, conventional, plural, local, and particular. Thus these critics too depend upon the legitimacy of the dichotomy I want here to call into question.

    Harding's "strong objectivity" (1991, Chapter 6) is an interesting attempt to reconcile "objectivity" and "situatedness" which is in some (but not all) ways quite like my attempt to reconcile universality and particularity. I regret that lack of space prevents me from attending to her discussion in more detail.

24. The following five paragraphs are taken, with changes and additions, from the originally published version of Chapter 10. They have been removed from Chapter 10 in order to eliminate unnecessary redundancies across the chapters of this volume.

25. For further discussion concerning the implications of the impossibility of achieving a God's-eye point of view, see Siegel (1987), Chapter 2; Rosenberg (1993), p. 203.

215

26. As Denis Phillips reminds me, some might deny these claims, and respond that (for example) while space curves within *our* scheme, it does not in schemes which do not ascribe that property to space. This move I think simply turns the issue on the table into that concerning the viability of epistemological (or metaphysical) relativism; on that question see Siegel (1987).

27. As indicated earlier, I here use "scheme-independent" not in the sense of being not embedded in any scheme, but rather in the sense of having legitimacy and point beyond the bounds of the scheme in which it is embedded.

28. It is worth pointing out that universalistic "Enlightenment" ideals, e.g. of the dignity of human reason and the commitment to decide matters on the basis of reasons, themselves can and should be understood in this way. These ideals arose and gained currency in particular historical/cultural circumstances (in ancient Greece, and in the "Age of Enlightenment" in Europe), but that fact in no way undercuts whatever universal validity they enjoy. Below I suggest that some such universal validity is necessary. For further general discussion, see Chapters 9–11 above.

29. The distinction is actually medieval in origin, and played an important role in medieval philosophy.

30. I hasten to note that I do not myself advocate the idea that truth should be understood in terms of ideal rational acceptability; I favor a conception, advocated by an earlier Putnam, of truth as "radically nonepistemic" and as unconnected to considerations of rational acceptability. For further discussion see Chapter 1 above.

31. I have been arguing only that the particular *can* be universal as well; that the two are not mutually exclusive. A stronger thesis, that universality is *required* for the justification of particular claims, is one that I endorse, although I haven't systematically defended it here. That strong thesis is defended by Habermas and Apel, and criticized by MacIntyre, in their selections in Baynes, Bohman, and McCarthy (1987). MacIntyre argues that rationality and rational justification are always relative to historical and contextual factors: in judging the rational adequacy of claims, "there are no general timeless standards" ([1987], p. 417);

> if some particular . . . scheme has successfully transcended the limitations of its predecessors and in so doing provided the best means available for understanding those predecessors to date *and* has then confronted successive challenges from a number of rival points of view, but in each case has been able to modify itself in the ways required to incorporate the strengths of those points of view while avoiding their weaknesses and limitations *and* has provided the best explanation so far of those weaknesses and limitations, then we have the best possible reason to have confidence that future challenges will also be met successfully, that the principles that define the core of a . . . scheme are enduring principles. (p. 419, emphases in original)

This view of rational justification is historicist and contextualist in the sense that the justification of a scheme depends on the comparative merits of the scheme vis-a-vis those of its historical rivals, but MacIntyre seems not to notice that this historicist/contextualist standard is *itself* a "general timeless," i.e. acontextual/ahistorical, standard of the sort he claims to eschew. The same can be said of his acontextual/ahistorical *defense* of that standard.

32. Of course not all universal claims are cogent; I am not suggesting that false, unjustified, or otherwise problematic claims are beyond reproach simply because they are universal. Fallibilism applies to these claims are well as to their particularistic cousins. My point, rather, is that their universality is not *itself* grounds for regarding them as defective.

33. To refer back to Rorty one last time, I should note Rosenberg's claim—which I endorse—that Rorty *needs* universality in order to make sense of his version of liberalism, however much he seeks to reject it:

> A bourgeois liberal democracy is positively interested in educating and informing its citizens, and a bourgeois liberal democracy is positively interested in being reasonable. That is, it wants its [universalistic] stories about what it's okay to *do* to people to hang together with its [universalistic] stories about what it's responsible to *believe* about people, about what people *are*. (Rosenberg [1993], pp. 212–213, emphases in original)

34. This is clearly suggested, for example, by McLaren (1994); among feminist writers, in addition to those cited below, see Dalmiya and Alcoff's (1993) contention that traditional epistemic standards are complicit in the practice of "epistemic discrimination" against women, and Code's (1991, 1993) similar claim.

35. I should note that the *way* in which "reason" is "male" differs significantly for these theorists. For general discussion, see (among many other sources) the essays in Alcoff and Potter (1993) and Antony and Witt (1993). Thanks once again to Barbara LeClerc for helpful suggestions concerning this point.

36. It should be noted that, on MacKinnon's view, "rationality" is synomymous with "objectivity"; she does not distinguish between the two, but rather rejects it/them both (Rapaport [1993], p. 129). MacKinnon understands objectivity as "the nonsituated, distanced standpoint" (1987, p. 50); as I hope is clear, this is not the understanding of it I am utilizing here, since situatedness does not preclude (on my understanding of it) objectivity. For what I hope is a more nuanced and defensible understanding of the concepts of rationality and objectivity, and their interrelationship, see Neiman and Siegel (1993).

37. Putnam (1982), p. 20. For more general discussion of the self-defeating character of the rejection of normative evaluation, see Siegel (1987) and (1995a).

38. For discussion of the general case, see Siegel (1987). Antony (1993, esp. pp. 190, 208–210) argues determinedly that radical feminists need to recognize and utilize a traditional conception of truth and traditional ideals of objectivity and

impartiality, and to recognize (more or less) traditional standards of philosophical and empirical argumentative quality, if they are to achieve the aims either of feminism in particular or of political radicalism in general.

39. It should also be pointed out that MacKinnon routinely appeals in her work to the very standards she seems to want to reject.

40. Israel Scheffler, throughout his work, has emphasized the importance to education (and philosophy) of the rational critique and improvement of standards, including standards of rationality and rational critique themselves. See, e.g., Scheffler (1973), pp. 79–80, 87.

41. Nor is it wise, as Nussbaum points out (1994, pp. 60–1), to reject a standard on grounds of its misuse. Concerning those who "have used the claim of objectivity to protect their biased judgments from rational scrutiny," Nussbaum writes: "More than a little perversely, some feminists have blamed this behavior on the norm of objectivity itself, rather than on its abusers."

42. I should also point out that the problem cannot be finessed by construing the relevant standards as "contextual" or "communicative," as Nicholas Burbules (1991, 1991a, 1995) suggests. As I argued in Chapter 7, this won't work: standards must have *epistemic* significance to be worthy of the name; without such probative force, the problem of justifying the standard of inclusion remains.

43. At least they often can. In cases in which participants cannot uncontroversially do this, the wise course is clearly to err on the side of inclusion. Thanks again to Roy Mash for his good comments here.

44. This point, concerning the extent of our abilities to acquire expertise and so escape our "epistemic dependence" on experts, is a surprisingly tricky and subtle one. For an introductory discussion and a brief guide to the relevant epistemological literature, see Siegel (1988c). It is a topic much discussed in current epistemology and, increasingly, philosophy of education; see, e.g., Goldman (1995), Hare (1995), and Norris (1995).

45. Roy Mash raises two general problems my discussion raises which I have not addressed. First, what should be said when the moral obligation to include conflicts with the epistemic obligation to seek truth? Second, shouldn't something be said concerning the sensitivity of the obligation to include to the *venue* of conversations, since (to use his example) "Joe Six-Pack" obviously has a rightful place in a conversation concerning race relations that takes place around the kitchen table, but equally obviously doesn't have a rightful place in a conversation on that topic that takes place among putative experts in a public forum or a scholarly journal? Both of these problems deserve extended discussion; I regret that I cannot pursue them here. Once again, I am grateful to Mash for his thought-provoking comments.

46. See, e.g., McLaren (1994). I of course deny the suggestion that analytic epistemologists inevitably represent or advance politically regressive interests; I recommend Antony's (1993) argument to the contrary. (With one proviso: I think

that Antony's defense slides between a defense of analytic philosophy in general, and of naturalized epistemology in particular. Her argument in my view succeeds in defending the former, but fails to single out the latter as the only defensible "analytic" position.)

47. This chapter was presented as the Presidential Address of the Philosophy of Education Society, at the Society's annual meeting in San Francisco, April 2, 1995. I am grateful to my commentators on that occasion, Sharon Bailin and Kathryn Pauly Morgan, to the members of the audience who heard and discussed it then, and to Don Arnstine, Nick Burbules, Michael Gilbert, Wendy Kohli, Barbara LeClerc, Roy Mash, Al Neiman, Denis Phillips, Hilary Putnam, Israel Scheffler, Kenneth Strike, Bruce B. Suttle, Audrey Thompson, and Mark Weinstein, for penetrating criticism, excellent suggestions, and supportive comments. Needless to say, they would not all endorse the finished product.

EPILOGUE

1. In the standard Kantian sense of establishing that something—in this case, a concern for the justification of inclusion in particular, and for matters of epistemic justification in general—is *necessary*, in order for something else—in this case, the justified serious valuing of inclusion—to be *possible*.

2. From here on I will limit my discussion to matters concerning inclusion. I am assuming that the points made will apply mutatis mutandis to broader but parallel questions concerning matters of social justice and moral appropriateness.

BIBLIOGRAPHY

Alcoff, Linda, and Elizabeth Potter, eds. (1993): *Feminist Epistemologies*, New York: Routledge.

Alston, William P. (1989): *Epistemic Justification: Essays in the Theory of Knowledge*, Ithaca, NY: Cornell University Press.

Antony, Louise M. (1993): "Quine as Feminist: The Radical Import of Naturalized Epistemology," in Antony and Witt (1993), pp. 185–225.

Antony, Louise M., and Charlotte Witt. (1993): *A Mind of One's Own: Feminist Essays on Reason and Objectivity*, Boulder: Westview Press.

Arcilla, René Vincente. (1995): "For the Stranger in My Home: Self-Knowledge, Cultural Recognition, and Philosophy of Education," in Kohli (1995), pp. 159–172.

Audi, Robert. (1988): *Belief, Justification, and Knowledge*, Belmont, CA: Wadsworth Publishing Company.

Bailin, S. (1988): "Putting Our Heads Together: Reason, Innovation and Critical Thinking," in James M. Giarelli, ed., *Philosophy of Education 1988: Proceedings of the Forty-Fourth Annual Meeting of the Philosophy of Education Society*, pp. 403–406.

———. (1992): "Culture, Democracy, and the University," *Interchange*, vol. 23, pp. 63–69.

Bar On, Bat-Ami. (1993): "Marginality and Epistemic Privilege," in Alcoff and Potter (1993), pp. 83–100.

Bartley, W.W. III. (1984): *The Retreat to Commitment*, Second edition, revised and enlarged, La Salle: Open Court Publishing Company.

———. (1987): "A Refutation of the Alleged Refutation of Comprehensively Critical Rationalism," in Radnitzky and Bartley (1987), pp. 313–341.

Baynes, Kenneth, James Bohman, and Thomas McCarthy, eds. (1987): *After Philosophy: End or Transformation?*, Cambridge: MIT Press.

Beyer, Landon E., and Daniel P. Liston. (1992): "Discourse or Moral Action? A Critique of Postmodernism." *Educational Theory*, vol. 42, #4, pp. 371–393.

Biro, John, and Harvey Siegel. (1992): "Normativity, Argumentation, and an Epistemic Theory of Fallacies," in Frans H. van Eemeren, et. al, eds., *Argumentation Illuminated: Selected Papers from the 1990 International Conference on Argumentation*, Dordrecht: Foris, pp. 85–103.

Blair, J. Anthony, and Ralph H. Johnson. (1987): "Argumentation as Dialectical," *Argumentation*, vol. 1, #1, pp. 41–56.

Burbules, Nicholas C. (1991): "The Virtues of Reasonableness," in Margret Buchmann and Robert E. Floden, eds., *Philosophy of Education 1991: Proceedings of the Forty-Seventh Annual Meeting of the Philosophy of Education Society*, pp. 215–224.

———. (1991a): "Rationality and Reasonableness: A Discussion of Harvey Siegel's *Relativism Refuted* and *Educating Reason*," *Educational Theory*, vol. 41, #2, pp. 235–252.

———. (1993): "Rethinking Rationality: On Learning to Be Reasonable," in Audrey Thompson, ed., *Philosophy of Education 1993: Proceedings of the Forty-Ninth Annual Meeting of the Philosophy of Education Society*, pp. 340–349.

———. (1993a): *Dialogue in Teaching: Theory and Practice*, New York: Teachers College Press.

———. (1995): "Reasonable Doubt: Toward a Postmodern Defense of Reason as an Educational Aim," in Kohli (1995), pp. 82–102.

Burbules, Nicholas C., and Suzanne Rice. (1991): "Dialogue Across Differences: Continuing the Conversation," *Harvard Educational Review*, vol. 61, #4, pp. 393–416.

Cherniak, Christopher. (1986): *Minimal Rationality*, Cambridge: MIT Press.

Code, Lorraine. (1991): *What Can She Know? Feminist Theory and the Construction of Knowledge*, Ithaca: Cornell University Press.

———. (1993): "Taking Subjectivity into Account," in Alcoff and Potter (1993), pp. 15–48.

222

Cohen, Avner, and Marcelo Dascal, eds. (1989): *The Institution of Philosophy: A Discipline in Crisis?*, La Salle, Illinois: Open Court.

Dalmiya, Vrinda, and Linda Alcoff. (1993): "Are 'Old Wives' Tales' Justified?," in Alcoff and Potter (1993), pp. 217–244.

Dostoyevsky, Fyodor. (1958): *The Brothers Karamazov*, tr. David Magarshack, Harmondsworth: Penguin Books, 1958. The novel was originally published in 1880.

Dummett, Michael. (1980): *Truth and Other Enigmas*, Cambridge, Massachusetts: Harvard University Press.

Ennis, Robert H. (1989): "Critical Thinking and Subject Specificity: Clarification and Needed Research," *Educational Researcher*, vol. 18, #3, pp. 4–10.

Feldman, Richard. (1993): *Reason and Argument*, Englewood Cliffs, New Jersey: Prentice Hall.

Feuer, Lewis S., ed. (1959): *Marx and Engels: Basic Writings on Politics and Philosophy*, New York: Anchor Books.

Finocchiaro, Maurice. (1981): "Fallacies and the Evaluation of Reasoning," *American Philosophical Quarterly*, vol. 18, pp. 13–22.

Firth, Roderick. (1981): "Epistemic Merit, Intrinsic and Instrumental," *Proceedings and Addresses of the American Philosophical Association*, vol. 55, #1, September 1981, pp. 5–23.

Fraser, Nancy, and Linda Nicholson. (1989): "Social Criticism Without Philosophy: An Encounter Between Feminism and Postmodernism," in Cohen and Dascal (1989), pp. 283–302.

Freemantle, Anne. (1956): "Introduction" to *The Grand Inquisitor*, New York: Frederick Ungar Publishing Co.

Giarelli, James M. (1990): "Philosophy, Education and Public Practice," in David P. Ericson, ed., *Philosophy of Education 1990: Proceedings of the Forty-Sixth Annual Meeting of the Philosophy of Education Society*, Normal, IL, Philosophy of Education Society, pp. 34–44.

Giarelli, James M., and J. J. Chambliss. (1991): "The Foundations of Professionalism: Fifty Years of the Philosophy of Education Society in Retrospect," *Educational Theory*, vol. 41, #3, pp. 265–274.

Giroux, Henry. (1988): "Postmodernism and the Discourse of Educational Criticism," *Journal of Education*, vol. 170, #3, pp. 5–30.

———. (1992): "The Habermasian Headache: A Response to Dieter Misgeld," *Phenomenology + Pedagogy*, vol. 10, pp. 143–149.

Goldman, Alan H. (1988): *Empirical Knowledge*, Berkeley: University of California Press.

Goldman, Alvin I. (1995): "Education and Social Epistemology," in Alven M. Neiman, ed., *Philosophy of Education 1995*. Champaign, IL: Philosophy of Education Society, pp. 68–79.

Goodman, Nelson. (1952): "Sense and Certainty," *Philosophical Review*, vol. 61, pp. 160–167. Reprinted in Goodman, *Problems and Projects*, New York: Bobbs-Merrill, 1972, pp. 60–68.

223

Govier, Trudy. (1987): *Problems in Argument Analysis and Evaluation*, Dordrecht: Foris Publications.

Green, Thomas F. (1971): *The Activities of Teaching*, New York: McGraw-Hill.

Haack, Susan. (1993): *Evidence and Inquiry: Towards Reconstruction in Epistemology*, Oxford: Blackwell Publishers.

———. (1993a): "Epistemological Reflections of an Old Feminist," *Reason Papers*, vol. 18, Fall 1993, pp. 31–43.

Harding, Sandra. (1989): "Feminist Justificatory Strategies," in Ann Garry and Marilyn Pearsall, eds., *Women, Knowledge, and Reality: Explorations in Feminist Philosophy*, Boston: Unwin Hyman, pp. 189–201.

———. (1991): *Whose Science? Whose Knowledge?: Thinking from Women's Lives*, Ithaca: Cornell University Press.

Harding, Sandra, and Merrill B. Hintikka, eds., (1983): *Discovering Reality: Feminist Perspectives on Epistemology, Metaphysics, Methodology, and Philosophy of Science*, Dordrecht: D. Reidel.

Hare, William. (1995): "Teaching and the Socratic Virtues," Memorial University (in press).

Harman, Gilbert. (1986): *Change in View*, Cambridge: MIT Press.

Haslanger, Sally. (1993): "On Being Objective and Being Objectified," in Antony and Witt (1993), pp. 85–125.

Kekes, John. (1989): "Rationality and Logic," in Shlomo Biderman and Ben-Ami Scharfstein, eds., *Rationality in Question: On Eastern and Western Views of Rationality*, Leiden: E. J. Brill, pp. 3–17.

Kim, Jaegwon. (1988): "What Is 'Naturalized Epistemology'?," in James E. Tomberlin, ed., *Philosophical Perspectives, 2: Epistemology, 1988*, Atascadero, California: Ridgeview Publishing Company, pp. 381–405.

Kitcher, Philip. (1983): *The Nature of Mathematical Knowledge*, New York: Oxford University Press.

Koertge, Noretta. (1981): "Methodology, Ideology and Feminist Critiques of Science," in Peter D. Asquith and Ronald N. Giere, eds., *PSA 1980: Proceedings of the 1980 Biennial Meeting of the Philosophy of Science Association, Volume Two*, East Lansing, MI: Philosophy of Science Association, pp. 346–359.

Kohli, Wendy. (1993): "A Feminist Rethinking of Reasonableness: An Experiment in Translation," in Audrey Thompson, ed., *Philosophy of Education 1993: Proceedings of the Forty-Ninth Annual Meeting of the Philosophy of Education Society*, pp. 350–354.

———, ed. (1995): *Critical Conversations in Philosophy of Education*, New York: Routledge.

Kozol, Jonathan. (1991): *Savage Inequalities: Children in America's Schools*, New York: Crown Publishers.

Kripke, Saul. (1972): "Naming and Necessity," in Donald Davidson and Gilbert Harman (eds.), *Semantics of Natural Language*, second edition, Dordrecht: D. Reidel, pp. 253–355 and 763–769.

Lipman, Matthew. (1988): *Philosophy Goes To School*, Philadelphia: Temple University Press.

Longino, Helen. (1990): *Science as Social Knowledge: Values and Objectivity in Scientific Inquiry*, Princeton: Princeton University Press.

Lyotard, Jean-Francois. (1984): *The Postmodern Condition: A Report on Knowledge*, Minneapolis: University of Minnesota Press. Translated by Geoff Bennington and Brian Massumi from Lyotard, *La Condition Postmoderne: Rapport sur le Savoir*, Paris: Editions de Minuit, 1982.

MacIntyre, Alasdair. (1987): "The Relationship of Philosophy to History: Postscript to the Second Edition of *After Virtue*," in Baynes, Bohman, and McCarthy (1987), pp. 412–422.

MacKinnon, Catharine. (1987): *Feminism Unmodified: Discourses on Life and Law*, Cambridge: Harvard University Press.

Martin, Jane Roland. (1982): "Excluding Women from the Educational Realm," *Harvard Educational Review*, vol. 52, May 1982, pp. 133–148.

McCarthy, Thomas. (1988): "Scientific Rationality and the 'Strong Program' in the Sociology of Knowledge," in E. McMullin, ed., *Construction and Constraint: The Shaping of Scientific Rationality*, Notre Dame, Indiana: University of Notre Dame Press, pp. 75–95.

McGrew, Timothy J. (1995): *The Foundations of Knowledge*, Lanham, MD: Littlefield Adams Books.

McLaren, Peter L. (1994): "Foreward: Critical Thinking as a Political Project," in Kerry S. Walters, ed., *Re–Thinking Reason: New Perspectives in Critical Thinking*, Albany: State University of New York Press, pp. ix-xv.

McPeck, John. (1981): *Critical Thinking and Education*, New York: St. Martin's.

Misgeld, Dieter. (1992): "Pedagogy and Politics: Some Critical Reflections on the Postmodern Turn in Critical Pedagogy," *Phenomenology + Pedagogy*, vol. 10, pp. 125–142.

Missimer, Connie. (1988): "Why Two Heads Are Better Than One: Philosophical and Pedagogical Implications of a Social View of Critical Thinking," in James M. Giarelli, ed., *Philosophy of Education 1988: Proceedings of the Forty-Fourth Annual Meeting of the Philosophy of Education Society*, pp. 388–402.

———. (1990) "Perhaps By Skill Alone," *Informal Logic*, vol. 12, #3, pp. 145–153.

———. (1995): "Where's the Evidence?," *Inquiry: Critical Thinking Across the Disciplines*, vol. 14, #4, Summer 1995, pp. 1–18.

Moser, Paul K. (1985): *Empirical Justification*, Dordrecht: D. Reidel.

———, ed. (1986): *Empirical Knowledge: Readings in Contemporary Epistemology*, Totowa, NJ: Rowman & Littlefield.

Moshman, David. (1990): "Rationality As a Goal of Education," *Educational Psychology Review*, vol. 2, #4, pp. 335–364.

Moulton, Janice. (1983): "A Paradigm of Philosophy: The Adversary Method," in Harding and Hintikka (1983), pp. 149–164.

Nagel, Thomas. (1986): *The View From Nowhere*, Oxford: Oxford University Press.

Neiman, Alven, and Harvey Siegel. (1993): "Objectivity and Rationality in Epistemology and Education: Scheffler's Middle Road," *Synthese*, vol. 94, #1, pp. 55–83.

Norris, Stephen P. (1995): "Learning to Live with Scientific Expertise: Towards a Theory of Intellectual Communalism for Guiding Science Teaching," *Science Education*, vol. 79, #2, pp. 201–17.

Nussbaum, Martha. (1994): "Feminists and Philosophy," *The New York Review of Books*, vol. 41, #17, October 20, 1994, pp. 59–63.

O'Hear, Anthony. (1980): *Karl Popper*, London: Routledge & Kegan Paul.

Paul, Richard. (1982): "Critical Thinking in the "Strong" Sense: A Focus on Self-Deception, World Views, and a Dialectical Mode of Analysis," *Informal Logic Newsletter*, vol. 4, #2, pp. 2–7.

Peterson, Michael L. (1983): "Recent Work on the Problem of Evil," *American Philosophical Quarterly*, vol. 20, #4, October 1983, pp. 321–339.

Pike, Nelson, ed., (1964): *God and Evil*, Englewood Cliffs, New Jersey: Prentice-Hall.

Popper, Karl. (1962): *The Open Society and Its Enemies*, Volume 2, Princeton: Princeton University Press.

———. (1970): "Normal Science and Its Dangers," in I. Lakatos and A. Musgrave, eds., *Criticism and the Growth of Knowledge*, Cambridge: Cambridge University Press, pp. 51–8.

Post, John F. (1987): "The Possible Liar," in Radnitzky and Bartley (1987), pp. 217–220.

Pratte, Richard. (1990): "Philosophically Useful Kibitzing," in David P. Ericson, ed., *Philosophy of Education 1990: Proceedings of the Forty-Sixth Annual Meeting of the Philosophy of Education Society*, Normal, IL, Philosophy of Education Society, pp. 45–50.

Putnam, Hilary. (1981): *Reason, Truth and History*, Cambridge: Cambridge University Press.

———. (1982): "Why Reason Can't Be Naturalized," *Synthese*, vol. 52, #1, pp. 3–23.

Radnitzky, Gerard. (1987): "In Defense of Self-Applicable Critical Rationalism," in Radnitzky and Bartley (1987), pp. 279–312.

Radnitzky, Gerard and W. W. Bartley III, eds. (1987): *Evolutionary Epistemology, Rationality, and the Sociology of Knowledge*, La Salle, IL: Open Court.

Rapaport, Elizabeth. (1993): "Generalizing Gender: Reason and Essence in the Legal Thought of Catharine MacKinnon," in Antony and Witt (1993), pp. 127–143.

Rescher, Nicholas. (1988): *Rationality: A Philosophical Inquiry into the Nature and the Rationale of Reason*, Oxford: Clarendon Press of Oxford University Press.

Robertson, Emily. (1991): "Reason and Education," in Margret Buchmann and Robert E. Floden, eds., *Philosophy of Education 1991: Proceedings of the Forty-Seventh Annual Meeting of the Philosophy of Education Society*, pp. 168–180.

———. (1995): "Reconceiving Reason," in Kohli (1995), pp. 116–126.

Rorty, Richard. (1989): "Solidarity or Objectivity?," in Michael Krausz, ed., *Relativism: Interpretation and Confrontation*, Notre Dame: University of Notre Dame Press, pp. 35–50.

226

———. (1989a): *Contingency, Irony, and Solidarity*, Cambridge: Cambridge University Press.

Rosenberg, Jay F. (1993): "Raiders of the Lost Distinction: Richard Rorty and the Search for the Last Dichotomy," *Philosophy and Phenomenological Research*, vol. 53, #1, pp. 195–214.

Ross, Stephen D. (1969): *Literature and Philosophy: An Analysis of the Philosophical Novel*, New York: Appleton-Century-Crofts.

Russell, Bertrand. (1957): *Why I Am Not a Christian and Other Essays*, London: George Allen & Unwin Ltd.

Satris, Steven. (1986): "Student Relativism," *Teaching Philosophy*, vol. 9, #3, pp. 193–205.

Scheffler, Israel. (1960): *The Language of Education*, Springfield, Illinois: Charles C. Thomas.

———. (1965): *Conditions of Knowledge*, Glenview, Illinois: Scott, Foresman and Company.

———. (1973): *Reason and Teaching*, London: Routledge & Kegan Paul.

———. (1985): *Of Human Potential*, London: Routledge & Kegan Paul.

———. (1995): *Teachers of My Youth: An American Jewish Experience*, Dordrecht: Kluwer.

Searle, John R. (1993): "Is There a Crisis in American Higher Education?," *Bulletin of the American Academy of Arts and Sciences*, vol. 46, #4, pp. 24–47.

Shapere, Dudley. (1984): *Reason and the Search for Knowledge: Investigations in the Philosophy of Science*, Dordrecht: D. Reidel.

Siegel, Harvey. (1980): "Justification, Discovery and the Naturalizing of Epistemology," *Philosophy of Science*, vol. 47, #2, pp. 297–321.

———. (1983): "Genderized Cognitive Perspectives and the Redefinition of Philosophy of Education," *Teachers College Record*, vol. 85, #1, Fall 1983, pp. 100–119.

———. (1983a): "Brown on Epistemology and the New Philosophy of Science," *Synthese*, vol. 56, #1, pp. 61–89.

———. (1983b): "Truth, Problem Solving and the Rationality of Science," *Studies in History and Philosophy of Science*, vol. 14, #2, pp. 89–112.

———. (1984): "Empirical Psychology, Naturalized Epistemology, and First Philosophy," *Philosophy of Science*, vol. 51, #4, pp. 667–676.

———. (1987): *Relativism Refuted: A Critique of Contemporary Epistemological Relativism*, Dordrecht: D. Reidel Publishing Company (Synthese Library, volume #189).

———. (1988): *Educating Reason: Rationality, Critical Thinking, and Education*, New York and London: Routledge (Philosophy of Education Research Library).

———. (1988a): "Epistemology and Philosophy for Children," *Analytic Teaching*, vol. 8, #2, pp. 32–42.

———. (1988b): "Rationality and Ideology Revisited (Reply to Cato and Selman)," *Educational Theory*, vol. 38, #2, pp. 267–274.

———. (1988c): "Rationality and Epistemic Dependence," *Educational Philosophy and Theory*, vol. 20, #1, pp. 1–6.

———. (1989): "The Role of Reasons in (Science) Education," in W. Hare, ed., *Rea-*

son in Teaching and Education: Three Essays in Philosophy of Education, Halifax, Dalhousie University School of Education, 1989, pp. 5–21; reprinted under the same title in M. Weinstein and W. Oxman-Michelli, eds., *Critical Thinking: Language and Inquiry Across the Disciplines*, Upper Montclair, NJ: Institute for Critical Thinking, Montclair State College, 1989, pp. 7–21.

———. (1989a): "Philosophy of Science Naturalized? Some Problems with Giere's Naturalism," *Studies in History and Philosophy of Science*, vol. 20, #3, pp. 365–375.

———. (1989b): "Farewell to Feyerabend," *Inquiry*, vol. 32, #3, pp. 343–369.

———. (1990): "Must Thinking Be Critical to Be Critical Thinking?," *Philosophy of the Social Sciences*, vol. 20, #4, pp. 453–461.

———. (1990a): "Laudan's Normative Naturalism," *Studies in History and Philosophy of Science*, vol. 21, #2, pp. 295–313.

———. (1992): "Education and the Fostering of Rationality," in R. Talaska, ed., *Critical Reasoning in Contemporary Culture: Theoretical Perspectives on the Meaning, Conditions, and Goals of Critical Reasoning*, New York: SUNY Press, pp. 89–112.

———. (1992a): "Justification By Balance," *Philosophy and Phenomenological Research*, vol. 52, #1, pp. 27–46.

———. (1992b): "Rescher on the Justification of Rationality," *Informal Logic*, vol. 14, #1, pp. 23–31.

———. (1992c): "Naturalism, Instrumental Rationality, and the Normativity of Epistemology," invited address, Eastern Division meeting of the American Philosophical Association, December 1992.

———. (1995): "Reason and Rationality," in J. J. Chambliss, ed., *Philosophy of Education: An Encyclopedia*, New York: Garland Press, 1995 (in press).

———. (1995a) "Naturalism and the Abandonment of Normativity," in W. O'Donohue and R. Kitchener, eds., *Philosophy and Psychology: Interdisciplinary Problems and Responses*, London: Sage (in press).

———. (1995b): "Naturalized Epistemology and 'First Philosophy'," *Metaphilosophy*, vol. 26, #1, pp. 46–62.

———. (1996): "Education and Cultural Transmission/Transformation: Philosophical Reflections on the Historian's Task," *Pedagogica Historica* (in press).

Siegel, Harvey and John Biro. (1995): "Epistemic Normativity, Argumentation, and Fallacies," in Frans H. van Eemeren, et. al., eds., *Analysis and Evaluation: Proceedings of the Third ISSA Conference on Argumentation*, Volume II, Amsterdam: Sicsat, pp. 286–299.

Sorensen, R. A. (1991) "'P, therefore, P' without Circularity," *The Journal of Philosophy*, vol. 88, #5, pp. 245–266.

Sosa, Ernest. (1987): "Serious Philosophy and Freedom of Spirit," *The Journal of Philosophy*, vol. 84, #12, pp. 707–726.

Stone, Lynda. (1995): "Narrative in Philosophy of Education: A Feminist Tale of 'Uncertain' Knowledge," in Kohli (1995), pp. 173–189.

Strike, Kenneth A. (1990): "Response to Lisman," *Studies in Philosophy and Education*, vol. 10, #4, pp. 355–60.

Sutherland, Stewart R. (1977): *Atheism and the Rejection of God*, Oxford: Basil Blackwell.

Taylor, Charles. (1992): *Multiculturalism and "The Politics of Education,"* with commentary by Amy Gutmann, editor, Steven C. Rockefeller, Michael Walzer, and Susan Wolf, Princeton: Princeton University Press.

Toulmin, Stephen E. (1950): *The Place of Reason in Ethics*, Cambridge: Cambridge University Press.

———. (1958): *The Uses of Argument*, Cambridge: Cambridge University Press.

Trigg, Roger. (1973): *Reason and Commitment*, Cambridge: Cambridge University Press.

Tymoczko, Thomas. (1979): "The Four-color Problem and Its Philosophical Significance," *The Journal of Philosophy*, vol. 76, #2, pp. 57–83.

Weinstein, Mark. (1990): "Towards a Research Agenda for Informal Logic and Critical Thinking," *Informal Logic*, vol. 12, #3, pp. 121–143.

———. (1992): "Reason and Refutation: A Review of Two Recent Books by Harvey Siegel," *Studies in Philosophy and Education*, vol. 11, #3, pp. 231–263.

———. (1992a): "The Forest and the Trees: Reply to Siegel," *Studies in Philosophy and Education*, vol. 11, #3, pp. 285–291.

———. (1993): "Rationalist Hopes and Utopian Visions," in Audrey Thompson, ed., *Philosophy of Education 1993: Proceedings of the Forty-Ninth Annual Meeting of the Philosophy of Education Society*, pp. 25–36.

———. (1994): "How to Get from Ought to Is: Postmodern Epistemology and Social Justice," *Inquiry: Critical Thinking Across the Disciplines*, vol. 13, #3–4, pp. 26–32.

Williams, Bernard. (1985): *Ethics and the Limits of Philosophy*, Cambridge: Harvard University Press.

Yates, Steven. (1992): "Multiculturalism and Epistemology," *Public Affairs Quarterly*, vol. 6, #4, pp. 435–456.

229

INDEX